Sheryl M

Hand *for* Hand

WANASOMA
BooKs

CALIFORNIA

Hand for Hand

First printing WanaSoma Books trade paperback edition: August 2020

ISBN # 978-0-9822085-5-7

PRINTED IN THE UNITED STATES OF AMERICA

Cover by Maurice Scriber

All WanaSoma Book titles are available at special discounts for bulk purchases for sales promotion, premiums, fund-raising, educational, or institutional use. For more information visit www.sherylmallory-johnson.com.

BOOKS BY SHERYL MALLORY-JOHNSON

The Hand She Played
Love & Regrets
Sense of Love

Young Adult Books
L.A. Summer

To My Daughter
Mallori Taylor Johnson

You were born together, and together you shall be forevermore, but let there be spaces in your togetherness, and let the winds of heaven dance between you.

—Kahlil Gibran

Part Four

Prologue

A t the West Hollywood Sheriff Station, two cops sat me in a small room and left me alone. There wasn't a clock to keep track of time, pictures on the white walls to admire, or a window to gaze out of, just a square table, three metal folding chairs, and a camera recording every move I made.

The door opened, hastening my heartbeat. Through jumpy eyes, I watched a black man in a suit and tie and a white man in a golf shirt with khaki pants walk into the room. Detective Sergeant Carter and Detective Lazarus, they called themselves. Lazarus, the white detective, sat across the table from me and read my Miranda rights.

I exercised my right to remain silent. Silence came easy for me. I had upheld my vow of silence out of shame and guilt for many years. This silence I upheld out of loyalty, knowing anything I said or did could be used against Vangie in a court of law.

Carter, the black detective, said, "Call anyone you'd like to call—on me. We'll step out of the room." He held out a cell phone and smiled, an overly friendly smile that made me question his sincerity.

I thought of calling my mother. She was the only person I could call under the circumstances, but I knew she wouldn't understand my decision to trade my life for Vangie's freedom. I knew no one would understand it, and so I chose not to call anyone.

"Don't let my size intimidate you," Carter said. "I'm not the bad cop, here to beat a confession out of you; I don't even care about the evidence stacked against you. You know what I care about, Vangie? The truth. So does the victim's family. They want answers and it's our job to give them those answers. Wouldn't you agree?"

If I had answers to give, I would do everything in my power to clear Vangie's name and prove her innocence. With six years and an ocean standing between Vangie and me, I knew very little about her life nowadays, no more than I knew about her life in the old days. The little I did know I'd learned from our mother. Vangie had recently graduated from law school, lived in Hollywood somewhere, and was wanted for murder.

One

Feeling reckless, Vangie left her hideout and walked the streets of Lyon, numb to the briskness of France in fall.

Every pub and shop along the boulevard had closed, and there wasn't a police car on patrol for Vangie to look out for. The most she had to worry about, according to the locals, was getting her pockets picked, which didn't worry her either. Nothing worried Vangie tonight, neither life nor death. Living was her self-inflicted punishment of sorts, her misery a constant reminder that she didn't deserve to live happily ever after.

She took dawdling steps in stilettos, her coal-black hair draping her face and shoulders haphazardly, her eyes as dark and lifeless as the night.

She wandered into Club Vingt-Et-Un, a trendy spot for the twenty-five and up crowd. Friday nights, before 11:00 PM, ladies entered free and men paid 20 euros. Vangie squeezed her way through the crowd of happy drunks and stationed herself at the lively bar.

"French Blonde," she ordered.

The Bartender served up a tall cocktail and kissed her cheeks. "*A la votre!*"

"Cheers!" Vangie threw back a mouthful of the citrusy gin, then stared out into the smoky atmosphere. People mixed and mingled, lounged on the velvet sofas, or danced on the floor flashing with flamboyant lights. She envied the vacationers who had traveled to this romantic country for its many charms and to hang out with the locals. To be young and free had forsaken her.

After her third cocktail, a toasty feeling spread through her stomach, crept into her bloodstream, and deadened her senses. She floated onto the dance floor at the hand of a dark-haired Frenchmen. The floor swayed beneath her feet as she and her partner moved among partiers grinding, jumping, and bouncing to electro-pop music. Or was she the one grinding, jumping, and bouncing? Vangie was too drunk to know or to care. She danced the night away, hoping to forget.

Regarding her with his bedroom eyes, the Frenchmen swerved his pelvis against hers suggestively. She thought she might puke right onto his Topsiders. She peeled his groping hands from her hips and shoved him off her.

"*Ou'allez-vous,*" he shouted after her as she made her way toward the door.

Waving a tired hand over her shoulder, Vangie said, "I'm going home!"

Somewhere in her inebriated brain she thought, *I don't have a home.* She would've cried had she not laughed out loud. It was all Vangie could do—laugh to keep from crying.

The Frenchmen followed her out of the club and into the chilly night. "We have danced close. We will sleep close, yes? I have dreamed of sleeping with an angel."

"I'm no angel."

"You have fooled me."

Vangie laughed dryly. "You're not the first man I've fooled."

"I love you black American girls. You have a wicked sense of humor."

"I'm getting married."

"Yes, of course. Who's the lucky mate?"

"The love of my life." Reality bit into her heart with sharp teeth.

"I will give you the best bang of your life. Yes?"

Vangie contemplated the Frenchman's proposition. Sleeping with a stranger tonight could be a welcome change to sleeping alone. She didn't need to know his name, and she certainly didn't want him knowing hers. The possibility that he might be an undercover cop wafted through her mind like smoke from his vapor cigarette and drifted off.

The Frenchman followed her through the ornate double doors of her medieval apartment complex and helped her climb the four flights of wooden stairs that led to her flat. When she reached the landing, she would have stumbled backward had the Frenchman not braced her from behind.

Regaining her equilibrium, Vangie squinted to make certain she wasn't hallucinating. *It can't be*, she thought, *but who else could it be?* No one else knew where or how to find her.

Tears of joy filled her eyes as she rushed down the narrow corridor toward Ronnie Livingston, the tapestry carpet seemingly stretching with each wobbly step she took.

"Ron!" she squealed, disturbing the peaceful building.

Ronnie, who had been sleeping at her doorstep, bound to his feet. "You scared the shit out of me!"

Staring nostalgically into his melancholy blue eyes, Vangie stroked Ronnie's five-o'clock shadow that lay around his chiseled chin and upper lip as if someone had sketched it on with a fine pencil.

"It's really you," she said dreamily.

"It's me. And who is this?" Ronnie said, referencing the Frenchmen.

"This is the love of your life. Yes?" said the Frenchmen to her.

Vangie laughed and threw her arms around Ronnie's neck. "He's my lifesaver!"

"She gets this way when she's zonked. I'll take her from here. Thanks, bro." Ronnie shook the Frenchmen's hand, who in turn shook his head disappointedly as he wished them both *au revoir* and walked away without causing a scene.

Vangie couldn't stop staring at Ronnie or control her silly grin. Seeing him felt surreal; the three months since she had seen him last seemed more like three years. He had shaved his ash-blonde hair down to an Ivy League style, and he looked to Vangie like he had slimmed down too, making him look taller. She noticed too how his pecs and biceps defined the baseball Tee he wore with jeans and high-top tennis shoes, as if he'd been hanging out at the gym 24/7.

"Look at you," she said sentimentally, mussing Ronnie's moussed hair. "You sober up nicely."

Frowning, Ronnie brazenly assessed her body in her hip hugging, breast-enhancing black dress and six-inch stilettos with straps that wrapped sexily around her legs.

"Definitely. Club it up. Get plastered. I'm just the accomplice," he said.

Vangie couldn't control her laughter. "You're jealous."

"I'm not jealous."

"You shouldn't be here, Ron."

"I have a good excuse."

After unlocking the door, Vangie staggered into her flat, slumped down on the leather sofa, and freed her feet from her shoes. "What's your excuse?"

"You've been arrested, Van."

She laughed harder. "You're high. Tell me you're not, Ron. One of us has to stay sober." She waited for Ronnie to say, "high as a kite." His commitment to sobriety was tenuous at best.

"Totally abstinent. Five months, twenty-two days, and some hours..." He took in a long breath. "It's your twin. She showed up...in jail."

The shoe in Vangie's hand hit the floor with a thud. She dug her nails into red leather, bracing herself for heartbreaking news, ready to collapse under its inevitable weight.

"She's dead, isn't she?" She spoke with what felt like the last breath in her weakened body.

"Did you hear what I said? Your twin is in jail! They think she's you or that you're her or... What difference does it make? We're fucked." Ronnie ran his fingers through his hair and paced the room.

"Don't play with me, Ronnie."

"I wouldn't dick you around about something this serious." He handed his cell phone to her.

"Woman arrested in Hollywood Stabbing Case," an Internet source read.

Vangie broke out in cold sweat when she saw the photo of armed police officers, who looked ready to shoot Angie first and ask questions later. The image alone hadn't stopped Vangie's heart from beating as much as seeing her twin again for the first time in years. Angie's hair, once as long as her own, was cut into to a short, curly 'fro; but her dark round eyes defining exaggerated cheekbones, her curvy, full lips, golden complexion, and five foot six stature still mirrored her own.

Six years of restless nights and grief stricken days, six years of feeling half alive and fearing she would never see her twin again assailed Vangie. Not even the alcohol she had drowned herself in could insulate her from the chill icing her blood like a cold day in Michigan, even the coldest day she could remember growing up there.

"This isn't happening," she muttered.

Ronnie was talking, but Vangie couldn't hear him above the whooshing in her ears. Her impulse was to run, run to her twin's rescue. As she sprang to her feet and bolted toward the front door, the room suddenly spun like a Ferris wheel and her stomach was in her throat before she knew it. She flew to the kitchen and vomited violently into the sink.

"That brings back brutal memories," Ronnie said.

Two

"In the murder case that shook Hollywood, the police have apprehended Vangie Cooper, 26, at the Los Angeles International Airport. Cooper will be arraigned on a charge of first degree murder," the article read.

Vangie read on, scanning the inflated history of Todd's assent to stardom, from his Ivy League education, to his off-Broadway success and two Tony Award nominations.

Like most articles she found on the Net, this one was brief and nondescript, a good gage of where the police were at in the investigation process. However, a colorful story of Annette Cooper, the mother she had killed off in a figurative sense, would soon surface, followed by a nationwide search for her missing twin, presently in police custody, in a clear case of mistaken identity.

Vangie handed Ronnie his phone back. "When're we leaving?" she asked in a fit of desperation as she looked at him helplessly.

"Give it a few days. Maybe less. It's complicated."

"How complicated could scheduling a flight on a private jet be, Ron?"

"Extremely complicated. My dad is notorious for being a major pain in my ass. Do you want my advice?"

"I don't need advice; I need you to stop playing with your stupid phone and get me home."

Ronnie took his eyes off his cell phone to look at her. "I'm not playing with my incredibly smart phone; I'm profiling tech companies. Check this one out. A tech guru I know designed this powerful new app…"

Vangie pushed the phone away from her face. "Never mind. I'll fly commercial." If it weren't for Ronnie forcing her to lie down in the first place, she would've caught the first commercial flight she could find back to the states. Based on her calculations, the length of the flight from Europe, factoring in the time difference, gave her only a few hours leeway if she left right now.

But when Vangie went to stand, the room spun again, and she fell back onto the bed. She wanted to cry. A hot shower hadn't thawed out her raw nerves, and she felt like ants were crawling beneath her skin. Since birth, seemingly, she had stood on her own two feet, pulling herself up by her bootstraps whenever life pulled her down. She had thought no deadly storm, raging fire, or earthly disaster could break her at this point. She had never been so broken.

"My advice…if you fly commercial, you'll be delayed in Customs. If you would chill out, I'll have you home in twelve hours flat." Ronnie wrapped his arm around her shoulder. "Will you trust me?"

Vangie sighed resignedly. She knew Ronnie was right. Customs on a commercial flight would be a fugitive's nightmare. She groaned and curled into his arms.

"I don't know what I'd do without you."

"You'll never do without me. I missed the shit out of you." Ronnie pulled her closer and gazed down at her.

"I missed you too," she breathed, watching the flames of desire dance in Ronnie's eyes like blue fire. A magnetic force inched their lips closer together. Vangie couldn't resist her own kindling desires.

"Are we really going to do it this time?" Ronnie said.

"Are we?" Vangie's eyes challenged his.

"What're the rules of engagement?"

"No rules." She had nothing to lose or gain from sex for the first time in her life.

Bending forward, Ronnie wrapped her lips in a mouth-watering kiss that brought an instant pulse to her groin. Giving into his kiss, Vangie slid down the mattress until she was lying face up, Ronnie rigid and ready between her burning thighs.

He pulled out of their kiss with a show of reluctant passion in his eyes. "Are you one hundred percent good with this? If you're not..."

Vangie curled her lips and tongue around his. She didn't want to talk or to second-guess her decision; she wanted to forget. She slipped off her tank top, tossed it aside, and raised her hips, assisting Ronnie as he slid off her panties. She in turn helped him wrestle out of his boxer shorts.

Leaving little to chance, Vangie straddled Ronnie and took him inside of her, whole and recklessly. His initial thrust stole her breath away. She gasped to catch it.

Their indulgent and deliberate trot began, as if to make up for the years of celibacy between them that had defined their friendship. With each stroke, warm waves crashed against her inner walls, lapping deliciously at her pleasure zone.

She was certain now. She needed this. Wanted this. Wanted Ronnie. Wanted to stay warm and liquid inside. Holding fast to her fleeting ecstasy, she slowed her ride, but Ronnie's impatient penetrating vanquished her. She matched him thrust for thrust, his heart drumming against the palms of her moist hands that clawed into his bare chest.

At the height of her intense delight, milliseconds before their respective explosions, life for Vangie was blissful. Afterward, she slumped forward and caught her breath.

"I'm not objecting, not by a long shot, but what just happened?" Ronnie panted.

"A great bang." Vangie fell onto her back.

Ronnie rolled on top of her and stared lovingly into her evasive eyes. "Is this a good time to say I'm totally in love with you?"

Vangie squirmed from beneath Ronnie and then fixed her eyes on the ceiling.

"Nice shot to the ego. If I was too quick with the gun, give me a minute. I want more of you." He dove for her neck and suckled.

She shoved him back with gentle force. "You don't love me."

"That's complete bullshit."

"You don't, Ron."

What more could she say? Ronnie loved her persona, not her, and now that she had entrusted him with her dirty little secret, she couldn't hardly look him in the eyes.

His staring burned into the side of her face with the intensity of a magnifying glass. She dared to look at him again, only to be confronted by his flushed face contrasting ice-blue eyes.

"For Christ's sake, Van. Are you capable of honesty?"

"What does that mean?"

"You're mourning your fucking ex-boyfriend after you just did me. Is that honest enough for you?"

"He wasn't my *ex-boyfriend*. We were getting married..." Her voice faded off.

"Right. Keep lying to yourself. Gotta love your integrity."

"Get out!" she spat at him.

"Is that what you really want? You want me to leave?"

No... She didn't want him to leave, but as it stood, she felt as if she had betrayed Wade—yet again. Making love to Ronnie hadn't helped her to forget, and in truth, only made matters worse. No man other than Wade Fitzgerald the Fourth had reached that undamaged place deep inside, but Ronnie had gotten close. Dangerously close.

"Just leave, Ron. Go!"

"I've met my bullshit quota for the night anyway." Ronnie hopped out of bed, crammed his legs into his jeans, and tugged them on.

Though Vangie yearned for him to stay, she said nothing to stop him from storming out of the room. Feeling like a motherless child, she curled into a ball beneath the sheet and took in the totality of her life. Nothing was out of place or out of the ordinary in the room that served as her private prison cell for the past three months. Pairs of shoes littered the wood flooring, her clothes, the few items she had taken with her on the run, buried the lone chair, and empty wine bottles collected dust on the nightstand and bureau.

She wondered how she'd arrived at this place, not France or this suffocating room, but this place in her life. Thoughts of Angie drove her deeper into sorrow and regret.

She reflected on their final days together Christmas break her freshman year at Stanford. She had dreaded going home for the holiday only to be reminded of why she left. If only she could turn back the hands of time.

Twenty minutes later, Ronnie slipped back into bed and wrapped his arms around her so lovingly she almost cried.

"I'm sorry," she whispered.

"It's my crap, not yours. I'm in a bad headspace. You don't need it."

Vangie turned over to face him. "It's not you, Ronnie. It's me. I'm selfish. I'm evil…"

"You're none of those things, Van. You're a great person. You're a badass and ballsy as shit, but you have an enormous heart. Did I mention that you're beautiful?"

"Go home, Ron. You really shouldn't be here."

"I'm not leaving without you."

"You don't get it! My sister is locked up because of me!"

"I fully get it. One hundred percent."

"If you're arrested too… I couldn't handle it. I can't…"

"I got the clearance," Ronnie announced.

Vangie submitted to the smile that so wanted to escape. "I really do love you, Ron."

"Very charitable of you." He reached over the side of the bed, came up with his backpack, and pulled an envelope from it. "I nabbed it from the cottage before the cops ransacked it."

Vangie looked at the certified mail in Ronnie's hand and recoiled. She had been careful to forward her mail to a private mailbox. The State Bar of California, however, knew where to find her.

"Don't you want your results?"

"What gave you that impression?"

"Total speculation." Ronnie placed the envelope on the bed and went back to playing with his phone. " Zeke the Great shit a brick when he found out his tenant was a murder suspect…"

While Ronnie talked, Vangie leered at the envelope, wishing she had X-ray vision. There were several reasons she hadn't logged into the California State Bar's secured server to find out her test results. For one, if she had actually passed, her eligibility for state bar membership would soon be revoked. Two, the FBI would've tracked her down in an instant. Three, she just didn't give damn if she passed or not.

"Would you like me to do the honors?" Ronnie said, side-eyeing her.

Vangie snatched up the envelope and ripped it open. Her eyes jumped past the preamble, down to the first sentence. "Congratulations! I'm happy to inform you that you have passed the June 2016 California Bar examination…"

"What's the verdict?" Ronnie asked.

Dismissing her short-term feelings of achievement, Vangie crumbled the sheet of paper into a tight ball. If she had a match, she would've incinerated it.

Zeke Livingston's Learjet doubled as a two-bedroom luxury high rise. Cradled in Italian leather seats, Vangie watched the city of Lyon diminish. The sun stole glances through milky white clouds under the dawning sun as the plane leveled off in God's great blue territory.

Ronnie feasted on a spread of breakfast breads, Canadian bacon, and an assortment of fruit served by the lone flight attendant, while Vangie reminisced about her very first trip outside of Detroit with Antonio Moretti. A mere teenager at the time, she felt bold and free, awed by the New York lights lighting up the sky above streets as white as cotton.

With Antonio and Jacob Stein she had discovered a hidden world filled with luxury hotels, botanical gardens, fine restaurants, and private dinner clubs, and had eventually learned to carry her own weight in a world determined to hold back a poor black girl.

Now she was back to square one, a thought that made her cringe. Her stomach dipped with the aircraft as it hit some turbulence. In twelve hours flat she would arrive back in Los Angeles—not as Vangie Cooper but as Daniela Silva.

Three

My transfer from the holding cell to a women's detention facility in Los Angeles was due to the serious nature of Vangie's suspected crime.

Long after the cell door, reinforced by two loud clanking bolts, slammed shut and stopped my heart cold, my ears were still ringing. I was a deer in a lion's den; the lion was my cellmate. Pictures of kids taped to the wall, books and whatnot on the desk, and a pair of wet socks hanging out to dry gave me the impression that she had been locked up long enough to make herself at home.

She sat crouched on the bottom half of the twin bunk, twisting a mass of woolly hair into a thick French braid, her legs as long and as thick as tree trunks.

We had the freedom to sleep, read a book, listen to music, or do nothing while locked up; I decided to make good use of the three sheets of paper and single pen issued to new inmates by inventing recipes. As I categorized dishes in either sweet or savory flavors, the walls around me came down and delicious scents overtook the smell of hopelessness.

"You sittin' in my seat."

My cellmate and I hadn't yet exchanged a hello. Her mean mug had shut me up before I could choose to talk or not. I'd been careful not to incite her territorialism, playing a silent game of Simon Says by reading her threatening cues before I used the sink or the toilet, which also belonged to her. I'd forgotten to read her cue before I took the liberty to sit at the desk.

To avoid a fight I'd inevitably lose, I gathered my sheets of paper and stood.

Her hardened eyes seemed to laugh at me. "You better woman up, cuz," she said.

I returned to the top bunk and stared at the ceiling. Apart from the slamming doors, the shuffling of feet up and down the hall, the random shouting, and the overall unnatural sounds around me, I heard only my shallow breathing and pounding heartbeat.

I couldn't lie to myself. Jail terrified me. I knew people who went to jail, had overheard their drunken tales whenever they hung around our apartment, partying until the sun circled. They had all lived to tell their stories.

I pray I live to tell Vangie's story, and mine, someday.

Later, a guard took me to a small conference room and sat me at the table, across from Detective Sergeant Carter and Detective Lazarus. Their eyes persecuted me, as if they'd decided Vangie's guilt without the benefit of a trial.

"We're giving you another chance to talk before the judge throws the book at you," Carter said.

I continued to exercise my right to remain silent.

"I don't think she understands, Sergeant," said Lazarus. "You're looking at first degree murder and life without parole. Do you have anything to say to the charges?"

I had nothing to say.

"Can you account for your whereabouts on the twenty-seventh of June at around 10:00 PM?" Carter said.

I said nothing.

"This ought to jog your memory." Lazarus slid an 8x10 glossy photo across the table, practically placing it under my nose.

The man lying in a pool of his own blood, his eyes frozen for all eternity, and hands welded to the knife in his stomach, shocked me to tears. I shied away from the gruesome photo.

"Do you know what your tears tell me?" Lazarus continued. "They tell me you're not a coldhearted killer. They tell me you're capable of remorse, and your remorse tells me that you have a guilty conscience. Do you know why you have a guilty conscience, Vangie?"

"Because you're guilty," added Carter.

I didn't feel remorse or guilt. I felt ashamed for questioning my heart and mind. I knew Vangie like I knew myself. We were from one egg, one womb, twins always and forever. Vangie wouldn't kill a fly unless she had to.

Lazarus leaned back in his chair, his elbows winged over his ears and hands clasped on his head, flattening out his buzz cut. "Just for shits and giggles, I'll tell you a story about an old case I had. Nice girl, pretty too, from the inner city, rough and tough place, mother drugged out, father locked up, the whole shebang. You know the drill. She made it out, had her whole life ahead of her…"

"This is where the story gets really interesting," Carter interjected.

"This girl, see, was banging her boyfriend's homeboy. When the homeboy threatened to rat her out, she killed him with a blunt object. It wasn't a premeditated act, meaning she didn't plan to commit murder. As I said, she's a nice girl...intelligent too. She took the rap, got time off for good behavior, and the rest is history." Lazarus drummed the table. "Is that how it went down, Vangie? Things just got a little out of hand?"

I responded to his question with resounding silence.

"That's one theory," Carter said. "Here's another. You weren't the one doing the banging."

"Your fiancé was banging his homeboy."

"Happens every day," Carter added.

"You find out the actor is blowing the doctor, go apeshit, and gut the poor guy like a fish. Correct me if I'm way off base here."

Silence...

"I think you're getting warm," Carter said.

"I think you're right, Serg." Lazarus cracked his knuckles.

"You're how old, Vangie?" said Carter. "Twenty-five? Twenty-six? I have a daughter your age, and let me be the first to tell you, you're too young to spend the rest of your life in the penal system. You don't want to go down that road. It's in your best interest to confess while you have the chance. A judge might go easier on you."

"We have substantial evidence that places you at the victim's home at the time of his murder, enough to charge you with a capital offense. That's the death penalty in the state of California." Lazarus smirked at me.

I swallowed a mouthful of dust.

"You see that camera right there?" Carter pointed to the wall. "It's recording everything you say and everything you don't say. A jury may see your lack of cooperation as a sign of guilt. I think you'd better start talking."

"The more you talk, the quicker you'll get home," said Lazarus, swiping sweat from the back of his neck.

At some point during my interrogation, Carter left me alone with Lazarus. He took over Carter's chair next to me and leaned close enough for me to see the white specks in his gray eyes.

"The chicks you'll be bunking with aren't your doctors, lawyers, or college cohorts; they're bangers, Crips, Bloods, Aryan Nation bikers, sociopaths... Do you know what they hate more than baby killers? Uppity chicks who think they're above the law." He grinned. "Or they may love you to pieces."

My silence continued to fill the room like a wall of stones.

Lazarus suddenly snapped, leaping out of the chair that flipped onto its back. "You killed him!" he screamed in my face. "Say it!"

I lifted my head, raised my eyes, and stared at him in silent defiance.

She didn't do it! My eyes screamed.

Four

A startling alarm awakened me.

We had ten minutes to dress and lineup. I only had three because my cellmate hogged the sink and toilet. When my turn came, I splashed my face with rusty water, glossed over my teeth with bitter toothpaste, dressed quickly, and hurried out of my cell.

Simultaneously, my cellmate and I stepped into the white painted box and waited to be counted present. The chance to shower came next. I skipped the opportunity.

Breakfast came in a paper bag delivered directly to our cells. I couldn't remember a time when food didn't excite my taste buds. Food was my life, mostly for the love of it but also the lack of it growing up. Back when our unwelcomed houseguests would eat us out of house and home, I would get to school early enough to catch the free breakfast, then eat the heaviest meal at lunch to hold myself over until the next day.

While my cellmate complained about the quality of the food here, I finished off the imitation cheese stuffed between two slices of dry, spongy white bread, the stale fruit bar, and drank the carton of warm milk without a complaint.

Following breakfast, a guard entered the cell.

"Cooper-58," the guard said. "You have a visitor."

I hopped down from my bunk, landed squarely on my feet, and stood at attention. "Do you know who it is?" I squeaked like a nervous mouse.

"Your lawyer."

"I…don't…have…one."

"You do now."

She marched me through a series of heavy steel doors until I arrived at the visitor's section of the compound, then placed me inside a chilly room with no more than a table and a few chairs. A lady in a red dress and high heels flew forward and gave me a bear hug. After squeezing me nearly to death, she stepped back and stared me down with large brown wet eyes.

"Oh, my God, Van! You've lost weight. And your hair! Who butchered it?" She gave me another squeeze. "My poor roomie, you've been through it."

"Why're you here?" I said, digging for her identity.

"To get you out of this, bitch! Tell her, Ross."

The dude, Ross, was tall and of medium build. He had swirls of dark hair, skin the color of a just ripe banana, and wore a nice suit and tie. In all, he was nice to look at.

"I'm here to represent you," he said.

"Oh. Thanks, but I don't need a lawyer." I was holding out hope Vangie would come to my rescue, and soon.

"You're not serious?" the lady said, frowning. "Anyone charged with a criminal offense needs to lawyer up. You of all people should know that. Right, Ross?"

"It's par for the course." Ross pulled out a chair for me.

We sat on opposite sides of the table.

"I shouldn't have to remind you of the penal code for aggravated assault, and I won't ask if you're guilty or innocent. If you didn't sign a confession, you're good," the dude said.

"Vangie's not a layperson, Ross."

"I've seen lawyers sell out their mommas in an interrogation room on a dime," he told her, and then he turned back to me. "Did you sign a confession or make one? That's all I need to know."

I shook my head, deciding not to speak again unless I had to.

"When you were interrogated for *six hours* and jailed without being *formally* charged, did you say anything?"

I shook my head.

"Good. Don't talk to anyone but me."

"And me," the lady added. "Whatever you disclose outside the confines of attorney-client privilege, the DA will use to prosecute you to the full extent of the law."

I stared at them both blankly.

"Your arraignment is Tuesday," Ross continued. "If you want me to represent you, I'll need a signed consent." He set a piece of paper on the table, spun it around, and slid it toward me. *Ross E. Lewis and Associates, Contract for Legal Services,* the heading read.

The lady leaned forward and whispered, "We quit the Public Defender's Office and opened our own firm. We kept it low key. You know people."

"We just moved into a premium office downtown," Ross said.

"You're our first client." The woman turned her smile upside down. "I mean... That isn't anything to brag about, right."

"Don't get it twisted," said Ross. "We got prospective clients lining up."

"I'm the paralegal slash legal assistant slash glorified secretary." The woman chuckled, her face turning into a chocolate covered strawberry. "Just until I'm *officially* sworn in, quote, unquote."

I scrunched my forehead and twisted my mouth.

"Oh, my, God!" she exclaimed. "You don't know." Her body deflated. "How could you know? We haven't talked since Todd..." Her eyes turned wet, again. "I passed, Van. Third try. Pathetic, right?"

"The state doesn't care how many times you sit for the bar exam, Clarissa. You passed, baby. Be happy," the dude said.

In my excitement to put a name to a face, I came close to jumping up and calling her by name. Clarissa had been Vangie's roommate at Stanford. I remembered her face— Pretty brown eyes, cheeks like chocolate pastry puffs, and her perfect smile—was once scattered throughout Vangie's cell phone photos. Worried she might recognize something about me distinct from Vangie's poise, beauty, and grace under fire, like my overall dazed look and lack of sophistication, I dropped my eyes to the table.

"Well...?" Clarissa said with a question mark in her tone.

I glanced up to catch her staring at me as if I'd buried a bone, as my mother would say.

"Are you actually going to make me ask?" she pressed.

I blinked my eyes innocently.

"You passed, first round, didn't you?"

Knowing Vangie, who never failed at anything she set her mind on accomplishing, she was probably right. I smiled modestly.

"I hate you!" Clarissa said with a big smile.

"Can we get back to business?" Ross handed me a pen to sign the contract.

"I can't pay you," I said.

He cleared his throat. "I expect to get paid and I don't come cheap."

Clarissa swatted the air. "We'll talk compensation later, Van. I know you're good for it."

I signed the agreement with Vangie's name. Somehow, I would find a way to repay them for their kindness.

"If anyone can get an acquittal, I can. You're looking at the best." Ross tucked the contract into a file folder and studied me for a long minute. "You disappeared for three months. What's your alibi?"

"Maybe it was cold feet, Ross."

"Having cold feet isn't an alibi, baby."

"Constitutional Law 101: presumption of innocence until otherwise disproven."

"What're you getting at, Rissa?"

"Taking a three-month hiatus after law school isn't an element of a crime. Loyola actually encouraged us to travel abroad and gain perspective on the world after graduation. Second point, Vangie is a world traveler. Her dad lives overseas. She visits him once or twice a year. Right, Van?"

Not wanting to contradict Vangie's lie, I nodded.

"If she can't substantiate a three-month hiatus, your argument is baseless, baby."

Clarissa arched her perfectly arched brows. "Is there evidence contrary to my argument?"

Ross stroked his goatee and turned back to me. "You turned yourself in, showed up to face this charge of your own free will?"

I nodded.

"No one coerced you?"

I shook my head, following his lead. He wasn't asking me questions, I realized, but directing my answers.

"Whatever you remember about the events that took place the day of the alleged crime, tell me."

"I don't remember anything," I blurted out

Ross chuckled, but I got the impression he didn't find me very funny. "Here's the thing, Vangie. If I know you're lying, nine times out of ten, the jury will know too."

"Maybe she's telling the truth, Ross."

Ross took his frustrated gaze off of me and shifted it to Clarissa. "Baby. Please. Take notes and let me handle this."

Clarissa folded in her ruby red lips and went back to taking notes on her fancy iPad.

"Since you know the game, you should know amnesia is not a sustainable defense," Ross said to me.

I didn't know the game, didn't know anything about being a lawyer. My feelings of inadequacy returned like an old habit. I laid my head between the bend of my elbow on the table and cried.

"This is breaking my heart," Clarissa whispered.

"She'll live."

"She's in shock, Ross. You didn't have to be so hard on her."

"This is softball, baby. Hard is when the prosecution goes at her, guns blazing, in front of the judge and jury. I'm not trying to go there. Know what I'm saying?"

Before leaving, Clarissa gave me a long hug, and Ross told me to stay out of trouble.

∼

I walked the cellblock in my royal blue jumpsuit, feeling curious eyes watching. When I was young, I would make myself small, hiding behind my silence and Vangie's courage. In jail, being small could get me killed.

During social hour we had the choice to play dominoes, chess, spades, blackjack, backgammon, visit the library, or watch TV. I watched the prison scene play out like I had the high school scene at lunchtime, hoping to blend in with the forest green walls like water-colored paint.

The longer I sat alone, however, the more noticeable I became, mainly to a Mexican girl who was no older than eighteen from what I could tell. She hadn't taken her eyes off of me since I sat down, as if I interested her more than her friends.

She walked over to me, her prison jumper sagging on her tiny body. "You're that killer bitch," she said matter-of-factly, then slid across the bench until her thigh pressed against mine. Now she was staring at me with large doe eyes that gleamed like pretty black marbles.

"How'd you fake out the cops?" she said.

"She's smart, that's how." A second girl walked up and sat to my left, sandwiching me between the two of them.

"If she was smart, she wouldn't be locked up with us," said a third girl, who stood over me. She was the biggest and most boyish of the three.

"You a lawyer?" said the second girl.

"I hate lawyers, dude," said the first girl. "Mines didn't do nothin' but take money and make money, and I didn't kill nobody."

"Me too."

"Me three."

They all laughed and slapped high-fives.

I knew they were bangers. The teardrop tattoo staining each of their right eyes told me they had killed and could kill again.

"You know what we call lawyers in the pen?" said another.

"Jailhouse lawyers!" someone answered from a distance.

"Welcome to the pig pen, baby!" said number three.

"I think she's ignoring us," said banger number two.

"Are you ignoring us, *la puta*?" said the first.

I thought to turn the other cheek, like the Bible warned, but my cheeks were burning, my mouth watering to defend Vangie's name against their lies.

"She's mad dogging you, homey," number three said.

The first one placed her nose inches from mine. "You mad dogging me, killer bitch?"

That was the first big mistake I made in jail, mad dogging someone. Hair pulling was usually the first line of attack new inmates were told and encouraged to wear ponytails or buns. Since I wore my hair boy-short, they would likely snatch me baldheaded and tear me apart, limb by limb.

The first blow came out of nowhere and landed squarely on my left eye. Then came the kicks and punches meant to crush every bone in my body. Instinctively, I fought back like a hyena. The fight ended when a guard put me in a chokehold just before I was beaten within an inch of my life, or so it felt.

Five

Hell is said to be a place of eternal damnation where darkness reigns over light and evil outranks good. Restrictive Housing was my personal hell. Other than the freezing cold, I wouldn't know the difference.

I'd been on restriction around the clock, without a book to read or a piece of paper to write on. No visit to the nurse's unit either, or questions asked about the fight that landed me in here.

I'd lost track of the hours in the day. Time lived and breathed in these walls like a parasite, sucking the life out of me, each second a reminder of each minute that stretched into an entire life.

Nights in here, there wasn't sufficient light to even see the outline of my hand. Usually, after dinner, my cell neighbor beat the walls with what could be her fist or her foot. She kept up her banging for hours. She was quiet now, so I put the time in the vicinity of midnight.

With only my thoughts to occupy endless time, I thought of what was and what may never be again, people I loved and may never see again.

My heart beat like a drum roll as I lay on the hard cot staring into pitch darkness. The darkness stared back, stubborn and spiteful, like the devil himself trying to make me regret my decision to trade my life for Vangie's freedom.

Sometime during the night or early morning, a flood of light rushed into the cell, shocking my eyes back open.

"It's your lucky day. You're going to court."

I didn't know which made me happier—the chance to shower or the chance to see the sky and take in a breath of fresh air. There was time in my life when I lived comfortably in my grimy skin and unwashed dreaded hair, but nowadays, I looked forward to the feel of hot water trickling down my body and the fresh scent of soap.

I found my shoes, held out my arms and spread my feet. First came the clamp of cold metal around my wrists, then the chain around my waist, and finally the handcuffs around my ankles.

Outside the shadows and the darkness, the officer wasn't the personification of a grizzly bear, nor did he act like he enjoyed carrying a gun. He held me gently by the arm as I shuffled through the gloomy cave. Behind each steel door I pictured hopeless eyes sunk into long faces, uncombed, matted hair and un-brushed teeth, bodies shrunk into corners, balled up on a cot, or walking in circles. I knew their torment, and I felt their pain. I cried the tears I hadn't cried for myself.

"You have five minutes to shower and dress," he said.

Turned out the water wasn't hot and didn't trickle; it sputtered out of the corroded showerhead, lukewarm, wetting my body and hair with just enough water to gather lather. I showered as fast as my sore arms and legs let me, avoiding the black and blue bruises that stood out clearly in the bright lights.

The officer stood just outside the bathroom door, watching me from the other side of the plastic shower curtain that left my feet, head, and shoulders exposed. Privacy in prison is like privacy in a homeless shelter; there isn't any.

"Times up!" he yelled.

I shut off the water, and still soapy, covered myself up with a towel.

The jumper and socks left out for me were clean. I dressed and brushed my teeth. In county jail, mirrors were hard to come by, most ripped off the wall or defaced. This one was intact, reflecting back my disfigured face. The bruise around my left eye, spreading from my cheekbone and rounding up to my forehead, was the shape and color of an eggplant.

To avoid my reflection, I bent forward and rinsed the dried blood caked at the corners of my cut lip, then spat a fresh red stream into the sink.

"Times up!" the officer yelled.

White bread stuffed with cold cheese, a fruit bar, and a carton of milk was breakfast. After breakfast I was put out to pasture, so to speak. "The Dog Run," they called it, a concrete box the size of a small backyard.

"Walk, run, do jumping jacks, make snow angels...but whatever you do, you have fifteen minutes to get it done," the officer said.

The slip-on tennis shoes I wore weren't made for running. I used my time to walk.

"Times up!" the guard yelled.

In the wee hours of the morning, four of us, all chained together, were loaded into a van and driven beyond the concrete walls. The van moved through the quiet streets like a prowler in the night. Concealed from the world behind darkly tinted windows, I watched the sun clip the mountaintop, reminiscing about the great outdoors, when freedom was mine to claim.

We pulled into an underground parking lot for Superior Court, were unloaded and then led into the bowels of the courthouse. They placed us each in our own holding cell. We had plenty of time to think about our alleged crimes before going before the judge

Some hours later, Ross and Clarissa walked in, or started to walk in before they stopped and stared at me as if they had encountered a monster. Clarissa, her hand pressed to her neck, looked as if it pained her to see me.

Ross cleared his throat. "You'll be alright," he said, as though to convince himself that I would be okay, and if not today, some day.

Clarissa sat next to me and clutched my hand. "We're going to do everything we can to get you released on bail. Stay strong."

Ross hitched up the legs of his suit paints and squatted before me like a coach preparing his team for a big game. I listened to him explain the arraignment process with little hope I'd wake up a free woman tomorrow, little hope I'd ever feel the sun again.

When Ross and Clarissa left the cell, I waited for my turn in court. Eventually my number was called, and two guards escorted me upstairs by elevator.

My hands and feet shackled, I hobbled into the court-room. Clarissa warned me not to look around. I should've listened. At a glance I saw people packing the court benches. I was a seventh grader in a classroom full of laughing heads all over again, unable to put two syllables together to form an audible word and feeling like a freak of nature.

The two court officers stood me between Ross and Clarissa.

The bailiff called the court to order and the Honorable Margaret Jimmerson, a regal black woman with silver hair, took her seat at the bench.

Another black woman stood on the opposite side of the courtroom wearing a pants suit that loosely fit her tall, lean body, and her short, tapered hair parted to one side. My eyes jumped back into their sockets when I caught sight of her serious mug.

"Kimberly Fitzgerald for the People, Your Honor," she said.

Ross fastened a button on his suit jacket and cleared his throat. "Ross E. Lewis for the defense, Your Honor."

After reading to me my constitutional rights, the judge asked me to state my full legal name for the record.

I heard a pen drop in my silence that filled the courtroom.

"Do you need me to restate the question, Ms. Cooper?"

"No, ma'am. My name is Vangie Annette Cooper," I lied.

"Can you speak up so that I can hear you please?"

"Oh. Sorry, Your Honor. Vangie Annette Cooper!" I said it as loudly as my voice would carry, which wasn't very far.

"Thank you, Ms. Cooper. I must advise you that there has been a complaint filed against you alleging the crime of murder. The complaint alleges that on or about June 27, 2016, in violation of section one, eighty, seven of the state penal code, that you, Vangie Annette Cooper, committed a felony by willfully, unlawfully, and with malice and forethought, murdered Todd Ethan Bryant; a crime punishable by imprisonment for a term of twenty-five years to life , or life without the possibility of parole, or by death. How do you plead to the charge, Ms. Cooper?"

Not guilty, not guilty, not guilty, Clarissa had told me.

"I plead not guilty, Your Honor," I said, strongly.

The prosecutor and Ross argued.

"Your Honor, the proceedings are founded on assumptions and not the facts," Ross argued. "We respectfully request that this Court dismiss the murder charges against Ms. Cooper. She's suffered enough."

"Mr. Lewis, you have brought several requests before the court. Motion to dismiss is denied. As for your motion to recuse the assistant district attorney from prosecuting this case, on grounds that she has a conflict of interest, I am aware of the prosecutor's personal relationship with both the defendant and the victim in this case and have read your brief in support of your motion. Motion is denied."

The vein in Ross's neck pulsated.

"Ms. Fitzgerald, what is the People's position on bail?" asked the judge.

"Your Honor, due to the nature and seriousness of the alleged crime, we believe the defendant is a danger to the community and a flight risk. The People respectfully asks the Court to hold the defendant in custody without bond, pending the disposition of these charges."

"With all due respect, Your Honor, my client is a law school graduate and an upstanding citizen in the community with no prior criminal record," Ross said.

"*Pa-lease.*"

"Are you making an argument, Ms. Fitzgerald?" asked the judge.

"Not at this time, Your Honor."

"You may continue, Counsel."

Ross cleared his throat. "As I was saying, we respectfully ask the Court to consider a reasonable and fair bond based on my client's lack of prior criminal history and her good standing in the community. Ms. Cooper deserves a fair and reasonable bond be set so she can remain out of custody as we prove her innocence."

The prosecutor fired back. "The evidence of guilt in this case is overwhelming, Your Honor, and rebuts any argument for release on bond based on the defendant's community standing and lack of criminal history. As argued by the defense, Ms. Cooper has the legal training to understand and comprehend these proceedings and the adeptness to obstruct the very law she purports to uphold. She is a flight risk and danger to the community..."

"Where's the evidence supporting your argument that my client is a flight risk?" Ross rustled through the papers on the table. "Because I don't see any."

"Save the theatrics for trial, Mr. Lewis, should it come to that," said the judge. "Your arguments have been heard. Bail is set at two million dollars, on the condition that Ms. Cooper surrenders her passport and that she is placed under home confinement for the safety of the community.

The preliminary hearing in the matter is set ten days from today." The judge banged her gavel. "Court adjourned!"

For obvious reasons, I didn't react to the judge's decision one way or another, given I didn't have two million dollars to bail myself out of jail.

Ross took the news like a coach winning the championship game, pumping his fist. The prosecutor didn't take the news so well; her mocha colored skin looked sun torched when, just after throwing me shade, she left the courtroom.

J etlag and two rounds of sangria last night had gotten the best of Vangie.

As she wrestled herself out of a dark sleep, opening her weary eyes, she couldn't remember which country she was in. The tranquil sound of ocean waves, the plush platform bed cradling her, one of the world's most expensive surfboards strung from the ceiling as a visual art piece, and the mega flat screen TV mounted to the wall above the enclosed fireplace jogged her memory.

Ronnie was a true minimalist and too impulsive to inhabit one residence for long periods of time, which kept him hopping Learjet's and traversing the globe. His tri-level bachelor's sanctuary was in Hermosa Beach, California, known as the Beverly Hills of the South Bay Coastline. From where Vangie lay in bed, she had a boardwalk view of the pacific through the glass doors that opened to the terrace.

Vangie didn't feel a smidgen of the peace and tranquility the ocean sounds usually brought her. She stared out into the horizon, watching the waves rush to shore and retreat back to sea. Kids chased foam while surfers rode the next big wave, seeking a thrill.

Reminded of Ronnie's love for riding waves, she rolled onto her back and looked to her left to find his side of the bed empty. She had a hazy memory of his body curved behind hers last night.

Minutes later Ronnie emerged from the bathroom fully dressed. Ronnie's typical wardrobe consisted of tank tops, sweats, cargo shorts, swim trunks, tennis shoes, Tees worn with skinny jeans, or a pair of flip-flops. But that was the old Ronnie. This Ronnie wore a blue slim-cut suit, a white open collar dress shirt, and fawn colored hard-soled shoes. Vangie scarcely recognized him.

She sat up. "You look great, Ron." *Fine* was the word she had in mind.

"Point taken. Stick to my sober look." Ronnie ambled toward her. "Are you good?"

"Are *you?*"

"I'm a bundle of pulsating fibers, but I'm definitely good; one hundred percent primed for the firing squad."

"You'll get a standing ovation."

"They'll lose interest before I surpass the ten-minute pitch threshold." Ronnie stood at the side of the bed, staring at her pensively.

"What?" she said, on guard.

"Give me the go and I'll make the call."

"No go."

"What's your objection?"

Tired of repeating herself, Vangie sighed. If hiring Ronnie's dream team of sharks was the simple solution to a legal night-mare, she would've turned herself in and set Angie free.

"Bye, Ron."

"If anyone stops by the house, you know what to do."

"Like one of your groupies?" She pursed her lips and rolled her eyes at him.

Ignoring her jealous remark, Ronnie said, "You'll be here when I get back?" His question resonated with skepticism.

She kept a straight face. "Where else would I be?"

"Right."

She waited for Ronnie to leave, but he dawdled, rocking on the heels of his dress shoes, his hands stuffed inside pant pockets. There was something else on his mind and Vangie didn't have the time to listen. She had overslept as it was.

"I've told you the story of Zeke the Great, haven't I?" he said, much to her impatience.

"Which story?" She figured she had heard them all.

"Bring your brats to work day."

Vangie frowned. "Brats? That's a new one, even for Zeke."

"My dad's way of being perversely humorless. Chockfull of himself, he stood big bro and I in front of his kiss-ass team of producers, studio heads, and directors and told us to pitch him a screenplay idea. Fucking incredible."

"So, what happened, Ron?" she pressed.

"Big bro, Johnny on the spot, killed it, and got offered a pilot deal. Little bro literally pissed his pants." Blood rushed to Ronnie's face. He ran his hand through his perfectly moussed hair and shook his head. "One of the finer moments of my life."

Knowing how important this meeting was for Ronnie, the chance to pitch his new venture to investors without his father's backing for the first time in his life, Vangie said, "You'll kill it."

"Killing it is overly ambitious. I'll try hard not to piss my pants." Ronnie put on his charming smile, but Vangie could see the terrified little boy behind his melancholy eyes.

Before he could walk off, she caught him by the hand, and in a moment of speechlessness, merely stared at him, refusing to shed a tear.

"You want to me stay? I'll stay. Screw the pitch."

She shook her head. "It's not that."

"What is it?"

She searched her mind for the right words to let him down easy. "I don't know how I'll ever repay you, Ron."

"That's bullshit. It was all my pleasure."

"I'm serious. You've been a great friend to me."

"It's great to know we're still great friends. For a minute I thought we had a future together..." The wounded look in Ronnie's eyes made Vangie want to recant her statement, but it was best to leave him with the wrong impression. By no small miracle, their longstanding relationship hadn't become public knowledge, not yet. If she hadn't put her Detroit cell phone number in her mother's name at the ripe old age of fifteen, her phone records could prove vital to the prosecution's case against her.

Ronnie bent forward and kissed her lips tenderly, hatching butterflies in her stomach.

An hour after Ronnie left the house, Vangie left too.

Camouflaged in a short, auburn wig and faux eyeglasses, Vangie walked into the five-star hotel, strutting confidently to discourage questioning glares. She passed rose petals afloat in an arrangement of soaring glass vases as she approached the check-in desk.

"I'll take what's available," she said to the lone reservationist. Steady handed, she removed her identification from her Gucci wallet tucked inside her Gucci handbag and presented her counterfeit ID and cash passport.

The woman batted her eyes. "Our rooms start at six hundred a night," she said.

When that didn't scare her off, the reservationist took a closer look at Vangie's identification. Vangie suspected trouble when the woman disappeared behind a door.

Trouble came in the form of a tall, freckled-faced man wearing a suit and a badge that said "Manager."

"Early check-in?" he asked nicely enough.

"Early flight."

"Visiting the area?"

"Business," she said, avoiding small talk.

"Family in town?"

Vangie was not going to answer another question. To boost her haughtiness, she had dressed very French and very chic in dark jeans rolled up at the ankle, flat sole shoes, a starkly white V-neck Tee, and a summer neck scarf.

The manager studied her identification and then said, "How many nights will you be staying with us, Ms. Silva?"

"Just one."

Barring any complications, she thought

He handed over her key. "Will you be needing assistance with your luggage?"

"No. Thank you."

Wheeling her Louie Vuitton duffle bag stuffed with her worldly possession, Vangie bee-lined to the business center.

Once alone, she logged on to the Internet using a hotel computer.

Seeing Wade, the man who had dominated her life and driven her every premeditated act for the past six years, would set her back years emotionally, and remind her of how deeply and insanely she loved Wade, enough to die for and kill over. But she had to know, something.

Heart thrashing, Vangie Googled Wade Fitzgerald. Finger trembling, she clicked the first link and breathed easier. The link had nothing to do with Wade but with Wade's grandfather, the patriarch of the Fitzgerald family. The links glorifying Wade Fitzgerald the Second's success as a real estate tycoon and well-respected defense attorney ran for pages.

Vangie entered a new query: Wade Fitzgerald, optometrist. Memories pummeled her as she read over Wade the Fourth's curriculum vitae, including his medical training at Johns Hopkins, where he specialized in neuro-ophthalmology and received the dean's award, numerous research awards, and was elected into the Alpha Omega Alpha Medical Honor Society.

The next link stilled Vangie's thumping heart for a split second before a cyclone whirled inside of her. Hypnotized by the face that stole her heart at first sight, she read the article hurriedly the first time, deliberately the second.

"I think I would know if my fiancé were capable of homicide," the article quoted Wade as saying. She could just imagine his dignified look of offense.

Vangie logged off the computer and rushed out of the room.

Four floors up, she sat on the hotel's king-sized bed, sorting out twenty, fifty, and one hundred dollars bills into neat piles. Tears fogged her eyes, ready to spill, but she held them at bay as she haphazardly counted out what was left of the fifty thousand dollars she had taken with her on the run.

After her fourth attempt, she felt confident she had enough on hand to get by until she could get her hands on the money in her bank account. She stuffed a large portion of the cash back into the manila envelope and placed it inside the hotel safe.

Coming out of a trance, Vangie found the minibar, snatched up a container of cashew nuts and a bottle of chilled water, and slammed the door shut with her foot.

The window had a bird's eye view of the corporate building across the street. Vangie peeked through the sheer drapery, watching those coming and going closely as she took slow sips of water.

When the mid-morning sun flickered against the glass façade, casting a picturesque light over the city's skyline, Vangie's mind was whisked back to Loyola Law School, which was just a short distance from where she stood. If she walked a few blocks, she would come across one or two fine dining establishments where she and Clarissa debated ethics and criminal procedures over glasses of wine.

More significant in her memories of the downtown Los Angeles area was her memory of one of the most sought after and swanky wedding venues in the city and around the country, a 35,000-square-foot cathedral with a luxuriant garden where she and Wade had planned to exchange their wedding vows. It was sure to be a fairytale held the perfect time of year for a wedding, autumn, when the air turned warm and crisp and the leaves colorful. That was before she crashed and burned, of course.

Pulling herself out of her depressing reverie, Vangie dressed in a hurry, exchanging her French attire for a pair of baggy boyfriend jeans, a black, faded hoodie, and the oldest tennis shoes she could find at the thrift shop. After removing all traces of makeup from her face, and brushing it into a bushy ponytail, she left the hotel.

Hands tucked in the hoodie's front pouch as if concealing a loaded weapon, she crossed the busy street, walking with her neck withdrawn into her shoulders as though to hide herself in broad daylight.

Vangie's undaunted determination ended once she entered the high rise on Grand Avenue. Each step she took thereafter she thought to turn back and devise another strategy. But there seemed no turning back at this point.

On the tenth floor, Vangie removed her sunglasses and her hood and then walked boldly into the office. Anything short of a show of confidence might tip off the occupants.

The signage, *Ross E. Lewis & Associates,* made a bold statement in bronze letters behind the receptionist's console. Aside from the two leather armchairs and glass coffee table, the room wasn't well thought out or, seemingly, ready to receive visitors, Vangie noticed. She could hear a printer grinding out paper in the back somewhere.

The phone rang, which didn't startle Vangie as much as when Clarissa barreled into the receptionist area as if a fire alarm had gone off. Vangie stared at her best friend, teary eyed. On an ordinary day she would've complimented Clarissa on her impeccable look. Not a hair on Clarissa's long, faux ponytail was out of place, and Clarissa's black and white dress perfectly matched her pumps.

"Oh. My. God!" Clarissa mumbled into the palm of her hand.

Vangie, looking as submissive as her overconfidence would allow, said. "Hi. I'm here about my sister, Vangie."

Clarissa fanned her eyes with her hand. "I'm sorry for being demonstrative, but when I heard Vangie had an identical twin, I couldn't believe it. How could she hide you from me, her BFF! Can I hug you?"

Classic Clarissa, Vangie thought, smiling to herself. She wanted to profusely apologize to her BFF for her deceitfulness, but she stayed in character, pulling back from Clarissa's hug quickly and keeping her hands inside the pouch of her hoodie, her eyes evading direct contact with Clarissa's. No one knew the complexities of Angie's demeanor better than her.

"Excuse our mess. We just moved in, so to speak." Clarissa picked up an artificial tropical floor plant and moved it to the corner of the room, then proceeded to arrange magazines on the coffee table.

The phone rang again.

"I'd better get that. There's coffee, tea, and water. Help yourself." Clarissa snatched up the phone. "Ross E. Lewis and Associates. How can we help with your legal needs today?"

Keeping composed, Vangie prepared a single Styrofoam cup of coffee in a Keurig and stood nearby, waiting for Clarissa to wrap up her phone call.

When Clarissa hung up, she said, "I hope you don't mind waiting a few minutes longer. Our lead counselor is on his way and can answer any questions you have about Vangie's case. He shouldn't be long."

"I don't have long," Vangie said with some urgency. "Can't you help me?"

Clarissa placed her hand on her forehead as if to think over a difficult decision. "It couldn't hurt to get started without him, I guess."

Vangie certainly didn't think it would hurt. Clarissa had the makings of a great lawyer their first year in law school and the passion for the profession she never possessed. It was Clarissa's lack of confidence that concerned her.

They made their way to Clarissa's office, where Clarissa sat behind a white distressed vintage desk and Vangie sat in one of the two petite, paisley chairs swirling with brilliant colors. A stack of books waited on the floor to be shelved, and artwork leaned against the wall awaited being hung.

Hands clasped studiously on the desk, Clarissa stared at Vangie, her expression one of solidarity and trustworthiness. Before Clarissa could bombard her with questions, Vangie set a letter-sized envelope on the desk.

"That's fifteen hundred dollars to cover my sister's initial legal fees. I'll have more soon," Vangie said.

Clarissa looked ready to cry again. "Vangie is my best friend. I'd take her case pro bono if it was left up to me. I'm one hundred percent positive Vangie is innocent."

At that, Vangie said, "I have something to tell you, in the strictest confidence."

"Your confidences will not leave this office."

Vangie took a deep breath for courage. She hadn't thoroughly thought her plan through. To add to her trepidation, Clarissa and Wade were first cousins, and even though Clarissa's love for Wade had been tarnished over the years by what Clarissa perceived as family betrayal, "blood is always thicker than water" as her mother would say. For once, Vangie agreed with her mother. She could only hope Clarissa would not put her loyalty to family over their friendship.

Ultimately, Vangie put her faith in attorney-client privilege, which legally bound Clarissa to confidentiality, since technically she *was* the client and not Angie. *Here goes nothing...*

Seven

Clarissa expression was a synthesis of bewilderment, incredulity, and skepticism. "How do I know *you're* not the imposter?"

"You'll have to trust me." Attempting to convince Clarissa that she was telling the truth might only cast more doubt in Clarissa's mind, Vangie had decided.

Clarissa pushed back from her desk, walked around it, lowered herself to her knees, and began a frenzied search through the books spread out on the floor.

"Found it!" Clarissa handed Vangie a familiar book. "Recite the side note on the first page, sight unseen," Clarissa said, hands at her hips.

The Bluebook was a required text for first year law students. Clarissa still had the used copy she purchased back then. Clarissa had taken the crude drawing of a penis on the first page as an omen and swore it had cursed her life.

"If you're reading this, you're screwed," Vangie recited, her eyes never leaving Clarissa's resolute ones.

Clarissa's irises sparkled, but her pursed lips didn't curve into a smile. "That could be hearsay. Who was my first boyfriend?"

"Jonathan," Vangie said without hesitation. How could she forget Jonathan? No guy Clarissa dated after Jonathan could measure up, not even Ross.

Clarissa's arms dropped to her sides. She bunched her forehead and leered at Vangie like a familiar stranger. "If you can answer my next question, I'll be convinced that you're Vangie."

Vangie held her breath. Clarissa would likely ask her something so inconsequential that only a person with a photographic memory could call it up.

"What'd I score on my second exam?"

Vangie wanted to object to Clarissa's loosely framed question. "Second exam" was misleading and could have easily tripped her up if she hadn't known which exam Clarissa was referencing.

"You failed your second bar exam by three points and swore on your father's life you'd never sit for the bar again. I brought over a bottle of my best wine; you chased it with vodka and got so drunk you passed out on the floor. Did you pass third round?"

Clarissa nodded, tears welling in her eyes again.

Smiling, Vangie said, "I'm proud of you, Riss."

And she was proud her best friend for accomplishing her lifelong dream of becoming an attorney. If circumstances were different, they would dine at one of L.A.'s finest restaurants tonight and toast Clarissa's achievement with the oldest bottle of wine from the owner's personal cellar.

When Clarissa held out her arms, Vangie fell into them, bearing down on her friend's chest with the overwhelming weight of her own burdens.

"I can't believe you killed Todd," Clarissa whispered in her ear.

Vangie couldn't believe she killed Todd either. Numbed by the gravity of the moment, her knees caved, and she dropped into the chair.

Clarissa repositioned the empty chair, sat directly in front of her, and stared unnervingly at her. "Are we talking premeditated murder, Van?"

Vangie knew whether she profusely denied premeditation or cried self defense, her answer would be self-incriminating. She leaned on the law.

"It's your constitutional obligation to defend me, so does it really matter?"

"It's not *my* obligation, Van. Ross is your counsel and he's going to get real ghetto when he finds out you colluded with your twin."

"Angie didn't have anything to do with what happened to..." Todd's name jammed in her throat, discharging a foul taste in her mouth.

"I'm not throwing your twin under the bus, Van, but she is complicit in the eyes of the law. And, by the way, you haven't told me what happened or substantiated your story. You said you had business with Todd that night, and that one thing led to another. What *one* thing? And what business could you possibly have had with Todd-creepy-Bryant...?" Clarissa's doll eyes expanded. "Oh. My. God. You didn't, Vangie... Did you?"

Vangie felt a sharp knife to her gut. She couldn't bring herself to speak of that night. Tears pressed against her eye sockets again. She held them in check with a heart of steel, walked to the window, and stared at the city skyline. A sea of blood stared back.

Moments later Clarissa placed a hand on her shoulder and gave it a gentle squeeze. "I'm sorry for insinuating that you got with Todd behind Wade's back. I know how we both hated Todd... Wait. That's incriminating. Strike that." Clarissa sighed. "Forget what I think, Van. Consider what the twelve people in the box will think if this case goes to trial."

"Rissa! Who locked the front door?" someone yelled.

"Shit. It's Ross." Clarissa pressed a finger to her lips and whispered. "Stay here."

Baring her soul to her best friend paled in comparison to confessing her sins to Ross. She needed a few hours, a glass of wine, maybe two, before facing his judgment.

"I'm leaving," Vangie said.

"You can't leave. I could be charged with being an accessory."

"And sanctioned for violating attorney-client confidences if you tell Ross what I disclosed to you."

"God, Van. Do you really think I'm so dumb I don't know the rules of ethics? As your counselor, Ross is entitled to privileged information. And what about your twin, what is she entitled to?"

Vangie did not have an adequate comeback.

Clarissa raised the palm of her hand for her to stay put and closed the office door behind her when she left.

Ready to run like hell, Vangie waited a few minutes before peeking her head into the hallway. She could hear Ross and Clarissa's muffled conversation across the hallway. She made it as far as the reception area before retracing her steps.

If she was going to be crucified, Ross might as well pound the first nail.

~

The hotel room Vangie occupied across the street had been cleared of all traceable evidence, and it now sat empty, waiting for the housekeeper to make her rounds.

Vangie sat in the passenger seat of Ross's black Benz, feeling his silent condemnation that made the drive across town, in gridlock traffic, insufferable.

He pumped his breaks, coming short of slamming into the back of a pickup truck carrying a large, hazardous load.

"This stupid mo-fo!" Ross laid on the horn with a heavy hand.

Vangie suspected his anger was directed at her and not at the careless driver. She also suspected Ross cared more about his billable hours and blowing his chance to win his first big case and gain his five seconds of fame than he cared about disbarment for harboring a known fugitive.

Vangie stared at him. "If you don't want to represent me, feel free to withdraw."

"As of right now, this minute, you don't have representation. The contract your twin forged is null and void." Ross chuckled, humorlessly. "You and your twin colluded to mastermind a hell of a crime, I'll give you that."

"Collusion would be hard to prove; I haven't seen or talked to my twin for over six years."

"Your twin was in possession of your passport and driver license at the time of arrest; your twin failed to identify herself to the authorities; your twin didn't resist arrest; your twin said enough in court to perjure herself. Those are the facts." Ross side-eyed her. "Here's another fact the prosecution will attack us with. Your twin withheld information about a crime. If I was prosecuting this case, you can believe I'd prove collusion."

Vangie turned her tearful gaze back to gridlocked traffic. Years of being Angie's spokesperson, years without a social life, years of family obligations...she had longed for this day, prayed for Angie to speak to anyone besides her. On one hand, finding out Angie had finally broken her vow of silence overjoyed her, but on the other hand she felt cheated out of the most important moment of her twin's life and hers. A lone tear dropped from her eye. She swiped it away quickly.

They arrived at the home of Valentina Martin-Lewis, Ross's deceased mother. The initial sight of the little pink Spanish style house warned Vangie to lower her expectations, drastically. The stucco was soot stained and weathered, the front lawn patches of dirt sprouting more weeds than grass.

The small home, set in the heart of East Los Angeles, was Ross's prize possession. If Clarissa had her druthers, the house would've been sold to new owners or, at the very least, rented out. Ross refused to do either.

Clarissa and Ross had debated where to hide her. Clarissa lobbied for their Burbank condo, launching into a monologue about how little the Fitzgerald's knew about her life and how they had never taken the time out of their privileged lives to visit her, not once, so the risk would be extremely low. Ross said they couldn't risk the DA's investigative hounds discovering they had the wrong twin in custody.

So here she was, stuck in this dump.

Ross pulled his Benz into the driveway, easing toward the battered one-car garage door. The backyard lawn was in better shape than the front, from what Vangie could see behind her darkly tinted sunglasses. She slipped out of the car and through the backdoor. Removing her sunglasses didn't shed a better light on the depressing residence that reeked of everything old and nothing new.

They walked through the small kitchen reminiscent of another decade. Down the hallway, cluttered with dusty family photos, Ross stopped at the first room, which was presumably off-limits. He closed the door before she could look inside.

"This is you, right here," he said of the second bedroom at the end of the hallway. The room had enough square footage to hold a full-sized bed and chest of drawers, both in grave need of replacement.

Vangie frowned.

"Hey. It got me through high school. The ladies didn't complain."

After giving her a cursory tour, Ross's parting words were, "Don't leave, don't call anyone, and have your facts straight when I get back." He handed her a legal file bearing her name. "Look for discrepancies."

Vangie dragged herself to the leather sofa, the nicest and newest piece of furniture she'd come across so far, which was complimented by a leather recliner and a flat screen TV of substantial size.

She cracked open the file. The sight of Angie's mug shot stapled to the corner of the officer's report made her stomach ball into a fist so tight she couldn't breathe. She snapped the file shut and closed her eyes, but the image of Angie's grayed-out face and look of terror were permanently imprinted in her mind's eye. The stark photo spoke volumes of what Angie had endured because of her.

I'm so, so sorry, Angie.

Vangie took in a courageous breath and reopened the file. It didn't take her much digging to determine the prosecution's strategy—to conceal discovery. Much of the information had been redacted, of course. According to the officer's report, Angie arrived in Los Angeles from Detroit at approximately 10:00 A.M, at LAX. She had in her possession a backpack and suitcase, and she did not resist arrest.

Questions surrounding Angie's arrest plagued Vangie. Why hadn't Angie simply informed the police she had been misidentified? The court would've had no choice but to drop the charges.

Feeling a splitting headache coming on, Vangie set the file on the coffee table and walked to the kitchen in search of whatever she could find to drink. The refrigerator and cabinets were virtually empty, so she found a cup and filled it with tap water.

Returning to the living room, Vangie curled up on the couch. Her burner phone was on the table calling out for her attention. She wondered if Ronnie had killed his pitch. She even contemplated calling her mother, but that would be more trouble than it would be worth and leave a trail of crumbs for the prosecution to follow. She adhered to Ross's warning and refrained from calling anyone.

The fading afternoon sun strained through the blinds, offering slight light to the gloomy house. Vangie's eyes grew heavy. She drifted off to a dark place.

The front door slammed, rousing Vangie out of fitful sleep before she knew it.

"It's me," Clarissa announced. A light clicked on; heels clanked against the tarnished wood. "It took longer than I expected. Traffic, groceries, and the requisite Chinese food; I hope you're hungry. I'm totally starved."

"I'm not hungry," Vangie said. Two cups of coffee and cashews had satisfied her nervous stomach for the day.

"I know how you feel, Van. This is surreal for me too. I literally pinched myself driving here."

"Did you buy anything to drink?" Vangie called after her.

"Cabernet!" Clarissa said over her shoulder, reading her mind. "Plus, orange juice, breakfast supplies, munchies, and Pan Asian Kitchen. Our favorite!"

After banging around in the kitchen, Clarissa returned to the living area with a look of disgust. "I can't find a set of stemware in this shithole. Are you sure you'll be okay here, Van?"

"I'm sure. I've lived in enough shitholes."

"That's hard for me to believe."

"Believe it."

"Well, I don't believe it!" Clarissa shot back.

Ross walked into the house like he was late for an important meeting. "Let's huddle up."

Vangie took in a long breath, sat up, picked up her file, and walked to the table where Clarissa had a spread of kung pao chicken, sautéed vegetables, soft noodles, and sushi as if she was hosting a dinner party. This gathering to discuss her chances in a murder case and review the merits of the prosecution's case against her was a party Vangie could've skipped.

"Taste this, babe." Clarissa attempted to hand feed Ross a sushi roll.

He recoiled. "I hate sushi, baby."

"The philistine that you are, how could I forget." Clarissa rolled her eyes and popped the roll into her mouth. "I know how much you love great sushi, Van. Which would you like? Tiger or spicy salmon?"

"I'll take something to drink," Vangie replied.

"Every strategy meeting calls for a nice red." Clarissa uncorked the bottle of wine.

Before a word was spoken about the case, Ross streamed music through a wireless speaker loud enough to drown out their voices without disturbing the peace. Clarissa turned on her iPad, and Vangie concentrated on the cobwebs in the corner of the room while nursing her mug of wine.

"Our best-case scenario is an acquittal. Worst case, we'll tie the case up in pretrial and strike a plea deal. Right now, the DA doesn't have a case, as long as your twin doesn't get charged with battery before I come up with an exit strategy."

Clarissa shot Ross a cautionary glance that raised the hair on the back of Vangie's neck. "What battery?" she said, volleying her eyes between Ross and Clarissa.

"I thought you told her?" Ross said to Clarissa.

"I didn't have the heart to, Ross, before you opened your big mouth!"

"You didn't have the heart to tell me what?" Vangie snapped.

"Your twin got into it with some crazy ass females, got placed in solitary, and got a little busted up. Before you panic, she's alive," Ross said.

Vangie had exceeded panic. Fury rippled through her like a forest fire. When she opened her mouth to speak, an unrecognizable voice came through, deep and throaty. "Get her out!"

"Slow your roll and think about this for a minute."

Vangie slammed her fist on the glass table so hard wine splattered. "Get her out or I'm turning myself in!"

"And play right into the prosecution's hands too, a two for one deal; lock your twin up for five to twenty and throw you in the pen for life," Ross said.

"She'll be charged with a felony, Van," Clarissa added. "You can't help your twin if you're both in jail."

Vangie knew all too well the legal ramifications for Angie should she turn herself in at this point. She would have to cross that bridge when she came to it.

She shot for the front door and banged on the locked security screen with an iron fist. "Let me out!"

In an unexpected display of sympathy, Ross walked up and hugged her. Vangie wanted to sob into his hard chest like a baby.

"Get her out, Ross," Vangie said through clinched teeth.

"I got this."

"Team hug." Clarissa joined the embrace.

"Can we get back to business before somebody calls the cops?" Ross said.

Eight

Vangie hugged her knees and rocked from side to side. The last time she recalled rocking like this was when she and Angie were in a strange place, on what could've been a bed if it had a frame or box springs. Angie had lain next to her, sleeping soundly, while she listened to the grownups on the other side of the door party all night. Other kids were sleeping on the mattress with them, and one soaked her with pee.

When her mother finally showed her face the next morning, she swooped her and Angie out of bed with loving arms and carried them both home on her hips—wherever home was at that time—promising never to leave them alone again. Her mother was full of empty promises.

Rocking hadn't been an effective way to alleviate her anxiety back then and it wasn't effective now. Not even the six hundred thread satin sheets and goose down comforter Clarissa had been kind enough to bring from home could relax Vangie.

She had visited a maximum-security prison as a law student, witnessed firsthand what became of offenders locked in solitary confinement, people restricted to a black hole and left in dehumanizing conditions. She couldn't imagine Angie being placed in solitary. Angie was her better half, "the angel child," and she herself was the "devil's spawn," to hear her mother tell it. Angie could do no wrong and she could do no right.

She had hoped to God that Angie's life had turned out better than her own, but maybe she was expecting too much of Angie. God help her if Angie had lost her mind like their mother had lost hers.

Listening to the whistling winds outside her bedroom window, Vangie made productive use of her nervous energy, calculating various forms of bail bonds collateral available to her—cash, property, land, jewelry, etc.—which didn't come close to two million dollars.

She paid cash for her two-bedroom loft back in Detroit, and the row of abandoned and boarded up homes she had purchased, all depreciating in a slow climbing real estate market.

Her eighty thousand dollar Mercedes Benz, she hoped, had been dismantled by now and sold, part-by-part, so that wouldn't help her, either

Her diamonds, gifted to her by Antonio Moretti, appraised somewhere between $7,500 and $10,000 dollars per carat, making them highly desirable by most any reputable buyer. She could cash them in inconspicuously.

Then there was her diamond encrusted Tiffany engagement ring, all she had left to remind her of Wade's love for her. She would as soon cut off her ring finger than to part with it, but then, again…

Vangie sighed. What did it matter? She couldn't use her own assets to bail herself out jail anyway. If she could just gain access to her bank account, she could put up the ten percent cash bond needed to set Angie free.

She stopped rocking when she heard a door slam, and then she flew into the living room where she found Ross suited up and *swagged out*, as always.

"Did you file the motion?" she said breathlessly, as if she had just run a marathon to get from one room to the next.

Ross looked up from sorting through mail and stared at her with eyes that said, "Do something with herself. Take a shower. Comb your hair."

"Well, have you?" she pressed.

"Have I filed a bail modification motion? Bad call."

"It's not a bad call. It's practice. Two million dollars is excessive in any case."

"Judges aren't in the habit of granting bail for aggravated assault or handing out get-out-of-jail-free cards. I can live with two mil. It's not about the money; it's about the win. If I were in your shoes, I'd appreciate the court's leniency."

Vangie quietly agreed with Ross. The judge granting bail, in light of the murder charge, was nothing short of a miracle. But whether the court was on their side remained an open question, as did Ross's aptitude to defend her effectively. He may dress the part of a high paid lawyer, but at twenty-eight years old, the graduate of a third rate law school, and having little felony trial experience, Ross's curriculum vitae didn't measure up to Kimberly Fitzgerald's. A Yale Law alum with ten years of felony trial experience under her belt, Kimmy had the motive and aptitude to send her to death row.

"Speaking of paper..." He swished his fingers together. "I need that next installment."

Vangie cast a cynical eye on him. "How much more?"

"Two thousand."

"I just gave you fifteen hundred, yesterday. Cash."

"You gave Rissa fifteen, not me. That's the friends and family rate. Any other client would incur a five thousand dollar retainer coming out the gate for a capital offense. Do I have to break it down for you? There's a retainer fee and hourly fees, travel expenses, investigative fees, rent, *food* for my clients… Running a law firm ain't a joke."

Vangie knew, if she spoke her mind right now, she would do irreparable damage to a delicate relationship. She returned from the bedroom and slapped two grand into Ross's waiting hand, cash she desperately needed to bail Angie out of jail.

Ross folded the bills neatly, clamped them with a money clip, and slipped the money into his pant pocket. "You'll thank me when your case is thrown out of court."

Deciding to let Ross have the last word, Vangie sat on the couch and aimed the remote at the television. "When's Clarissa coming?" she said coolly.

"Later."

"Can you leave the key to the security door?"

Ross cocked his head to one side. "For what?"

"In case there's a fire; I'd like to get out alive, Ross."

Ross dipped his hand inside a brass container filled with loose change on the end table and handed her a lone key. "If there is a fire or any other emergency, call me before you make a move."

Vangie took the key from Ross without batting an eye. "Thanks."

The minute Ross left the house, she showered, put on jeans and a clean tank top, knotted her hair at the crown of her head, and returned to the living room to wait for Clarissa.

Clarissa showed up around sunset. If they couldn't dine out, Clarissa was determined to dine in just as finely if it meant bringing her own dinnerware and stemware to the party. They could've been dining in Beverly Hills, given the place settings. For Vangie, that would be a welcome venue change.

On the dining table covered with a white tablecloth, Clarissa set two white dinner plates, saucers of toasted baguettes with a side spices swimming in olive oil, two long-stemmed wine glasses, and a nice bottle of red wine. The fragrance of shrimp, clams, mussels, and calamari garnished with marinated linguini brought an appetizing smell to the old house.

Throughout dinner Vangie kept a watchful eye on the grandfather clock as she pushed food around her plate and took small bites.

"You're thinking about the bond, aren't you?" Clarissa said, obviously noticing her disinterest in their conversation. "If I had the money, I'd loan it to you, interest free. You know I would, Van."

"I know, Riss. Thanks."

"True confession. I'm broke."

Vangie kept Clarissa's true confession in perspective. "Broke" for Clarissa wasn't going without a meal or being evicted from her luxury two-bedroom condo. Broke for Clarissa meant no longer having access to the Fitzgerald fortune and a rolling bank account now that she had severed ties with her dear old dad, Gerald Fitzgerald, for good.

"Ross and I had to beg, borrow, and dang near steal money to start our firm…" Clarissa's eyes grew large as if a revelation struck her. "Did I tell you Granddad had a stroke?"

Vangie paused to catch her breath. "A stroke?"

"I know, right. It's hard for any of us to believe. Seventy-five years old and never been sick or hospitalized a day in his life." Glassy eyed, Clarissa shook her head. "If it wasn't for Granddad, Ross and I wouldn't have a firm. Do you know what he did?"

Vangie waited for the punch line.

"Took us out to lunch at *the* Captains Club in *the* executive suite. I've finally been granted access. I guess I'm worthy of something in that family." Clarissa rolled her doll eyes, which shone with pride.

Whether or not Clarissa meant to stir up painful memories that Vangie wanted to forget, Clarissa had done precisely that. Vangie was whisked back in the Captain Club's executive suite during a Fitzgerald family gathering, when she felt on top of the world as the city lights floated around her. She could practically feel Wade's large hand crushing hers nervously just before he stood to announce his decision to attend Johns Hopkins Medical School and leave her behind.

"In summation, he gave us the loan, but only after giving us a protracted sermon about running a successful law firm. I can't take Ross anywhere, girl. He's so *hood*." Clarissa chuckled fondly.

"How's he doing?" Vangie asked of Wade the Second, but she was thinking of Wade the Fourth and how much he loved and respected his grandfather.

"He's recovering, slowly. Thank God he has the money to hire a private nurse around the clock." Clarissa stood and started clearing dishes from the table. To hurry Clarissa along, Vangie helped, and then she escorted Clarissa to the front door.

"Ross's plan will work, Van, just be patient," Clarissa said.

No comment from Vangie.

"If you want me to stay the night, I don't mind." Even saying it, Clarissa couldn't keep a straight face, scrunching her nose at her own suggestion of staying the night.

"I'm fine."

"Are you sure?"

"Yes, Riss."

Clarissa gave her a pitying stare, and then hurried outside. "Watch my back," she said before darting into the night and toward her car as if being chased by a phantom.

After Clarissa drove off, Vangie left the house through the back door, feeling her way down the dark alley.

Two blocks or so later, outside a mom and pop grocery store, she called for a taxi, then waited an hour for it to arrive.

Fog had descended upon the Hermosa beachfront. Vangie paid the taxi driver and hurried up the boardwalk toward Ronnie's place. A Plexiglas wall enclosed the patio that led to his front door. She mounted a flight of cobblestone stairs to the second tier and rang the doorbell.

When she didn't get an answer, she pressed the doorbell again. The thought of startling Ronnie hadn't crossed Vangie's mind until she put the key inside the lock. During Ronnie's drinking, gambling, and fast life days that kept him bar and club hopping all night, Ronnie wouldn't be home on a Tuesday night. Now Vangie worried she might disturb his sleep.

She opened the door quietly and hadn't fully entered the house when some chick emerged from the kitchen sipping a bottle of beer and looking extremely comfortable in the man's shirt she wore like a mini dress. Vangie noticed the chick's tanned legs first, which took up a major portion of her thin frame, before she noticed the mess of short blonde hair haloing the chick's face.

"I must have the wrong house" Vangie said. Ronnie walked into the living room wearing only cargo shorts as she was closing the door.

"Hey you," he said, but not with his usual I-missed-the-shit-out-you look in his eyes.

Vangie slammed the door shut. She hadn't gotten far before Ronnie caught up to her, clutched his hand around hers, and pulled her across the boardwalk toward the black sea, his bare feet sloshing through cold sand as if it was a summer day rather than a frigid night.

They faced off near an abandoned bonfire with smoldering embers.

"What the fuck, Van?"

"You tell me?" Vangie crossed her arms tightly at her chest.

"She's just a friend. We're barely on a first name basis."

Vangie would've laughed if the two-headed, green-eyed monster hadn't reared its ugly heads. She never doubted Ronnie had women lined up in his cell phone contacts. A fine, sweet, charming thirty-three-year-old millionaire from a well off family was bound to be a great catch for most any groupie. But why should she care? Ronnie had his life and she had hers; that had always been their agreement, Vangie reasoned with herself.

Filing her feelings for Ronnie in the back of her mind where she filed every man in her life who had hurt or disappointed her didn't work, however. Her feelings toward Ronnie had been compromised, the lines defining their friendship blurred. Ronnie held a significant place in her heart that she couldn't easily dismiss.

"You're incredible, Vangie. You bailed on me without so much as a screw-you note."

"And you got what you've always wanted, free of charge. I guess we both got screwed."

"My bad. I forgot. You're so fucking glorious that I've tolerated your shit just to bang you. Stop me if I'm aggrandizing."

"Whatever, Ronnie."

They stood in somber silence for a spell, Ronnie staring at her while she stared at a hill of seaweed in the near distance. A couple strolled by with their dog. A band of cyclists, out on a late ride, zipped down the boardwalk. The tide ebbed. More intense in her memory banks than the sound of the waves was the scent of the sea. It took Vangie back to the days, not so very long ago, when she and Ronnie had a mutual need for one another, when on a whim they would whisk off to an exotic tropical island to lounge in the sun, finding strength in one another's company and respite from their troubled lives. Now Ronnie treated her like a rescue mission. If he thought he could save her from herself, he was twenty-six years too late. The damage had already been done.

"It'd really be awesome if you wouldn't include me in the same category with every dude who hurt you," Ronnie said, as if he had read her mind. "I'm not that guy, Van. I'd never hurt you." He took hold of her hand. "What more do you want from me?" He sounded weary, as if he hadn't anything more to give her.

What Vangie wanted from Ronnie no longer mattered. She couldn't bring herself to ask him to bail Angie out jail. She had asked enough of him. Besides, she wasn't one to beg.

"I don't want anything from you." Her hand slipped from Ronnie's when she walked off. Ten steps later she held her breath, expecting to hear the patter of Ronnie's footsteps behind her, hoping to feel his hand clasp hers and refuse to let it go.

She looked back. Ronnie was gone.

Nine

There were specific restaurants, nightclubs, and bars in town where rich men huddled, and groupies looking for their next sugar daddy frequented these same places. Vangie wasn't looking for a sugar daddy or just any man. Her type of man would be unassumingly rich. No brand names of any kind displayed on his person, except for maybe his watch: Cartier, Piguet, Constantin, or Philippe. Belt: expensive. Shoes: basic but pricey. Age: unspecified: Race: flexible. Bank account: loaded.

Beverly Hills, Melrose, and Hollywood had been her old hangout spots. Taking precautions, Vangie had chosen Carbon Beach in Malibu as her target marketplace.

She strutted up Pacific Coast Highway and into the high-end boutique hotel. The three-story façade, obscured by mature palm trees, gave off the impression of modesty, but Vangie knew better. Some of the richest men in the city were residents of the exclusive neighborhood that took up twenty-one acres of the Pacific coast shoreline a mile or so from the hotel.

Rich men were also busy men. Catching a late meal on the fly was their custom. A few business moguls and a brief rendezvous would set her cash on hand straight, she hoped. As with the past, she would get the deed done with her eyes closed and the lights off.

In the restroom, Vangie fastened her diamond earrings. She left her neckline and wrists bare—the more casual and elegant her appearance the bigger the catch. She looked herself over in the mirror. She had dressed in one of her oldies but goodies: a black tube dress that fit her like skin. Her makeup was flawless, her fragrance irresistible. For a finishing prop, Vangie slipped on her engagement ring. A flood of grief pummeled her. She braced the marble countertop, shut her eyes, and waited for her sadness to pass.

Stilted on six-inch snakeskin pumps, Vangie accosted the woman behind the reservation desk of the Carbon Beach Diner's Club.

"Mr. and Mrs. Silva," she announced.

"Hi." The woman looked her over and then over her roster. "Will your husband be joining you tonight, Mrs. Silva?"

"When he gets here, please tell him I'm inside," Vangie said in the take-no-prisoners tone the rich are prone to.

A hostess escorted her inside. The restaurant was an elegant space with sleek teakwood floors and white leather seating. Vangie's eyes scanned the room for the best seats in the house. Seating was everything; the best seats were typically reserved for the A-listers.

Real or imagined, Vangie felt all were eyes on her when she walked in. However jumpy she may have been on the inside, she maintained a poised façade, holding her chin high. In a city with over four million people, a wanted criminal would be hard to identify, she reassured herself. Besides nobody was actually looking for her. At last report, she had been apprehended and locked up.

Seated at a table for two, nestled in the circular bend of the patio overlooking "Billionaire's Beach," Vangie had an entrancing view of the dark sea. She watched the white waves crash softly against a mound of boulders below, taking leisure sips of wine, vying time. Every so often she glanced around the room as servers hustled to earn big tips from the rich and the famous before the night ended.

Her first target caught her eye when he walked into the restaurant. She examined him discreetly as he crossed the deck and took his seat two tables to her right. He appeared pensive, as if his day had been long and he needed a drink to unwind. When his drink was served, Vangie flagged down her server.

"The bathroom?" she asked

"At the end of the bar." The server pointed.

Her target hadn't noticed her until her hip gently brushed against his shoulder as she sauntered by his table. "Excuse me," she said, laying a soft hand on his shoulder. Their respective gazes connected. One good look into his eyes was all Vangie needed. She sauntered on, leaving him with her irresistible scent.

In the restroom, Vangie removed her engagement ring, wrapped it inside tissue paper, secured it in her handbag, and returned to her table.

Her target hadn't taken the bait, obviously. Not once had he looked her way or looked up from his plate since she sat back down.

Vangie flagged down the server, again. "Looks like I'll be dining alone," she said.

"Would you like me to take your order?"

She ordered an appetizer of ahi tuna tartare to bide time.

Not long later, her server presented her with the most expensive bottle of wine on the list. "From Mr. Steward… *Chris Steward*," he emphasized. The look of reverence on the server's face suggested to Vangie that Chris Steward might be her catch of the night. Her interest was now piqued.

She put on a smile. "Please thank Mr. Stewart for me."

"Definitely!" The server popped the cork, poured her a glass of Ark Vineyard 2012 Cabernet Sauvignon, and walked to Mr. Stewart's table. Her eyes followed him to a table of three men: two white men in suit and tie and a black man wearing a black T-shirt under a black leather jacket. All three men smiled and waved at her.

Now came the game of cat and mouse. Vangie smiled at the men delicately and turned her eyes back to the tranquil sea, then waited expectantly.

"Beautiful backdrop for a beautiful lady. You got it beat." The man slid into the seat across from her. His voice was deep enough to vibrate her eardrums. His eyes were dark and playful, his build large and broad, skin brown and smooth. Vangie almost shied away he was so attractive.

"Did I steal someone's seat?" His playful eyes pulled hers in and held them.

"What if you have?" she teased.

"I wouldn't be surprised. A beautiful girl like you can't be living single."

"I'm not a girl. I'm all woman."

"That you definitely are." He grinned. "I hope you don't mind my company."

"Should I mind?"

"Time will tell." He reached out his large hand and held her hand hostage until it grew clammy in his. "Chris Steward.".

"Daniela."

"How do you like the wine, Daniela?"

Vangie eased back in her chair, circled the rim of the goblet with her finger, and tasted the wine's oaky sweetness off the tip. "Nice and sweet. Thank you."

Chris Stewart grinned, replenished her wine glass, and then refilled his own.

The server shuffled up. "Ready to order, Mr. Steward?"

"I'll let the lady order first," he said.

They chatted over wine and dinner. While Chris Steward talked, Vangie watched him quietly and listened closely. There are two types of wealthy men, Vangie had found: those who bragged about their money and those who found ways to drop a hint as to the size of their portfolio holdings. Chris Steward was the former type and shocked to learn she had never heard of him or seen him on ESPN.

His claim to fame came by way of the NFL. He had retired years back, from what Vangie gathered, and he had invested his millions in a fleet of car dealerships. Vangie breathed easier knowing he wasn't born into one of America's most elite black families and likely didn't hang with men of the Fitzgerald caliber. He wasn't from California either. Even better.

"Do you live in L.A.?" he said.

"I'm in town on business?" she lied.

"I don't see nothing wrong with mixing pleasure with business." He grinned again.

Vangie didn't have a moralistic stance on one-night stands if it yielded her a great return on her investment.

But Chris Steward was a risky investment for more reasons than one.

Another lifetime…

She excused herself to the restroom and never returned.

Possessed by her goal of getting the cash she desperately needed, Vangie wasn't ready to call it a wasted night.

A block down the road, she strutted toward the Japanese restaurant off the waterfront, best known for its celebrity sightings and exquisite cuisine. She froze like a deer in the headlights as a car sped toward her. Its tires screeched to a stop in a nick of time.

Leaving the headlights shining brightly in her eyes, the driver jumped out of the car and accosted her before she could walk away. "I'm afraid I don't have a defensible excuse for my carelessness. Are you hurt?" the man said.

"I'm fine." Vangie attempted to walk off.

"I'd like to buy you a drink," he said, his tone that of an eager teen. "That's the least I can do. I'm Richard Walsh, by the way."

Vangie had no intention of sharing her name or any other personal information with Richard Walsh, who looked north of sixty, but she shook his hand and accepted his invitation for a drink nevertheless. He had silver hair and looked lean and fit in the casual trousers and open collar dress shirt he wore.

Inside the Asian inspired dining room, Vangie sat across from Richard Walsh. Feeling indifferent toward the ambiance and panoramic waterfront view, she hid her eyes behind her upturned glass, taking continual sips of wine.

She and Richard Walsh shared pleasantries over seafood ceviche and kelp chips. He spoke obsessively of his travels around the world and his love for diving. He told her he was a widower with three children and five grandchildren.

Three cocktails later, Richard Walsh really loosened up. Based on his confessions, Vangie ascertained that he was a retired physician and now formulated generic pharmaceutical products for a living.

She dazzled him with her knowledge of real estate, her travels abroad, and her love for rare artwork. Her personal life remained ambiguous, however. Whatever Richard Walsh didn't ask, she didn't offer.

"You sound very well educated. How old are you, if I may ask without sounding officious?"

Vangie's eyelids grew heavy at the thought of her and Angie's birthday. Another year gone by. Another birthday apart.

"Are you feeling old?" He smiled. "If I were to tell you my age, you'd have a reason to lament." He patted his perspiring forehead and neck with a napkin and looked around the room. "It appears we've shutdown the place. If you're not in a hurry, dessert here is worth a try."

Vangie raised her wine goblet and then finished off its contents, giving his suggestion halfhearted consideration. The night had been long and unprofitable. The stroke of midnight had come and gone. What she wanted was a bed and to lay her weary head down.

"Thanks, but it's late and I'm tired," she said.

"I have a better proposition. I'll have my private chef prepare an exquisite dessert at my place. It's just up the street."

That was Vangie's second glimpse into the doctor's portfolio. The first peek was when his canary yellow Maserati convertible coupe nearly killed her. In her right mind she would never accept the promise of candy from a stranger, but her mind hadn't been right for years. Despite her misgivings, she decided she couldn't go home empty handed.

Richard drove up Pacific Coast Highway at twenty miles an hour. With the top down, the ocean breeze cooled off Vangie's clammy skin. A mile down the road they drove through the private gateway to Billionaires Beach and then to the doctor's house. He parked inside a five-car garage that looked like a luxury car dealership.

Richard's cider-clad estate had pinewood covered vaulted ceilings and a front row view of the sea at every turn. Vangie followed the doctor throughout his mansion, feigning interest in his priceless artifacts, paintings, and collection of rare stones from around the world.

After the lengthy tour, complete with detailed descriptions, they stopped in the kitchen. Vangie didn't smell anything exquisite cooking, nor did she see a private chef. Richard poured himself a cocktail from a crystal glass container and offered her a glass. She accepted his offer and gulped.

The tour continued upstairs. Her senses fully awakened, Vangie kept her head on a swivel and her eyes on the doctor. The tour concluded in his master bedroom suite. Richard's lascivious gaze opened the door of opportunity. It was now or never.

"If you're looking to party, my base fee is twenty grand with a three hour minimum. An overnighter will cost you ten grand more," she said in no uncertain terms.

Richard Walsh raised both hands, shrinking back against her ambush. "You've gotten the wrong impression. I'm not looking to party." He lowered his hands. "I will admit, I would adore sex with you, but a bout with prostate cancer precludes that ability, I'm afraid. I'm looking for companionship. Just companionship. I certainly expect a lower figure."

Every rich man Vangie had ever known kept a vault full of cash nearby. She suspected Richard had cash on hand to burn.

She put on her lawyer's face. "My fee is non-negotiable."

The doctor looked as if he wanted to object. "But you are exquisite," he said as if to convince himself she was worth of his money. He left the room and returned with an envelope.

Vangie thumbed through the stack of crisp new bills, too nerve-wracked to actually count them.

"That's ten grand there," he said.

"I don't accept deposits." She handed him back his money.

"Hold on a minute. Deposits are routine in this business."

"Phone a call girl. I'm an independent contractor. Twenty grand or I walk."

"Fair enough."

When the doctor returned with her full fee, Vangie excused herself to his bathroom suite and locked herself inside. It was all there, thirty-five thousand dollars. She had pushed her luck and, seemingly, gotten away with it. On average a high-end call girl probably made five grand per two-hour minimum. She wasn't a call girl and had never solicited money in exchange for sex, not blatantly, anyway. Heart drumming in her ears, Vangie stuffed the money inside her handbag and called on her alto ego to fight her temptation to bolt.

Back in the bedroom she found the doctor sitting on the bed, stark naked, gliding his hands up and down his leathery thighs as if to warm them up for her.

"I do hope your fee includes a wardrobe change." He handed Vangie the article of clothing.

Vangie looked over the peculiar dress. Jacob stein had preferred bondage gear, Antonio Moretti sexy lingerie. Richard Walsh had a different predilection. The pure silk creamed-colored nightgown with puffed long sleeves and a lace bodice was made for a 1930s bride on her wedding night.

While the doctor watched, Vangie stripped out of her clothes in a sensual tease. The gown plunged to her feet when she put it on. She thrust her foot gently between his legs, making him grunt with pleasure. She then worked the garter up her thigh with the most sensuality she could stomach. No longer did she feel empowered or intoxicated when being desired by men willing to pay for her company. She felt low budget no matter how much money he might have paid her. Five or six more nights of this, for Angie's sake, she told herself, and then, she vowed, she would hang up her six-inch platform pumps for good.

Throughout the whole ordeal, she endured the eerie voice of Nat King Cole on replay, droning through the surround sound as he sang "I Love You for Sentimental Reasons." Vangie endured the smell of the doctor's bitter breath. His gruff hands exploring her crevices, she endured. His teeth clawing into her thigh as he removed the garter, she endured. His naked sweat drenching the fine silk fabric of the dress, she endured, all the while listening to the gushing waves of the dark sea, clinging to its pulsating rhythm, trying to find her center.

Richard Walsh apparently lied about his bout with prostate cancer. He was on the brink of full penetration when the fire in his hazel eyes turned them jade and lit up in the dark room. For Vangie, the present became indistinguishable from the past. She was outside of herself now, staring down from the ceiling, bearing witness to her own acts of violence she couldn't control. Her knee reared up and hand snapped back. She heard Richard Walsh yelp, saw him lose his balance, watched him tumble from the bed and hit the floor.

She watched herself scamper in the dark for her clothes like she had as a child, whenever Annette skipped out on a motel bill. She felt the spasms of her heart as she ran from his room and flew down the back steps that led to the kitchen.

Having returned to her full state of awareness, Vangie dressed hastily, and then bolted out of the house through French doors that led to a promenade. One phone call to the police by Richard Walsh, saying he had been robbed by a lone black woman, and security would be combing the ritzy neighborhood in search of a dangerous criminal. And in a neighborhood of this caliber, security cameras were everywhere. What was she thinking?

At least she had been smart enough to leave the money. She couldn't be convicted for a felony without evidence to show for it, could she? Running wasn't smart either. She would stand out all the more, so she walked up the beach carrying her pumps, hugging herself, and shivering more from fright than from the frigid air. The water roared onto the shore and withdrew quietly before reaching her bare feet.

Back to the East Side, Vangie entered the little pink house through the back door. She was almost certain she had turned off the TV. Did she leave the lights on too? She closed the door quietly and stood still, tilting her ear upward and listening intently. Her loud heartbeat threatened to drown out any other sound.

Then she heard soft footsteps as an opaque figure formed a forbidding shadow on the hallway wall and moved stealthily toward her.

When Ross's scowl came into her full view, Vangie pressed her hand to her chest. "Don't scare me like that," she said like a child facing an angry father.

"I told Rissa you couldn't be trusted. If we get found out, it's a wrap."

"I had business to close out."

"I'll tell you what. The next time you have some business to take care of, you'll be leaving in a squad car. I'll be got'damned if I lose my law license for you or for anybody else." Ross registered anger in his flat tone, anger that was off the Richter scale.

Vangie retreated to her room.

N ow that I'd "woman-upped," the black inmates loved me to a fault. I stuck close to them mainly out of fear, but also for protection. If I turned my back on them, they would turn their backs on me, and the Mexican Mafia would find a way to send me to an early grave. The skinheads at least respected me for going down with a good fight, even if they still hated me. I envied the inmates who dodged the color lines altogether and found peace in quiet corners.

Geneva, my cellmate, was a bona-fide ex-member of the Crips, who walked and talked with the kind of authority that made me shrink inside. She had spent more time on the inside than the twenty something years she'd spent on earth for one crime or another. Her latest crime had been petty, stealing diapers and baby food for one of her three kids, but she was sentenced to a year in county jail for violating her probation—for forty-five dollars and seventeen cents worth of stuff her kids needed.

During free time and before lights out, Geneva and I played dominoes, a skill I'd picked up playing with my mother and her houseguests. That was the second big mistake I'd made in jail. In the snap of Geneva's fingers, I was thrown into the middle of a domino competition without any say so.

Winning at dominoes was worth everything to Geneva, but her hunger to win had more to do with collecting items than being crowned the next domino queen. Winners took all: cigarettes, sanitary napkins, candy, chips, stamped, envelopes, soda, toilet paper, toothpaste and what not. The loser had to pay up or possibly suffer deadly consequences.

I sat across from Geneva, my spine as stiff as a lead pipe. Our opponents sat on either side of us, their faces so hard a smile couldn't crack them. Half the cellblock stood around us, including a few guards, either to watch the competition or prevent a blood bath. Anyone with eyes could see the potential for violence and feel the intensity around the pod.

The "bones" were tossed out, signaling the start of the game. Slouched in her seat, Geneva gnawed on a pen and washed the bones simultaneously, bringing to my mind bittersweet memories of my mother who could wash bones with one hand and hold a drink in the other hand while puffing on a cigarette dangling from her maroon-painted lips.

"What you holdin', cuz?" Geneva asked me.

I blinked back tears to make out the black and white polka dotted tiles in my hands, made out big six and made the first big play of the game.

Bleeding sweat as I studied the black and white tiles zigzagging across the table, I played my hand like a mathematician by keeping track of those tiles that had been played and those that hadn't, scoring off the opponent playing ahead of me while trying to shut down the opponent play-ing behind me, setting Geneva up for a big score.

Geneva glanced up from her hand every so often, her brown, upward slanted eyes subtly praising me like a mother when I scored or reprimanding me like father when I didn't. One wrong move could send me back to hell. The worst part, I thought: Geneva might kill me in my sleep. I prayed for a riot to breakout, for the alarms to sound, to get a contagious disease, anything to call off the game before it came to a bloody end.

A guard walked up to me. "Cooper-58. Time to go."

I walked out of jail in the same clothes I'd walked in wearing: skinny jeans, my pink "Sammy's Bakery" long-sleeved T-shirt, a hoodie, and my old running shoes. The blue sky was heavenly, the sun at the center shining brighter than I remembered the sun could shine. I drank the air and wanted to kiss the ground.

Escorted by a plain-clothes police officer with a gun at his waist, I stepped onto the running board of the passenger van with a two-pound, bulky ankle monitor weighing down my right leg. With no other prisoners on this trip, I had my choice of seats. I chose to sit two seats behind the female driver. The male officer took the passenger's seat.

I kept my eyes on the concrete building until it disap-peared, and only then did I exhale or notice anything else, mainly the people, more of them driving than walking and some sitting at bus stops like time hadn't a beginning or an end. I'd bet they slept by their own body clocks, fell asleep watching TV, or ate at random times of the day.

I'd missed that most about living freely, eating food worth eating. I missed a whole host of things I valued more now after spending a week in jail.

I hadn't noticed that we were off the highway until we drove through an area of the city with cleaner streets, fancier buildings, and expensive cars driven by more white people than by people of color.

The driver made a sudden sharp turn, throwing me around in my seat. She then drove slowly through a quiet neighborhood I wouldn't feel comfortable walking through. Mesmerized by the size of the homes hidden behind iron gates and tall trees, I almost broke my neck trying to get a good look at their verdant lawns, sculptured gardens, and expensive cars parked in long or circular driveways.

The van jerked to a stop.

"Is this the place?" the driver said to the officer.

"This is the address, so I'm guessing this is it," said the officer.

They both turned their heads toward me as if I knew who lived there. I only knew what I'd been told, that an anonymous person posted my bail. My mind ran wild with what I thought could be the only possibility.

During Christmas break, back when Vangie was at Stanford and I was homebound, we took a trip to the place we spent our childhood dreaming of a better life. For me it was as good as a trip to Disneyland. I was finally going somewhere, even if it was just a fifteen-minute drive through the Detroit-Windsor tunnel. Vangie had dressed me up for the trip, and on that day we looked identical.

From Windsor we drove to Oakville, Ontario. Our final stop was on Lakeshore Road, in a neighborhood as beautiful as this one. Vangie had a way with people that I never had, and the smarts to finagle her way in and out of most uncomfortable situations. She finagled our way inside a stranger's home, fabricating a story about her fiancé, some kind of professional baller I'd never met or heard of, who was interested in buying the place.

Vangie's dream home had three levels, soaring ceilings, and too many rooms to live in comfortably. Impressed with Vangie's worldly knowledge, the homeowner invited us back to the summer kitchen and served us lemon butter-milk scones and loose-leaf tea. While she and Vangie talked about things I knew nothing about, I sat in my silence, nibbling on a slice of heaven. When we finally left Vangie's dream home, even I was convinced she could afford to buy a ten million dollar mansion in Canada.

The driver pulled away from the curb and into a long driveway, passing through a row of manicured cypress trees before circling the cobblestone driveway around a beautiful waterfall fountain. I leaned over and looked up to get a better view of the castle-like house. The windows were tall and arched, the columns white and stone, and the many peaks and valleys of the roof sprouted at least six chimneys.

The officer ordered me out of the van while the driver stayed seated. By the time I reached the fancy stained glass door my imagination had run rampant. I stood on jelly legs, ready to buckle at the sight of Vangie.

Eleven

The door opened slowly, answered by a Hispanic woman with plump hips and plump lips. The woman wore her sandy blonde hair in a ponytail at the crown on her head. Fear shown in her doe-like brown eyes when she saw me.

"Wait here. I get Mr. F. for you," the woman said with a heavy Spanish accent.

Inside the house, the corrections officer and I waited in the eye of a black and gold medallion engraved into the marble floor. Above our heads was a crystal chandelier suspended from the cathedral ceiling three stories high.

"Some place…," the officer said as he inspected a life-sized bronze of a horseman in the grand entryway.

Everything about this place was worth admiring. I admired the staircase, a work of art in and of itself, its wrought iron railing spiraling to the second floor. I wanted to believe with every beat of my thumping heart that the whole ordeal had been one big mistake, that Vangie wasn't wanted for murder, that this was her dream home and she was responsible for bailing me out of jail. In a flight of fantasy, I imagined her flowing down the marble stairs in a sequined gown, her arms outstretched, ready to take me in.

Blinded by the tears brimming my eyes, I hadn't noticed the elderly man roll up on me in a wheelchair. He wore a black silk and suede bathrobe over a white open collar dress shirt, black dress pants, and black leather house slippers on sock covered feet. His Afro was thick and silver, framing his face like a close-fitted cap, his burnished brown skin smooth for a man of seventy or eighty, which he otherwise appeared to be. I did my best to concentrate on his deep-set brown eyes and not his collapsed face or his hand that hung limply at his wrist, curled up like a useless tennis ball.

He appraised me with a frown that at first seemed to disapprove of me and then to question my identity.

"Thank you for bailing me out," I muttered. That was the least I could say to him on Vangie's behalf.

"Don't thank me yet," he said slyly, his words spurting out of his crooked mouth in measured syllables.

"This is your home?" The officer sounded suspicious, as if he'd never met a black person who lived so high above the poverty line. To be frank, I hadn't either.

The old man frowned at the officer and then wheeled away.

"You. Come with me." The officer wagged his curled finger at me.

Left totally in the dark, I followed the officer down a hallway with walls brushed in gold as he chased behind the man. The house had a museum feel. It was a beautiful place to visit, but I wouldn't choose to live here if I had the choice.

The old man wheeled into what looked like his office. Before I could enter, the officer stopped me and pointed to the leather bench against the wall.

"You sit and wait," he told me.

While the old man and the officer talked behind the closed door, I admired the intricate arched ceilings, and the three-star pendant chandeliers strung down a hallway wide enough to drive a small car through. It was like staring down a rabbit hole. I wondered what mystery lay behind the walls and arched doors leading to the unknown.

Did the old man live alone?

Did he have a wife, children, or grandchildren?

Why did he bail Vangie out of jail?

Where would I sleep tonight?

I still didn't move when the old man wheeled out of the office followed by the officer.

"You're in this man's custody," the officer said. "You know the rules. Break one and you're back in jail."

I nodded, understanding his warning clearly. The rules of home confinement were spelled out in the six-page document I had to sign before I left jail. I didn't plan to break any of them, if I could help it.

"She won't be breaking any rules in my house. Will you?" said the old man, and again I noted his sly tone and his measured syllables.

I shook my head.

After the officer left the house, the old man returned to his office and the housekeeper, who told me her name was Marisol, showed me to my room on the second floor. I stood in the hallway, my expression one big question mark.

Marisol half-rolled her eyes at me and pressed her back against the door, making space for me to enter the room ahead of her. She then backed out, closing the door gradually as she watched me curiously. I got the sense she didn't trust me. I didn't take it personally; after all, Vangie was accused of murder.

I looked around, stunned by the room's extravagance. My running shoes caught on the thick carpet and almost tripped me up. I caught my fall, snapping upright before my face met with the floor.

The décor was all things beautiful and Moroccan. Tan, white, gold, and various shades of brown ran through the comforter, lampshades, artwork, and whatnots. I noticed, in a cozy corner with a flat screen TV and fireplace, a place to lounge and eat.

I stared at the elegant canopy bed draped in lace fabric. Back home I slept on a convertible futon couch and had everything I needed at my fingertips in a studio apartment the size this entire room. Completely out of my comfort zone and scared to touch anything, I walked toward the open French doors in a dream state and stood in the ray of the sun, looking out at the neighborhood overtaken by palm trees.

A gardener stood on a ladder trimming the tall hedges surrounding the property. Smelling the freshly cut grass made me want to dig up dirt and plant something in the lovely garden below—something aromatic, sweet and green, to whisk my mind away from this place I felt undeserving of even standing within.

I heard a beeping sound and almost jumped out of my skin. There it was again, coming from an intercom system on the wall next to the bed. I crept up to it and pushed the receiver button as if it might bite.

"Dinner will be served at 6:30 in the main dining hall." The man spoke in a baritone, formal voice with an accent I couldn't place.

"Oh. Okay. Thank you."

I looked down at myself and frowned. Even if every stitch of clothing I owned hadn't been confiscated for evidence in a crime, I wouldn't have anything decent to wear to dinner in a place like this. The most I could do was try to clean myself up.

Everything in the bathroom sparkled: the brass faucets, the mirrors, the marble countertops, and marble floors. I sniffed and sampled the assortment of aromatic body sprays, perfumes, and body butters that smelled delicious enough to eat.

"If you can't look good for a man, smell good for him," my mother used to tell us. Vangie took our mother's advice to heart, wasting her fair share of hot water by taking two or three showers in one day. I kept up a hostile odor most days to keep our grimy houseguests away.

Out of habit, I glanced over my shoulder before undressing and hurried into the shower, which was large enough to accommodate six people comfortably. Six pulsating showerheads shot hot water at me from all sides, even above my head. I relaxed and enjoyed it.

I made good use of the dispensers mounted to the wall, lathering my body with citrusy body wash, washing and conditioning my hair in the same scent. I was already looking forward to showering tomorrow, or maybe soaking in the sunken bathtub that looked down on the garden.

Everything was thick, rich, and white: the fluffy towels I dried off with, the fluffy robe I put on, and the cotton house shoes I warmed my feet in. I examined my face in the brightly lit mirror, assessing what was left of the damage. Another week or so and there wouldn't be any trace of the fight that nearly took my life.

After shaping my hair into something presentable, I dressed in my old clothes and stepped outside the protection of my new room. To my right, a hallway of doors stood eerily, all closed. Seven steps ahead, I loitered in the bend of the staircase, staring over the railing, down into the eye of the gold medallion, waiting for a dinner bell to chime or something.

When I didn't hear anything after a few minutes, I got up the guts to go downstairs. With too many doors and directions to choose from, I felt like a lost lamb in a luxurious wilderness. I walked through the grand entryway and into an enormous sunken living room with soaring windows and a mesmerizing view of the setting sun. From that point, I didn't know if I should go left or right.

Taking a stab in the dark, I went right and got trapped in a maze of rooms. Each room led me to the next, and each had its own extravagant motif. In the middle of one enchanting room was a baby grand piano and a gilded harp basking in sunlight. I lingered for a second or two, imagining the beautiful music played here at a fancy party.

Worried I'd be late for dinner, I came out on the other side of the room and was back on course. The gray leather bench outside the old man's office was my marker. From there, I found my way back to square one.

I went left off the great entryway this time and walked into the dining room the size of a small banquet hall. Two chandeliers, their beaded crystals giving off a thousand points of light, hung low over a fancy marble table with the capacity to seat sixteen people. The table was formally set for two.

"You're early darlin'," the man I encountered said.

Standing face-to-face with what I recognized as a professional chef, I turned green from envy, I was sure. His baldhead shined like a cooper penny, and a trimmed beard covered the better half of his full cheeks. He wore black chef's crocks with black pants and a black chef's coat that fit tight against every inch of his pudgy stomach. His down-turned eyes, parted by a robust nose, danced and his fleshy lips twitched as if he was itching to say something but couldn't think of anything nice to say to me.

I couldn't decide if he liked Vangie or hated her. Standing in Vangie's shoes, I felt hated by most everyone.

"How have you been?" he said as if expecting a full report.

I gave him a non-committal shrug.

"I can see that, darlin'. I'll take care of that eye for you." He pulled out the armless chair for me.

"Thank you." I sat quickly, slid my feet under the table, and clasped my hands in my lap.

He then removed the head chair, placed it next to the lit fireplace that took up the entire wall, and uncorked a bottle of wine.

"You're a lover of red, if I remember," he said as he poured.

Vangie was the wine lover. I never found a love for wine and gave up drinking alcohol before it became a real problem for me.

"Chateau Latour. On the sweet side but pairs perfectly with the dish I've prepared tonight." He filled the glass halfway.

Thinking fast, I picked up the glass, swirled, sniffed, and sipped like I'd seen Vangie do back when she would sneak expensive bottles of wine into the house and lock them inside her hope chest filled with sacred and expensive things. Wine, whisky, beer, you name it, never lasted a day in our house with my mother and her houseguest around.

I smiled up at him and said, "It's delicious."

"Thank you, darlin." He left the room through a side door, glancing over his shoulder as if to get one last look at me.

I wanted to follow him into the kitchen, ask him his tricks of the trade, if he had any favorite tools, which spices he used and for which dishes. The list of questions I would never ask him were endless.

Alone, I salivated over the mini-skillet of plump golden pull-apart bread sizzling in butter and secreting a piney Rosemary scent, arousing the beast in me.

The old man wheeled into the room seconds later, pushed by a woman I hadn't seen earlier.

She parked him next to me. "If you need me, remember to *push* the green button." She picked up the old man's bad hand, uncurled his index finger, and placed it on the small portable device attached to his wheelchair. I assumed she was his nurse by the looks of the gray uniform she wore and the way she talked to him in a singsong voice like she would to a sick child.

Frowning, the old man yanked his hand away and his fingers withdrew back to their curled position.

"Use it or you'll lose it," the woman sang.

"I am not an invalid!" He shooed the nurse off with his good hand.

The nurse glanced at me, and in her eyes, I saw a cry for help. She hurried out of the room.

When he unfolded his napkin, I unfolded mine too and spread it across my lap. The chef returned to serve us bowls of soup topped with steamed clams.

"Mr. Big! How's the appetite?" The chef talked loudly and jovially, as though trying to cheer up the old man. He gave the chef a crooked smile and a thumb up.

I decided to call him Mr. Big too.

"Good! Good! Good!" The chef served us each a piece of the inviting bread before leaving us alone.

"How do you like your ac-com-mo-dations?" He garbled the last word into tiny bits as if he had trouble saying it.

I scoured my brain for the right words, something intelligent or witty that Vangie might say and came up blank.

Smiling, I nodded my head.

More questions seemed to assemble in the old man's squinted eyes. "You may eat," he said.

Jumping at the chance, I closed my eyes, blessed my food, and then peeked through one eye to make certain Mr. Big wasn't watching me. Playing food games was a habit I hadn't grown out of. I sniffed to guess the spices swimming in the red reduction, detecting the cloves, thyme, red pepper and garlic that tingled my nose and made my stomach rumble embarrassingly loud.

When I opened my eyes, Mr. Big wore a disapproving scowl. He cupped his chin with his good hand and wrinkled his forehead as if to say, "What has gotten into you?"

I used the uncomfortable moment to admire the slate blue dinnerware trimmed in gold. Jim Mahoney believed the more life skills "we girls" at Roxy's House learned the more likely we were to succeed in life. He was accurate twenty percent of the time. If not for life skills classes, I wouldn't know which of the three forks, the knives, and the spoons to use for what.

I picked up my soupspoon and devoured my first bite. The savory flavor left a lasting impression on my taste buds, teasing my insatiable appetite. To keep it contained, I mentally counted to ten between bites, nearly dying of starvation before I reached five.

When Mr. Big's napkin slid from his lap to the floor, I jumped to pick it up and then spread it across his lap.

"I never thought I would need help un-fold-ing a napkin?" he said jokingly, again stumbling through a word, but his sad eyes tugged at my heartstrings. I worked with the elderly, volunteering at the senior center run by the church. Many of them didn't have family or visitors, so I would listen to their childhood stories, compete with the men at board games, and style the women's hair like I had my mother's. They were the grandparents I didn't have, the family I had lost.

I watched Mr. Big struggle to guide the spoon into his mouth because of limited dexterity in his left hand and wanted to wipe the soup dribble from his chin.

After fighting with his soup, he eventually called it an early night and left the table before the main course was served. I happily ate alone, feasting on rib-eye steak with truffle-roasted potatoes and multi-colored ginger-lime baby carrots grilled to perfection.

The chef sent me off with a cold compress to apply to my black eye. I fell asleep dreaming about the decadent warm fudge cake with a mascarpone cream center I'd demolished for dessert.

D awn spread over the horizon like a blaze of fire under purple skies. It was 5:37 A.M. Back in Colorado Springs, I unlocked the doors of Sammy's Bakery around this time of morning, excited to start my workday.

During the four years I had worked at Sammy's Bakery, I'd never called in sick, never missed a day of work, or been late—not once, until now. All hell had probably broken loose. Floe would've been the first person to notice I'd gone missing and sound the alarm, and I didn't want to imagine Sammy's reaction when I didn't show up for work last week or what she thought of me.

Some days, before the regulars lined up and the crew arrived, I had the kitchen to myself and would test out my recipe ideas. Those were my favorite mornings. Every day at Sammy's Bakery gave me a chance to be daring.

Here, I didn't know what to do with myself with a full day ahead of me without a routine to guide me. Unmotivated to leave bed and the mattress made of soft feathers, I dozed off again.

I slept two hours more before hunger woke me up and got me out of bed. For a good five minutes I stared at the intercom system, afraid to disturb the peace of the house for a measly glass of orange juice or cup of coffee and buttered toast I could get for myself.

"Mornin' darlin'," the chef said as soon as I pressed the talk button.

"Hi…um…What time is breakfast?" I squawked.

"8:00 o'clock in the sunroom." The chef's voice was like sunshine, his words music to my ears.

Eager to eat, I freshened up like I had done when bathing everyday wasn't an option for me, kept on the Tee I'd slept in, put on my comfortable jeans, and then slipped my bare feet into house shoes.

I'd made it halfway down the stairs when the doorbell rang as loud as church bells summoning the neighborhood to morning prayer. Marisol came rushing out of nowhere to answer it, then stopped to straighten out the apron she wore over black pants with a white frilly shirt, muttering something in Spanish before opening the door.

When the prosecutor charged into the house like a bull let loose from a pen, I slipped on the marble stairs, almost tumbling headfirst to the bottom before grabbing the railing and holding on. The prosecutor wore the same style pants suit she had worn in court and the same serious mug. "Where is he!" she barked at Marisol.

"I get him for you, Misses Kimberly."

I turned and crept up the stairs.

"If you have the temerity to step foot in *this* house, have the decency to face me!" The prosecutor's commanding voice reverberated off the cathedral ceiling.

Heat traveled through my body like an inferno. Forced to face her, I turned around slowly. In a blink of my eye the prosecutor scaled the stairs and got in my face. Flinching, I took a step back and bumped into the railing.

"You're pathetic!" She gave me a slow once over, her eyes an icy breeze, and then pointed her index finger at me. "If you *think* I'll stand by while you luxuriate here after your scheme backfired, you've fucked with the wrong family. I'll personally see to it that you're executed by lethal injection before I let that happen. Do you hear me?" I could almost see venom seeping from between the prosecutor's clenched teeth. I thought she might spit it right in my face.

Mr. Big rolled up to the bottom of the staircase. "Kimber-ly. I've been expec-ting you."

She spun around to face him. "What in the hell's going on? I get a call from the D. A. informing me you posted bail for this conniving bitch!"

"We can talk in private." Mr. Big wheeled away. The prosecutor stomped down the stairs after him.

I shivered like a wet dog in the wake of her threat. When my feet finally cooperated, I flew to my room, closed the door, and fell against it. In search of somewhere to hide, I zipped my eyes around the room, and then shot through the French doors to the balcony. A flock of birds soared across the cloudy sky toward the breaking sun. I watched their black wings flap in unison and fought a strong impulse to take off with the wind and return to the underground world. I wrapped my white knuckles around the white column barrier and stared over the balcony, thinking nothing of the two-story drop or the injuries I might sustain should I jump and make a run for it.

I wouldn't make it past the tall hedges surrounding the property, I reminded myself. My ankle bracelet would send a silent signal to the police, and within minutes the house and surrounding neighborhood would be swarming with police.

A knock on the bedroom door saved me from a split second decision that would've landed me back in jail with broken bones. I tiptoed back into the room and waited for whoever it was at the door to leave, careful not to breathe.

The person knocked harder. "Breakfast!" It was Marisol.

I opened the door and peeked out.

"From the chef. Bernard," Marisol said. She pushed open the door with her black loafer, pushed past me, set the trey on the table in the sitting area, and left the room quickly.

Breakfast was beautifully plated—strawberries cut into rose petals with a whip cream center, scrambled eggs mixed with bits of pancetta and sprinkled with chives, and a huge crispy Belgium waffle.

I cleaned my plate with guilty pleasure, stretched out on the chase lounge and feel asleep watching TV.

"Van, wake up. It's me," I heard whispered.

I opened my eyes to see Clarissa standing over me, shaking me by the shoulder. Happy to see her, I leapt from the chair and hugged her like a long-lost friend.

She surveyed me. "This isn't going to work," she said, picking at my hair with her manicured nails. "Ross is working on reclaiming your property. In the meantime, I bought you a few things."

I looked over at the bed covered with shopping bags.

"I know you're not a charity case, but I won't take no for an answer. You need clothes and that's what friends are for." Her voice was firm. "We need to talk, but not here. Outside. Get dressed. I'll wait for you."

I looked down at myself. *I am dressed*, I thought.

"Don't forget your new clothes," she said before I dashed off to the bathroom.

I dug through the bags of clothes—underwear, bras, shoes, and whatnots—all with pricey tags attached. Everything was fancy and perfect—for Vangie. I chose something I felt comfortable wearing and hurried into the bathroom to shower and dress.

"Now you look like the Vangie that I know," Clarissa said with a smile when I walked out of the bathroom in dark skinny jeans, a nice white top made of soft spandex, and a pair of running shoes five times more expensive than any I could afford, and ten times more comfortable. I felt brand new.

"Thank you so much," I said.

"I'm not the person to thank." The look in Clarissa's eyes said much more than the words she spoke.

I stuck close to her when we left the room, keeping watch for the prosecutor as we descended the stairs. Clarissa seemed unhurried, her face a mask of mutiny, as if she wanted beef with somebody. She led me through the front door and down the pathway made out of flagstone, passing rows of colorful perennials and sculptured shrubs. We made it safely to the back yard, a paradise that overlooked the city. I didn't have a chance to take in the beautiful scenery on account of Clarissa pulling me by the hand so fast.

When we entered a quaint pool house, Clarissa closed all the shutters before turning on the TV and raising the volume to blast. When she was done making her rounds, she led me to the rattan and leather sofa by the hand and sat me down. The suspense regarding the words she had yet to speak was killing me. So as not to bite my nails, I tucked my hands under my thighs. Then I waited on the edge of my seat, sure I was busted.

"Is there anything you want to tell me?" she said.

It sounded like a trick question, so I didn't say anything at all. I turned down the corners of my mouth, raised my brows, and shook my head with a look of innocence.

"Nothing important transpired this morning that I should know about?" she pressed.

"No," I said, shaking my head emphatically.

Clarissa sighed. "I heard the assistant DA came by the house and got belligerent with you. Is that true?"

In the event the prosecutor retaliated against Vangie, I maintained my lie. Something in the prosecutor's eyes told me she would make good on her promise.

"She didn't come by the house or she didn't get belligerent with you? Which one?"

"Oh, yes, she came by, but no, she wasn't belligerent."

"Did she mention your case?"

"No."

"Did she make any inflammatory statements?"

Only that she wanted Vangie to die by lethal injection. I shook my head fast and hard.

Clarissa took a long pause and then smiled softly. "Thanks for being honest with me, Van. It's important that Ross and I know these things." She reached into her purse, pulled out a basic black cell phone and handed it to me. "I've programmed our numbers. Call Ross or me immediately if anyone from the District Attorney's office, a detective, or a private investigator tries to interrogate you. Tell them you will not speak to them without your attorney present. Be explicit." She flashed a smile. "But you know what to say. Because you're a lawyer, right?"

I nodded slowly.

"We're going to get you out of this. I promise." Clarissa pulled me into a bear hug.

Thirteen

Vangie flipped from one local news station to another. The assault and battery of a Doctor Richard Walsh in Carbon Beach, and subsequent hunt of a black female assailant, had yet to air. She thanked God for small miracles, but Richard Walsh was the least of her worries.

Hearing a car approaching the house, Vangie rushed to the living room window and peeked through the blinds for the third or fourth time in the past hour. When Clarissa's red BMW turned recklessly into the driveway, Vangie released a long sigh—and not out of relief. She needed to slow her heart rate before she had a heart attack.

"I swear on my grandmother's grave I hate my cousin," Clarissa professed in a low growl as she stormed into the house. She passed Vangie like a lamppost in her way, flung her handbag onto the dining room table, and helped herself to the last swallow of Vangie's wine.

Vangie stood by, watching and waiting. Surly Clarissa could sense her angst. She crossed her arms at her chest and tapped the toe of her flip-flop.

"I'm sorry, Van. I'm dumb. Your twin is perfectly fine."

"How does she look?"

"Ten times better than she looked days ago."

Vangie let Clarissa's exaggeration stand. She didn't want to know the extent of Angie's injuries and didn't ask for the graphic details. She just might seriously kill someone. She stuck with surface questions.

"What about the clothes?"

"She's been upgraded. I couldn't tell the two of you apart in a line up, down to your beauty moles, which is downright eerie. I hate you both for being to-die-for *perf*."

"Thanks, Riss, for everything." Feeling like a wrung-out mop, Vangie withered down onto the dining chair.

"Okay. True confession," Clarissa said contritely, putting Vangie on guard just when she had begun to lighten up.

Vangie squared her shoulders. "What is it?" She didn't mean to sound threatening, but there was always a crucial piece of evidence missing in Clarissa's true confessions.

"I almost told her the whole friggin' story."

"What do you mean by *almost?*"

"Meaning I upheld your gag order, not because I agreed with it but because I was out-voted two to one. Don't look at me that way. I didn't divulge anything. God only knows how badly I wanted to tell Angie." Clarissa raised a pointed finger. "And I still contend that, if she knows that we know, she'll protect our interests as well as her own. Think about it, Vangie."

"The less she knows the better." Vangie's tone was uncompromising.

Clarissa took liberty with the bottle of wine, refilling the glass. "I have your change. Remind me to give it to you. I don't want to forget."

"Apply it to my billable hours."

"Are you sure, Van?"

Vangie pursed her lips. Clarissa mirrored her expression. They both knew Ross would come for another installment soon—and for her life savings next.

They moved to the living room, kicked back on the sofa with their feet propped on the coffee table, and shared sips of wine.

"How can you stand it, Van?"

"Stand what?"

"Not seeing your twin in all these years. I can't image how you feel."

Anyone who hadn't shared their DNA with a twin, hadn't experienced the frustration of never being singular, the quiet agony of never feeling whole without their twin at their side, seemingly taken on the responsibility of their twin before either of them could walk or talk, or made extreme sacrifices for their twin, prompted as much by their undying love than their own will to survive couldn't understand how she felt or imagine her suffering. A slow chipping away at her heart with an ice pick might best describe her inner turmoil.

"I can't stand it," Vangie said as she snatched the glass from Clarissa hands and swallowed the lump in her throat.

"Don't take offense when I say this…"

"Say what?"

"Is it natural for identical twins to be so…different?"

"Different how?" Vangie said, trying not to sound offended by Clarissa's innocent question.

"Angie acts so young, and you've always been mature. Take that as a compliment. Why do you think I stopped going home during breaks? I wanted to prove to you, or maybe to myself, that I wasn't dying of homesickness. You set a high bar, Van."

Vangie took an indulgent sip of wine while reflecting on her first year of college and first time away from Angie. She had her own reasons for staying on campus during breaks and proving she did not suffer from homesickness wasn't one of them.

"My maturity came with a high price," Vangie mused aloud.

Clarissa gazed at her interrogatively, making Vangie regret her offhand remark. "Can you elaborate?"

"Another day, Riss."

"You can't keep avoiding the hard questions, Van. The more candid you are the better our chance to build a solid defense."

If she had been standing in her own shoes at her arraignment, Vangie thought, she would've plead no contest and taken a plea deal for lesser jail time. A trial in a felony proceeding would drag on for months on end of sworn testimony and reveal mounds of dirt that would publicly expose her chest of secrets.

"Oh, my God!" Clarissa sat straight up. "I just remembered what I wanted to tell you when I walked in. That ball buster had the unprincipled gull to go to Granddad's house and harass your twin."

Vangie's protective antennas went up. She never had a reason to dislike Wade's sister until now. She sat up too. "Define harassment."

"Let me put it this way. Whatever mandate Kimmy violated scared poor Angie into lying. I should file a complaint with the state and have Kimmy disbarred for egregious prosecutorial misconduct!"

As much as Vangie would love to see Kimmy disbarred for her benefit, filing a complaint with the state board would be wasting the court's time and Clarissa's.

"Did Mr. Fitzgerald have anything to say?" Vangie asked with a low note of cynicism.

"Granddad, you mean?"

Vangie swallowed the tart taste on her tongue. "Yes."

"'How I spend my money is my business.' That's what he said to his *own* granddaughter. Can you believe it? I can't put a finger on his motive. He's never been wasteful with his money. I'm not saying bailing you...I mean Angie out of jail was a waste of money, but it is risky, Van. What if your twin skips out on bail, theoretically speaking?"

Vangie couldn't honestly say she didn't have the same concern. However grateful she was that Angie had been set free, not knowing Wade the Second's motive was disconcerting, to put it mildly.

"We can't expect him to have sound judgment, can we?" Clarissa went on. "You should see my poor grandfather, Van. You wouldn't recognize him. He's aged ten years in one month. I remember when he couldn't be tied down with a lasso and would buck anyone who tried. Now he's confined to a wheelchair and slurs when he talks. It's so sad." Clarissa eyes glistened. "If he dies, the thin line between love and hate I have for that family will be permanently erased. I swear to God!"

Clarissa's ringing phone interrupted her manifesto. Ross ended all talk about the events of the day, summoning Clarissa back to the office to handle what he perceived to be an emergency—the new receptionist went home sick and someone needed to answer the phones while he took care of business.

Clarissa hurried off.

Alone, Vangie's thoughts ran rampantly through her head. The very idea of Angie sleeping in the same house as Wade's grandfather, unsupervised, compelled her to pace the room. She always suspected where Wade the Second fit into one of her three categories of men—those with the money to pay for their desires outright and the power to get away with most anything.

And it wasn't a family secret that he had a predilection for younger women, a few too young, in Clarissa's opinion. Over the years, she had visited Wade the Second's lavish Beverly Hills estate to attend family gatherings.

On one particular occasion, Wade the Second had kissed her on the lips in a way that no well-meaning grandfather would or should. "There's something about you," he said to her with a sly glint in his eyes. "I hope my grandson knows what he has." Vangie had come close to vanishing from Wade's life then, certain he would one day find out exactly what and who she was.

Fourteen

Ross held another strategy meeting over dinner—greasy Mexican take-out that didn't sit well on Vangie's nervous stomach. They convened in the living room around the glass coffee table. Ross sat on the couch with his elbows on his knees, the sleeves of his powder blue dress shirt rolled up and the collar open wide enough to see his wife beater underneath. Clarissa sat on the floor Indian style, and Vangie sat in the recliner, doing her best to act as a silent partner in their duo, giving Ross's ego room to roam.

As he talked, Ross's enthusiasm bled through the armpits of his dress shirt. Clearly, obstructing justice to leverage his career agreed with him. However skeptical Vangie may have been, she made no objections to Ross's unscrupulous strategy to win. Having Ross—the ex-used cars salesman, ex-thug, and a general shyster type who applied to law school on a dare and passed the bar on a prayer—as her defense attorney just might work in her favor when coming up against Kimberly Fitzgerald.

"Is this your best laid Johnny-Cochran defense strategy, Ross?" said Clarissa with a quivering voice.

"It's the best I got with what I'm working with." Ross looked at Vangie. "What physical distinctions between you two do I need know about, besides your hair... Any birth marks, tattoos, scars?"

Vangie stood, raised her shirt and lowered the waistband of her leggings to reveal the tattoo just above her left hipbone.

Ross leaned in and stared too long. "What is it?"

"The Chinese symbol for twins." Vangie lowered her shirt and sat quickly.

"What about it?"

"We have the same tattoo. Angie's is on her right side." A scratch settled in Vangie's throat. Their matching tattoos symbolized her and Angie's inseparability. Not a day went by that she wasn't reminded of her broken promise to Angie.

"What else?" Ross said.

"The black butterfly tattoo on my lower back."

"That could be a problem."

"Why?" Vangie was afraid to ask.

"In case we go with plan B."

"What friggin' plan B, Ross?" Clarissa snapped.

Ross moved along, stressing the importance of executing plan A expeditiously. The strategy meeting concluded. They retreated to their respective bedrooms. Vangie lay on a bed of thorns, watching a shadow of trees dance on the wall as the bed next door squeaked and squawked. Ross apparently needed to work off his excitement.

When all was quiet, Clarissa opened the bedroom door and peeked her head inside the room. "Are you sleeping?"

"I wish I could." Vangie sat up and hugged her knees.

Clarissa closed the door and meandered toward her in a mini tank dress and flip-flops, then lay at the foot of the bed, propping herself on one elbow. Back at Stanford, whenever Clarissa barged into her dorm room unannounced, Clarissa would talk her into a coma. Vangie hoped that would be the case tonight. She needed something to stop her mind from racing. Two glasses of wine hadn't done the job.

"I can't sleep either," Clarissa said.

"Yeah. I heard," Vangie teased.

Turning red in the face, Clarissa whispered, "Oh, my God. I'm officially embarrassed. Ross gets so friggin' loud. The more I tell him to shut up the louder he gets."

They laughed like they had in their college days, when the future was years ahead of them and they were in no great hurry to seize it. Vangie appreciated the comic relief.

"Our two-year anniversary is this March. If he asks me to marry him, what should I say?"

Vangie mused over Clarissa's question.

"I know what you're thinking. By my own prediction, Ross and I wouldn't last two months let alone two years."

"That never crossed my mind," Vangie asserted. She envied the look of love that shone in Clarissa's blissful eyes and her after-sex glow. She thought back to the day Wade proposed to her—a day that culminated with a nightmare.

Truth be told, she had never questioned Clarissa's choice in men. She assumed Clarissa was attracted to Ross's good looks and wanted to prove to the Fitzgerald family that she didn't want their approval.

"I'll admit Ross is not *Jonathan*, but he's driven and ambitious, and rest assured, he would never, ever leave me for a plastic chick or neglect his own kids like the spineless sperm donor I used to call daddy." Clarissa raised her index finger pointedly. "Exhibit A! Every rich man isn't worth marrying. I can name ten reasons why not."

Vangie, remembering when Clarissa could name ten reasons in favor of only marrying rich, laughed.

The mood of the room turned melancholy then.

"Don't tell Ross, but I'm really scared," Clarissa whispered. "We're committing the most egregious professional misconduct in the law book."

Vangie wished she had the privilege of fear. Fear belonged to other people. For her there was only survival driven by desperation. But Clarissa had every right to be scared. If Ross's scheme to outmaneuver the legal system derailed, Clarissa would be disbarred before she was officially sworn in.

The upside was, if all went as planned, Clarissa would soon return to Burbank where Hollywood stars could be sighted entering Warner Bros Studios and upper middle class executives could raise their two-point-five children in a relatively safe neighborhood. Her own housing prospects, however, weren't so promising.

"I don't know how I feel about anything anymore, Riss, but if you decide not to go through with it, I understand."

Clarissa's brows shot up. "And let Kimmy win? Hell no!"

Vangie smiled, grateful for their friendship. After her botched attempt to bail Angie out on jail had put them all at risk of indictment, she thought Clarissa would never speak to her again. Clarissa had even taken up temporary residence at the little pink house to act as her round-the-clock warden. She only hoped she would be as great a friend to Clarissa one day, if given the opportunity.

A moment of heavy silence followed Clarissa's outburst before Clarissa followed up with, "There's something else, Van; Something I've been wanting to tell you but couldn't bring myself to. It's about Wade."

A chill ran up Vangie's spin. Heart hammering against her chest cavity, she told Clarissa, "Whatever it is, I don't want to know." She wasn't mentally or emotionally prepared to talk about Wade.

"I think you should know this, Van. It might help you."

"Help me how?" Vangie challenged.

"To let go of my asshole cousin."

Vangie's stomach plummeted. "I know enough."

"You're right. Forget I ever mentioned Wade. I'm just the step-cousin in this family, anyway, and no longer privy to family business. It's probably social media fake news."

Clarissa had piqued her interest and now she regretted avoiding social media like the plague. "What fake news?"

"Wade and Cameron Calloway hooked back up," Clarissa rattled off as if the faster she spoke the words the less heartbreaking the news. "Cameron is an opportunistic slut. I just thought you should know."

Hugging her knees, Vangie rocked, her heart throbbing in her ears.

"You have my shoulder if you need to cry."

"I need to go to sleep." *And never wake up...*

The rickety bed rocked, and the old door shrieked open and then closed as Clarissa left the room without speaking another word.

Sleep was lost to Vangie. No sooner than she closed her eyes than it seemed they were open again, burning with tears. Homicidal thoughts of Cameron Calloway grew in her mind like an evil plot.

Then came the memories...

~

The sweet aroma of red wine infuses the air of the French restaurant nestled in the heart of downtown San Francisco.

"You two are a young couple," the server says in a French accent commensurate with the romantic atmosphere.

Wade orders a French beer and presents the server with his driver's license. "She's what you call young," he teases about her freshman status while tacitly boasting of his seniority over her.

"How old are you?" asks the server.

She remains cool as she whips out her fake ID. "I'm old enough," she says, displaying her fake driver's license. After the server's approving nod, she stuffs her license back into her wallet before Wade can glimpse her home address from across the table. She orders a three hundred dollar bottle of burgundy to bring home her point: She is rich!

"Great choice," the server says. He presents them with the chef's top menu choice, tells them to take their time with their dinner selections, and then departs.

When the server is out of earshot, Wade laughs. "When did you turn twenty-one? Let me check it out."

She ignores his gesturing hand beckoning for her to hand over her license to inspect. "Check what out? There's nothing to check," she teases.

"Your counter-questioning won't work this time. Your license, that's what? I want to see how beautiful you look in your fake ID photo."

"Well, I look ugly. I hate my picture."

The server returns with their drinks. While he's pouring her a glass, Wade is laughing, his gaze piercing.

Ignoring him, she takes a sniff, and then sips. The wine passes over her taste buds and down her parched throat without a trace. Once its calming properties take effect, her heart rate finds a steadier beat.

"Why do you keep staring at me?"

"I'm just wondering..."

"Wondering what?"

"What else about you is fake?"

Her heart beats as if she had sprinted around the room.

"Everything about me is fake," she says in a playful jest.

"I thought those were too perfect to be real." Wade drops his eyes to her breasts, glances up, and winks his eyebrows.

She laughs, albeit nervously, and vows to be completely honest with him from here on.

Vangie never found the courage to be completely honest with Wade. A small part of her wished she had never peered into his piercing eyes, but mostly she didn't know how she would live another day without seeing him, touching him, loving him.

Fifteen

It took the will of two elephants for me to skip out on dinner tonight. Around midnight, on top of other things keeping me awake, my hunger pangs got me out of bed. Guided by floor lighting, I tiptoed down the stairs and through the quiet house on cat's feet. Each step on the marble floor, my heart jumped, and sirens went off in my head. If I got caught, what excuse could I give for breaking into Mr. Big's study? It was inexcusable, but I did it anyway, I opened the door quietly and closed it soundlessly.

My eyes gradually adjusted to the darkness. Making out a freestanding lamp near the desk, I clicked it on. It burned low, lighting half of the room. The room dizzied me with its floor to ceiling red wood theme and the encyclopedia-size books taking over the wall-to-wall shelves.

I checked the desk first, appreciating the beauty and timelessness of its mahogany wood finish and curved claw foot legs. West would call it Victorian. Thinking of West made me think of the beautiful writing desk he had given me for my nineteenth birthday, the desk now burned to cinder with the rest of Cambridge Heights Apartments.

Caught up in love and loss, I forgot for a moment what I was risking my freedom to find. *Oh! A certificate, nameplate, or anything that identifies Mr. Big...*

A rustle in the bushes outside the window sent me scampering for the door like a scared cat. I left the study in a hurry, forgetting to turn off the light.

When the new day dawned, I leapt out of bed and changed out of my pajamas and into shorts and my old T-shirt.

I'd discovered a way to run. The house was as quiet as church on Monday mornings. My heart racing, I trotted down the stairs in my new tennis shoes, listening for signs of life and keeping my eyes in motion while I power walked down the main hallway.

Mr. Big's all-inclusive home gym was at the very end of the hallway, next to a room with a pool table and full bar. There were apparatuses of every kind, a mini refrigerator supplied with drinks, a water dispenser, and handy face towels in a bowl of melted ice. I disregarded it all, heading directly to the state-of-the-art treadmill, following the splinter of light shining through the glass-plated back door.

One light touch and the monitor lit up in the semi-darkness. The belt cranked up, accelerating my speed. My feet glided smoothly, geared up for takeoff.

The miles fell away as my speed increased, my feet pounding the belt in an effortless stride. In time, the pressure of trying to fill Vangie's high-heeled shoes melted away and I disappeared into thoughtlessness.

Fifty-five minutes in, while rounding the digitalized track at full speed, relaxing music suddenly filled the room and the recessed lights popped on. Through the mirrored wall, I saw a freckled face white dude wheeling Mr. Big into the room behind me.

At this point I couldn't stop the machine and didn't know how. Without thinking, I yanked off the emergency stop key.

From that point on, I couldn't remember what happened. Thrown from the treadmill, I landed on the floor like a wet rag.

Whooaaa!" The dude stared down at me, looking more interested in my ankle monitor than whether I was alive after my wipe out. I leapt to my feet in one swift move and stood there, unable to put one foot in front of other to walk away.

"Get her a glass of water," Mr. Big ordered, as always, enunciating like his life depended on it.

"Yes, sir." The dude hurried over to the water dispenser and returned with my ice-cold cup. "Here you go."

I took an excessively long gulp not to answer any questions about what I was doing in here or how I could be so clumsy. In my peripheral vision, I watched the dude help Mr. Big out of his wheelchair and stretch him out on a padded table. He then manipulated Mr. Big's legs, bending them to his chest and stretching them this way and that.

When my face finally cooled off, I slinked off, returning to my room to hide out.

I discovered something magical that day. If I skipped a meal, Chef Bernard sent it special delivery through Marisol. Today's menu: buttery, flaky biscuits with strawberry marmalade, Spanish frittata, seasonal fruit, and hot coffee—comfort food after my humiliating morning.

Later that morning Marisol returned to deliver another message. "He wants you. Mr. F," she said.

I gave Marisol a long, confused gape and pointed to myself.

"He is waiting for you. In his room."

"His room?" I croaked.

Marisol half-rolled her eyes at me. "*Si.*" She slammed the door in my face.

I felt like I'd been summoned to the boss's office for a reprimand. What if I'd blown my cover somehow? What if the prosecutor had returned and brought the police with her?

My fear of getting found out suddenly took a back seat to being alone with Mr. Big. I never believed the stories my mother told about Vangie or the whispers about Vangie at school, all of which passed through one of my ears and out of the other. I saw only what I wanted to see and closed my eyes to the rest. But the streets, where grimy men dished out money to have sex with teenage girls, had matured me faster than time could.

But Vangie was different. She never had a pimp that I'd met and had never done drugs that I knew of. But she had money, enough to fill our empty cabinets when food ran low, enough to pay the bills and keep the lights on when our mother couldn't, and enough money to pay her way, and my way, through college. The thought that Vangie might have lived here as the old man's concubine made my stomach turn inside out. I came close to hyperventilating.

Thirty minutes went by. To keep Mr. Big waiting a minute longer would be rude of me. Facing my overwhelming fear, I wandered through the house without a guide. In the isolated east wing of the house, I stumbled on Mr. Big's private suite and peered inside the massive room with soft brown walls and a deep blue color scheme.

"You may come in," Mr. Big said.

The sun, pouring in through the picture windows that overlooked the pool, blinded me as my tennis shoes screeched against the wood floor. I felt sure I would trip over my own two feet at any point now. The knot in my stomach tightened when I approached Mr. Big where he sat upon a blue suede comforter on his throne. He was wearing his fancy robe and silk pajamas bottoms, and even in his feebleness, he looked rich and powerful.

I reached the foot of the sleigh bed and stood behind the wooden frame for added protection.

"You asked to see me, sir?" I squawked.

Mr. Big stared over his eyeglasses that sat on the tip of his nose. "Do you know why you are here?"

Afraid to find out, I shook my head.

"Jail is not a place for a young lady of your cal-i-ber. I don't need to know the sordid details; Kim-ber-ly will get to the bottom of it." He wagged his index finger, pointing toward the sitting area. "See that box. Bring it to me."

I rushed across the room. The black box sat atop a brown, bearskin area rug near the three-sided fireplace. It weighed on my arms as I carried it to him.

"You handled white-collar crimes as an intern?"

I almost shook my head before nodding slowly.

"Review the contents for me. Tell me your findings. Between you and I. Un-der-stood?"

I didn't understand, but I nodded anyway.

Mr. Big stared at me over his eyeglasses again. "It's a nice day. Go for a swim. You're not in jail."

"Oh thanks...but I don't have a bathing suit," was the first excuse that came to mind.

"Mar-i-sol will take care of you. To-mor-row is Sunday dinner. Dress ap-pro-priate-ly. Family tradition."

Maybe he caught my puzzled expression, but he answered my question when he told me to dress semi-formal and to check my closet.

"Thank you so much, sir," I said, bowing as I backed away. He watched me retreat with a peculiar expression on his face, again.

I left the room as fast as I could without running. Behind the locked door of my bedroom, I removed the lid from the black box. I didn't know what to do with the heap of documents inside or what I was supposed to look for. It was easier to hide the box under the bed and pray the old man forgot about it.

Around lunchtime the intercom system buzzed. Lunch would be served poolside, the chef revealed.

At noon, I found Marisol waiting out back by the pool. Her skin reddened when I walked up, giving me the impression that I'd gotten under it again, somehow.

"Mr. F. He says it's okay for you to swim." A question mark hung at the end of Marisol's report. She glanced at my ankle monitor, frowned, and then handed me a beach tote.

"The towels. Over there." She pointed out the nearby towel container stacked with fluffy blue-and-white-striped towels. "Get one for yourself." She walked off, mumbling to herself in Spanish again.

The beach tote contained everything I needed: a bikini, a new pair of sliders, a sheer white mini beach dress, goggles, sunscreen lotion, dark sunglasses, and a fashion magazine. I locked myself in the pool house and changed into a tangerine string bikini, which I covered with the beach dress. Lunch was waiting for me poolside when I returned to the deck, and so was Chef Bernard, who stood under the gazebo with one hand behind his back.

"*Bon appetite.*" With a sweep of his hand, he gestured for me to take a seat at the long bar facing the blue sectional and brick fireplace.

Lunch was a burger on a golden pretzel roll with gooey cheddar cheese spilling over the edges, a side of artfully displayed French fries, and a lightly dressed spring salad, all presented on a gourmet wooden paddleboard. A saucer of plump chocolate chip cookies drizzled with chocolate sauce and garnished with a cherry, a glass of lemonade crusted with sugar, and a bottle of Voss finished off the five-star meal.

I stared at the chef with stars in my eyes. "It's beautifully plated," I said.

"Enjoy." He winked at me. When he waltzed away, I dug in.

The savory flavors of the juicy burger exploded in my mouth like fireworks. The beef was premium and perfectly cooked, making for a nearly orgasmic experience. Sadly, food was the only thing close to an orgasmic experienced I'd ever had.

Next, I tasted the homemade fries, crunching into crispiness, and then took slow bites of the delicious salad. There was a method to my madness when it came to food. Whichever taste I loved most, I finished with last. I stuffed the last bite of burger into my mouth and licked my fingers clean. Then I folded the cookies inside the napkin and placed it inside the tote bag in the event I succumbed to starvation in the middle of the night.

I left the Jacuzzi to give the freestanding hammock a try. Big, round and cushy, it swayed gently as I listened to the palm trees rustling in the breeze, the birds singing nearby, and the soft sound of water from the Jacuzzi drizzling over a mound of rocks.

Eventually I found the courage to take a swim. Taking baby steps across the pebbled surface, I crossed the shallow water until it covered my ankle bracelet. I then sat on the steps and dangled my legs over the pool's edge, worried my bracelet would somehow alert the police. The cool water lapped at my thighs and hips, warming me up to the idea of diving in. The water shimmered in the purest sapphire blue I'd ever seen, and after several minutes, I could no longer resist it.

On my own dare, I submerged myself in five feet of water and came up exhilarated, water dripping down my face. I swiped it away, took in a deep breath, and plunged again.

Now I was swimming around like an awkward fish rediscovering its habitat. I made it halfway to other side of the pool without coming up for air this time, then floated on my back weightlessly, staring dreamily at the clear blue sky.

I swam until my fingertips shriveled up like prunes before stepping out of the pool and then stepping down into the hot Jacuzzi whirling with bubbles. Resting me head against the headrest, I stared out into the flawless view of the city, enjoying the beautiful, carefree day while the time lasted.

Sixteen

A loud hammering at the front door rattled the little pink house. Ross moved stealthily toward the bookshelf, pulled a nine-millimeter from a hollowed out book and cocked it. Pressing a finger to his lips, he cautioned Clarissa to keep quiet while fanning the gun in Vangie's direction, instructing her to hide.

"Who is it?" he bellowed in a hostile tone.

Inside the bedroom, Vangie looked around frantically. Finding a place to hide was a joke. The old house held enough ancillary junk to jam the space underneath the bed and overstuff the small closet, and any chance she had of reaching the backyard to hide had been lost. This was the end of the line for her.

Vangie sat on the bed and waited out her fate. It wasn't the police who came bursting in, however.

"False alarm. Just a solicitor," Clarissa reported breathlessly, and then slammed the bedroom door behind her.

Vangie's chest collapsed, but her relief was temporary.

Clarissa's nerves were more wrecked than hers after learning Ross was a proud gun owner. Forget the obvious fact that they all could've been indicted for obstruction of justice.

Clarissa held out her hand, palm down. "I'm shaking like a leaf. This is a living nightmare."

Vangie concurred, a living nightmare she couldn't awaken from.

Ross peeked his head into the room. "What're ya'll waiting for?"

"Are you serious? You own a friggin' gun, Ross!" Clarissa ranted.

Ross laughed.

Their final strategy meeting never resumed.

Vangie woke to a headache and the smell of freshly brewed coffee. Needing a pick-me-up, she dragged herself out of bed and walked into the kitchen, intending to grab a cup of coffee and retreat back into solitude and misery

"Ew! Ew! Ew!" Clarissa shrieked. "Behind the coffee pot."

"What's behind it?"

"There! Right there!" Clarissa pointed at the wall, screeching and squirming as if her skin crawled with spiders.

"It's a roach, Riss."

"Oh, my God!"

"Just kill it."

"Kill it with what?"

"Your shoe."

Clarissa looked horrified at the idea of killing a cockroach with her designer sling backs that coordinated with her tan, black, and white dress.

"Kill it for me, Van. You know I'm a bug-a-phobe. Oh, my God! There it goes again! Up the friggin' wall!" Taking cover by the door, Clarissa pointed and cried. "Get it!"

The roach dashed for cover, but it was no match for Vangie. She grabbed a napkin and caught it before it could squirm into the crevices of the lime green tile.

"Is it dead?"

Van balled up the napkin and threw it into the trashcan. "It is now."

A look of complete disgust discolored Clarissa's face. Never in Clarissa's privileged life had she seen a roach let alone had to slay a rat or two. Vangie wanted to laugh. She thought it best not to tell Clarissa that there was a good chance more roaches were hiding in the walls, waiting to strike at midnight. Besieged by déjà' vu, her mood darkened a shade.

"Maybe I shouldn't leave you alone, today of all days," Clarissa said, striking up a serious conversation just as Vangie poured herself a cup of coffee.

"I'll be fine, Riss. Go home."

"Are you sure?"

"I'm sure."

"I wish you could come to church with us today."

"Me too." Vangie walked Clarissa to the front door.

"We're going straight to the office after church. Work is piling up and I have to fulfill my secretarial duties." Clarissa rolled her eyes. "I shouldn't complain, right? We need the money. Do you know most small firms fail in the first year? Granddad made that abundantly clear..." Clarissa paused midsentence and gave Vangie a long, somber stare.

They fell into a tight hug.

"Be strong," Clarissa said.

When Clarissa left the house, Vangie took a deep breath and kept a cool head. It had always been that way, her ability to compartmentalize in the face of debilitating fear, much like a traumatized child in a warzone. If Annette Cooper hadn't prepared her for anything else in life, she had prepared her for disaster.

Waiting was the hard part. To avoid any appearance of collusion and obstruction, they had all agreed there would be no contact between the three of them until further notice. Ross and Clarissa would return to their comfortable lifestyle and she was on her own.

She walked to her bedroom and found the pair of sharp scissors Clarissa had purchased, fought to remove them from the plastic package, and then sullenly entered the bathroom.

Her long hair had been the envy of other women and attracted the eyes of men for as long as she could remember. Wade wasn't an exception. He loved her hair long. She loved it too, and never imagined the day would come when she cut it all off.

With each snip strands of hair gathered around her feet, and the heaviness of her past seemed to fall off with it. Standing in a puddle of coal-black hair, Vangie studied her handiwork in the bathroom mirror. Her hair now framed her face in a short, natural style.

Without makeup, she was confident no one could tell her and Angie apart.

Seventeen

Now that daylight savings had come to an end, the sun was slow to rise and quick to set. It was 6:00 p.m. already, and I had less than thirty minutes to decide what was appropriate to wear for Sunday dinner. I thought up ways to lie my way out of attending, but guilt was a thorn in my side, prodding me to get up and get dressed.

Inside the walk-in closet were fancy coats and jackets, some fur, others leather or wool. There was a rack full of dresses—long sequenced ones, beaded ones, short ones, and simple or satin ones. Rows of stiletto pumps and beautiful purses covered the shelf space from floor to ceiling.

I closed my eyes and recited: "Eeny meeny miny moe."

My arbitrary pick turned out to be a long, black, overly tight dress with a neckline that fell too far down my shoulders and a split that ran too high up my right thigh.

I spent the next few minutes in a fit of frustration over what to do with my hair. Fed-up with it, I slicked it back and slapped on mounds of hair gel to hold it in place.

Thanks to Chef Bernard's cold compress the bruising around my eye and forehead had begun to fade, and the makeup Clarissa bought me helped to conceal what was left of it. Other than that, I went with my natural look.

At 6:25 I pushed my feet into black pumps. When I turned around, the gangly creature staring back at me in the full-length mirror caught me off guard. I could stare at myself until the cows came home, and Vangie and I would always be identical in everyone else's eyes but my own.

When I walked into the dining hall five minutes late, I came to a standstill. The chandeliers were dimmed, and the stretched fireplace flickered in a sequence of gold flames behind the glass screen. Three burning candelabras, set off by two bouquets of white chrysanthemums, decorated the dining table tonight.

Mr. Big was parked at the head of the table dressed in tuxedo style suit jacket and a white collared shirt; his hair looked newly cut and his face clean-shaven. But Mr. Big hadn't made me come to a hasty halt. The dude sitting in my assigned seat had.

"The bride has fin-a-lly arrived," I thought Mr. Big said, but could've been mistaken.

Lightheadedness made me realize I wasn't breathing. On wobbly knees, I sat down next to Mr. Big and across from the dude, grateful the wide table separated us. He didn't look happy to see Vangie, and since I was the object of his anger, I avoided eye contact as best I could.

But I sneaked nervous peeks. His skin reminded me of warm, sweet pumpernickel bread. He wore his curly hair shaved close to his head, his mustache and beard tracing his chiseled jaw line and rounding his lips, which reminded me of a nicely shaped heart.

I quickly lowered my head and stared at my own reflection in the shiny plate while nervously spreading my napkin across my lap.

The chef served salad with bacon and cheese cheddar biscuits as an appetizer. My mouth watered to taste just one cheesy biscuit, but I was too nervous to eat, to move or to look this dude directly into his eyes, which drilled into mine.

"I need to talk to you. Privately," Dude barked at me. He pushed off the table and stood. Standing six feet three or taller, he seemed to grow to an abominable size as he walked in my direction. To my relief and happiness, he walked right by me, stalking off in a silver-blue suit that narrowed at his long, muscular legs.

I looked at Mr. Big in silent appeal for help, but it was Chef Bernard who spoke up.

"Don't just sit there, darlin'." He was standing over Mr. Big, pouring him a glass of wine.

In no great hurry to meet with this dude privately or publicly, I stood slowly and left the room on two left feet. When I turned the corner, he was standing in the grand entryway. He stalked off when our eyes connected. I followed him down the main hallway, struggling to keep up.

When he turned into Mr. Big's study, I turned in after him. My knees on the verge of buckling, I dashed for the first chair in my path and leaned on its curved back to take the weight off my weak ankles.

He paced in front of the fireplace like a caged tiger in wingtip dress shoes. When he finally looked at me, I rolled my eyes over the wood beams and across the wood paneled walls so as not to make eye contact. The family portrait hanging over the fireplace mantel and above his head caught my attention. My roving eyes doubled back.

"The Fitzgerald's" the gold nameplate beneath the portrait read. The name sat on the tip of my tongue like a spice I could taste but couldn't name.

There were two men, three women, a boy in his teens maybe, and one toddler; all were dressed fancily and standing around Mr. Big, who sat in a throne-like chair and looked twenty years younger and in much better health. Mr. Big's perfect smile sat squarely on his face and stretched from ear to ear; and his irises twinkled like stars on a black night.

I stared at the youngest woman standing to Mr. Big's left. My eyes must have doubled in size. The prosecutor may have been younger in the portrait, but her serious mug was just as intimidating.

My eyes jumped from the prosecutor back to youngest dude in the portrait. Hypnotized by the same brown eyes, curved like half moons, I stared, first at the dude in the portrait and then at the man pacing before me. I finally put two and two together.

Wade Fitzgerald the Fourth!

I remembered now like it was yesterday. At the mention of his name, Vangie's eyes gleamed and her cheeks flushed. He was the only dude I'd ever known her to love, and one of the many secrets she'd kept from me. They were all related somehow, dude, the prosecutor, Clarissa, and Mr. Big!

"Is it true? Did you do it? Tell me you didn't, Van," Dude said.

I inspected the chair's fine leather, afraid if I looked up, he would know I wasn't Vangie.

When I peeked up, his breathing escalated, inflating and deflating his nostrils as he stared at me.

"What do you expect me to think? Huh? Huh, Vangie? You disappeared off the grid." His voice cracked and his eyes turned to glass.

"I'm sorry," I muttered for no other reason than to say something to console him.

"Sorry for what? For murdering Todd, for walking out on me, or are you sorry you didn't get away with it?" He screwed up his face. "Who are you? I don't even know you..." His heated voice had lowered to a simmer. He stuffed his hands back into his pants pockets as if to contain his rage. "On second thought, spare me another lie."

I wanted to plead Vangie's innocence, but he blew past me like a windstorm and left me in the wake of his sadness. Heart aching for reasons unknown to me, I rubbed the goosebumps covering my arms while hugging myself. I'd never needed my mother so much or missed home more.

I picked up Mr. Big's landline, the old kind, with dial by numbers. My heart stopped beating when the phone rang and revived when my mother answered. I wanted to tell her how much I loved her, apologize for abandoning her again, tell her not to worry about me, tell her I'd made it back to Colorado safely even if it wasn't true.

Choked up, I hung up the phone.

Eightteen

When I woke up the next morning, I wanted to go back to jail where no one knew Vangie intimately and I could get by with just being me. If I stayed here, I would be found out. I was sure of it.

I hopped out of bed and dressed quickly. Knowing the layout of the house by now, I took the back route to the gym. I made it to the gym safely, grabbed a sports drink from the mini-fridge and a power bar from the cabinet and demolished them both before takeoff.

Six miles in sixty minutes was my usual goal for the day. I cut it down to three. I hadn't seen Mr. Big since last night and wanted to beat the clock before his physical therapy got going.

I had run a mile when Marisol walked up and startled me half to death. I turned off the treadmill, safely this time, and hopped down.

"Hi," I said, breathily.

"A call. For you." She held a phone in her hand.

Something in Marisol's distrustful eyes made me hesitate to accept the call. Who would call me here anyway? Maybe it was Ross or Clarissa.

I reached for the phone and got caught up in tug-of-war with Marisol. Shooting daggers at me with her eyes, she held on tightly before relaxing her clutch on the receiver.

"*Vergonzosa*," she muttered under her breath as she walked away. I didn't know what the word meant, but I got the gist from her judgmental tone.

I brought the receiver to my ear. "Hello," I croaked out.

"Vangie," the man said in a baritone voice. "It's me. Douglas."

My mouth dropped open. I couldn't breathe. My emotions were whirling like a cyclone. Drenched in sweat, I took off running, almost mowing over Marisol as I sprinted by her. I leapt up the stairs two at a time. When I closed myself inside my room, I came back to my senses.

Douglas wasn't calling for me. He was calling for Vangie.

"Hello... Hello," Douglas said. "Vangie. Did I lose you?"

I cleared my throat to let him know I was listening.

"Before you hang up in my face, your mother asked me to give you a call. She said she received a call from this number last night. I hope what I've heard isn't true. I'll be blown away if it is. Out of the hundreds of students I've mentored over the years, you had the makings of success and an Ivy leaguers list of institutions to choose from. I'll leave it there. You don't need a lecture from me right now..."

Silence...

"I called the correctional facility and found out you've been released on bail. What's the situation? Is this where you live? What's the address? I'll be there to see you. Are you permitted visitors?"

I coughed to keep from chocking.

"You never want to see me again," he said to my coughing. "I haven't forgotten that slap. Trust me. What happened between Angie and me is on me; I take full responsibility for mishandling the situation and dishonoring your trust in me."

I pressed my hand over my mouth so as not to make a sound.

"Can you forgive me? You know I love you, Van. I'd hate to fly two thousand miles and get kicked to the curb." Douglas chuckled at his own joke. "I can be there as early as next week. Hello? Vangie? Did I lose you?"

I hated to hang up on Douglas, but I couldn't see him if I wanted to—and I couldn't let him see me. Douglas was one of the few people who could tell Vangie and me apart.

Memories of what happened between us came back, first like a flower blossoming on the first day of spring and then like a thunderstorm blowing through my life, leaving me out in the cold, homeless and alone.

I jumped into the shower to hide my crocodile tears.

Downstairs, breakfast was waiting when I walked into the sunroom. Its casual décor suited me more than the dining room's formal setting. The early morning sunlight streamed through tall curtain-less windows, offering a lovely view of the mountains.

The maple wood table for six was decorated with a bouquet of yellow mums, and Chef Bernard had set out an assortment of beverages on the antique buffet for me to choose from. I picked lemon tea and honey over my usual cup of coffee, then sat down to a quiet breakfast alone. Mr. Big preferred breakfast in bed.

A hot plate kept my meal warm. "Bon Appétit!" the tent card beside my plate read, giving me something to smile about.

I scarfed down my food so fast I regretted not taking the time to appreciate the incredible artistry of Chef Bernard's bowl of cheesy grits and poached eggs garnished with sautéed spinach and crisp bacon pieces.

When finished, I left the table in a hurry, carrying my empty dishes with me. I needed an excuse to enter the kitchen. Curiosity had emboldened me, either that or my sudden indifference toward everything. I reflected back to the night I sneaked into the kitchen at Roxy's House and thought nothing of violating the rules by baking a batch of cheesy biscuits. Filled with emptiness no amount of food could satisfy, I wanted to get caught that night. In a sense, today was no different.

I was feeling some kind of way, not toward Douglas but toward Vangie for her perfect beauty that emphasized my imperfections. I never made old men want to be young again, and girls, like the ones back in high school, hate me for just being me. Well, not me personally. I'd basically gone unseen and unheard my entire four years of high school, a boring shadow standing in the way of Vangie's golden light. Maybe it wouldn't hurt so much if I'd ever been loved by a man. I'd choose Vangie over me too if I were Douglas.

I walked boldly through the master kitchen's wide arched doorway. Seeing no signs of Chef Bernard, I set my dirty dishes on white marble countertop and crossed the gray wood floor in total awe of the kitchen's ultramodern machinery. The entire space outdid my wildest dreams and took my breath away. This kitchen was a chef's dream.

The Wolf range had ten burners, cast-iron grates, and a built-in griddle. I fired it up and watched the blue flames burn evenly and effortlessly.

The sub-zero refrigerator blended seamlessly with antique white wood cabinets. I flung back the heavy double doors and stood in the cool draft, investigating the racks of neatly arranged foods and marinating meats.

The food pantry was the size of a small kitchen, the white shelves so high that a wheeled ladder was used to reach the top shelves. Every great chef kept a handy supply of seasonings, I imagined. Chef Bernard kept his supply in pullout drawers, every kind of spice I could imagine alphabetized by name, from the basic to the most exotic.

I returned to the kitchen. After rinsing of my dishes, I placed them in the dishwasher to dry and then sat at one of the eight barstool chairs around the kitchen island to dream a little while.

I hadn't sat for very long when I heard the doorbell chime. Poised to run, I stretched my leg out to one side and listened closely for the prosecutor's voice. It wasn't a woman's voice that I heard, but a man's voice, deep and raspy and similar to Detective Carter's. Fear flashed through me like lightning.

I searched for an exit and found a narrow stairwell leading to the second floor. My room had been cleaned and smelled of citrus zest. I destroyed it looking for the cell phone Clarissa gave me to use in case of an emergency.

I searched inside the nightstand drawer and under the bed, crawling around on my knees. I turned the pocket lining of my jeans inside out and came up with lint. Now I was ringing my hands and walking the carpet, trying to think in a fog of fear. I was sure I'd tucked the phone safely between the box springs and mattress.

Marisol!

A sharp knock on the door stilled my heart.

"Vangie. It's Detective Sergeant Carter!" A second or two passed before he knocked again. "I'm coming in!" he announced while simultaneously entering my room without permission.

I remembered what Clarissa had explicitly instructed me to say, but I said nothing.

"Let's have a talk." Carter took me by my forearm and ushered me downstairs. I expected him to take me straight to jail, but he took me to a small parlor where two cops were posted at the door with their hands on their guns.

Mr. Big wheeled up at top speed with his nurse, who trotted behind him as if chasing after a runaway shopping cart. When Mr. Big reached the parlor, he turned sharply and blocked the parlor entrance with his wheelchair.

"I will be present during quest-ion-ing," he said.

"No need for that, Mr. Fitzgerald. You go get your rest. This is not an interrogation," said Carter."

"It had better not be!" Mr. Big said, stutter free, I noticed.

Detective Carter smiled thinly. "I understand you're a fine attorney, sir. Unfortunately for Ms. Cooper, she forfeited her right to have her attorney present when she failed to invoke Miranda. She should've spoken up when she had the chance. Now, if you'll move aside, sir..."

Mr. Big stared at me as if I must be the dumbest person on planet earth.

"This is still my house!" he fussed as his nurse wheeled him off.

Inside the parlor, Carter motioned for me to sit in one of the four wingback chairs huddled around a center-leg table. I sat near the window and focused my attention on

140 | Sheryl Mallory-Johnson

my tennis shoes. Carter sat adjacent to me, leaning on his knees as if we were about to have a heart-to-heart talk.

"If anyone understands how it feels to lose someone they love and to not have answers, you should." He pulled a folded sheet of paper from his suit pocket and handed it to me. "Is this the missing person's report you filed on your twin?"

The lump in my throat went down like a block of ice. Batting back tears, I looked over the report written in Vangie's handwriting. Based on the date listed, Vangie had filed the missing person's report one day after I ran from home.

I closed my eyes, tasting the salt of my tears as they drained down my face into the corners of my mouth.

"I have a very good lead from a reliable source on Angie's whereabouts as I speak," he said.

My eyes dried instantaneously.

Carter watched me as if my thumping heart was visible to the naked eye. Involuntarily, my hand flew to the nape of my neck and my fingers twisted the strands of my hair. My foot twitched out of my control. Guilt had to have been written across my forehead.

"False personation and obstruction of justice are felonies that carry a *long* prison sentence. Where is Vangie, Angie?"

Thunder cracked in my ears. I opened my mouth to ask for my lawyer. What came out was air.

"Here's what I believe. I believe there's more to this case than meets the eye. You're the law-abiding twin, aren't you? You want to do what's right. Your twin sister is the mastermind. She tells you to jump and you say how high. She tells you to commit perjury and you obey. You'd do anything for her, wouldn't you, even premeditate a plot to cover up her murder?"

No!

"Well, unfortunately, you got the short end of the stick. If you're waiting for her to step forward, you're kidding yourself. She's living it up somewhere, sipping a Mai Tai on the beach. She's off the hook and you're on it. You'll die in jail for a crime she's guilty of committing and she won't give a damn."

I was drowning in fear and tears.

"Here's what I'm willing to do for you. Help me close this case and I'll do all that I can to get the judge to agree to a lighter sentence for your cooperation. Deal?"

I pondered my options. If worse came to worse, I could tell him I planned everything, stealing Vangie's driver license and passport and faking her identity. I would make him see that Vangie wasn't a killer.

Then the simplest solution came to me. If I confessed to the murder, I could get Vangie a lighter sentence and time off for good behavior.

Be smarter, Angie...

As always, Vangie's warning to "be smarter" breezed through my mind in a ghost whisper. I wished I had been smarter and had upheld our vow to one another—maybe life would've turned out differently for the both of us.

I heard a commotion in the hallway outside the room before the shouting started.

"That's my client in there!" Ross yelled.

"Let him in," Carter said.

Ross strolled into the room and up to Carter. "Don't you ever talk to my client without coming through me first."

When Detective Carter stood, his height surpassed Ross's by a mile. He stared down at Ross bull-faced with flared nostrils. I feared he would crush Ross in the palm of his massive hand. Ross didn't back down though. Eventually, Carter did and left the room.

I threw my arms around Ross's neck.

"You need to chill," Ross whispered in my ear, delicately pushing me off him. He straightened out the knot of his tie and raised his index finger, warning me not to speak.

"Did you make any self-incriminating statements?"

I shook my head.

He opened his attaché and pulled from it a piece of paper that looked similar to the contract I signed back in jail.

"Sign—*your* name." He handed me a pen.

I scribbled my name on the line as fast as my trembling fingers could write.

"Here's what you're going to do. Go straight to the pool house, lock the door, and don't open it for anyone except Clarissa. Got it?"

I bolted into the hallway where the two officers idled. When I saw the prosecutor talking to Detective Carter, I flew past them both without stopping.

Nineteen

Sometime around 8:00 A.M. an anonymous caller tipped off the district attorney's office that the police had arrested the wrong twin. It was now 10:30 A.M.

A bundle of raw nerves, Vangie filled up on coffee, cookies, chips, and mixed nuts. Her stomach churned as she walked the house, rehearsing her lines as if preparing for a final trial closing argument. Preparation outfoxed the smartest student in class was a doctrine she acquired from mock plea negotiations in her first year of law school.

At 10:45 A.M., Vangie sat at the dining room table, now geared up for the performance of a lifetime. Her cell phone had been carefully placed on the table right next to her second cup of coffee.

At 10:57 A.M., her nerves were crawling, her heart beating in time with the old grandfather clock.

At 11:00 A.M., Vangie called Ross. He answered on the first ring in a voice that held both excitement and a touch of strain, which could've indicated any number of results, thought Vangie.

"Ross E. Lewis speaking!"

A beat passed while Vangie gathered her nerves. "This is Vangie Cooper—the real Vangie Cooper. The Court arraigned the wrong person. I'm offering a plea bargain."

"Hold on…"

Vangie heard a pause on the line, rustling and muffled conversations in the background, and suspected Detective Sergeant Carter was trying to trace her untraceable phone.

"I have you on speaker phone," Ross chimed back in.

"Hello, Vangie. This is Assistant District Attorney Kimberly Fitzgerald. You may remember my brother, the one you left standing at the altar."

Kimmy had stepped on Vangie's Achilles heel and weakened her with her first blow. White noise filled her ears. Whatever her rehearsed lines were, she couldn't recall them.

"We need identification, some form of proof that you are who you say you are," Ross said.

"I am. Trust me."

"Trust you? This is absurd! Prove your identity or this plea offer will be taken off the table now!" Kimmy snapped.

"Hold up. In the best interest of my client, I'd like to hear what she has to offer, if I can," Ross said.

Vangie chimed in. "I'm turning myself in under one condition…"

"Let me guess," Kimmy interjected. "Under the condition that I don't slap your colluding twin sister with a felony for fraudulent identification, obstructing justice, and being an accessory after the fact."

"Now that we're on the same page," Vangie said, regaining her bearings. "My twin must also receive complete immunity in return for my surrender or I will walk off into the sunset. That's my offer."

"My constitutional and ethical responsibility are to the victim's family and *friends* whose hearts have been ripped out because of your heinous crime. You must plead guilty to murder one. That's the only offer I'll entertain."

"This is an all or nothing deal," Vangie said, her tone uncompromising.

"You're not calling the shots! I am! Rest assured you *will* be apprehended. I'll use all the resources at my disposal to find you if it takes me the next twenty-five years while your twin sister serves out her sentence in a maximum-security prison. I'd tread very lightly if I were you, Vangie."

Vangie knew she was indeed on slippery ground, but she also knew, if Kimmy got the impression that she was willing to lay down her life for Angie, all bets would be off the table.

She hung up the phone.

She would let Kimmy sweat it out and leave the impression Kimmy had let a fugitive slip through her hands. God knew she herself was sweating and unraveling like cheap fabric. Her ability to compartmentalize and focus on the issue at hand had waned and her fear now ventured in the territory of the irrational.

What if the police had traced her burner phone through some advanced form of technology and were, at this very moment, en route to the little pink house? If she were apprehended, her attempt to subvert the criminal justice system wouldn't go over well with a judge or jury. They would throw the book at her, and Kimmy would invoke all the power of the state to make certain she never saw daylight again.

A siren sounded nearby and sent Vangie rushing to the window. She peeked through the blinds wildly, expecting to see a fleet of police cars, but the siren faded in the distance.

Thirty minutes later, when her stomach got off its rollercoaster ride, she regained her composure and called Ross back.

"We're ready to negotiate a plea deal," Ross said when he answered, putting on a great show for Kimmy's benefit.

Vangie didn't take her small victory as a win. She knew the plea-bargaining process had only just begun.

Kimmy set an uncompromising tone. The DA's office would recommend a lighter sentence for Angie, eliminating the charge of obstruction of justice if, and only if, she pled guilty to first degree murder.

"Let's be real," Ross told Kimmy. "The probability of this case going to trial is slim to none. We all have something to gain from this deal."

"Who exactly are you representing, Counselor, the killer or her diabolical twin?" Kimberly said suspiciously.

"I'm representing myself," Vangie made perfectly clear.

"The folly of every rookie attorney. You're a fugitive wanted for first degree murder with the aggravating factor of obstructing justice. That's an inherent problem to start with in any *backdoor* plea-bargaining procedure. My offer stands."

"I have one dog in this race, my client," Ross said. "She's willing to accept the lesser misdemeanor charge of fraudulent identification and a small fine if the DA's office agrees not to pursue felony charges against her."

Vangie waited with bated breath for Kimmy to either accept or reject Ross's offer. If Kimmy called her bluff, she didn't have a counteroffer.

Kimmy accepted the plea deal with the caveat that Angie serve six-month's probation in exchange for Vangie's guilty plea. Ross said he would confer with his client, but he was confident Angie would take the deal.

Now that the dust had settled between Ross and Kimmy, Vangie was left with a difficult decision—pleading guilty to the charge of murder in the first degree or being certain that she was setting Angie free. If she pled guilty, she would forgo a trial, relinquish her day in court, and the murder charge against her would seal her fate. She didn't have much choice.

"I'll turn myself in, but I will not plead guilty to murder one. That's my deal. Take it or leave it," she said sternly.

Her decision to reject Kimmy's offer rested on two crucial factors: First, Kimmy was in line to become the next county district attorney and aspired to be the next Attorney General for the state of California. If Kimmy rejected her offer, Kimmy knew that an onslaught of bad press might follow and have ramifications for her career. And second, the prosecution had yet to establish a motive for the murder and there was the added burden of mistaken identity. If the real killer remained at large, the district attorney's case would be trashed and Todd's murder would go unsolved and unpunished, from their perspective, since they really had no idea what happened.

Her hard line with Kimmy was a shot in the dark and maybe suicidal. The most she could do now was to hope that Kimmy wouldn't put up a fight. However, disappointment after disappointment had taught her that hoping for miracles didn't guarantee a happy ending.

~

I stayed locked in the pool house, afraid to open the door for anyone but Clarissa. When she showed up, she told me about the plea deal I was being offered, saying that if I confessed to impersonating Vangie I would only have to serve six-months on probation and pay a small fine.

"It's the best possible plea deal we can get for you. I strongly advise that you take it," Clarissa said.

I questioned Clarissa's legal advice on account of the contradiction in her eyes. She spoke as if she might not take her own advice if our places were reversed. What if I accepted the deal and it ruined Vangie's chances of being found innocent someday? In that case, I'd rather go back to jail. I shook my head, rejecting the deal.

Clarissa moved from the chair and sat next to me on the couch. Taking both my hands into hers, she looked me directly in the eyes. "What I'm going to show you cannot leave this room under any circumstances. Okay?" she whispered.

I gulped and nodded.

She then reached into the small front pocket of her dress, pulled out piece of paper and pressed it into the palm of my right hand. I uncurled my fingers. The paper was yellow and folded into quarters.

I looked up at Clarissa inquisitively.

"Go ahead. Open it."

Nervously, I peeled back the edges of the paper and read the words—*No stretch of the sea or the circumference of the earth will ever come between us.* Tears filled my eyes, blurring everything. The vow Vangie and I had made to one another was forever written on my heart.

I peeked up at Clarissa. She smiled faintly, the only confirmation I needed to know that Vangie was alive. I lend over my knees, crying and clutching Vangie's note in my hand. A rainbow had been painted over my heart and I could finally see a silver lining in a dark cloud.

"You're making me cry." Clarissa sniffled.

When I could pull myself together, I sat up and looked at Clarissa as if my life depended on her answer to my question. "Can I see her?"

Clarissa wiped a tear from her face, pinched her mouth, sucked in a breath, and sighed loudly. "I'll have an answer for you as soon as I get a call from Ross." She squeezed my hands again. "Angie, you have to accept this plea deal."

Clarissa had never called me by my name. Ross must know, too. I wondered if Mr. Big knew as well. What about Wade Fitzgerald the Fourth, Chef Bernard, and Marisol? I'm sure my face turned all shades of red, partially out of embarrassment but mostly because of the undeniable fact that I could never be Vangie.

I nodded my head, accepting the plea deal.

When Clarissa's cell phone rang, we both jumped as if something had bitten us.

Twenty

The defense had outfoxed the prosecution in the first round, but the prospect of dying in prison overshadowed Vangie's victory. Kimmy's instructions were unambiguous. If she didn't turn herself into the authorities within 24 hours, the plea deal would be withdrawn, and the district attorney's office would proceed with an indictment against Angie for two felony counts and instigate an all-out man hunt to locate the real killer.

Once taken into custody, she wouldn't have the chance to see Angie outside the confines of a closely monitored visitation room or have a private moment with Angie after their years of separation. She would be lucky if she could reach out and touch Angie ever again.

Vangie reflected on the note she had written to Angie, a note she implored Clarissa not to read. Their sisterly vow was theirs alone, a pact they made when they were too young to fully comprehend its significance. Now, more than ever, Vangie hung on to her promise to Angie.

Instinctively she knew the exact moment Angie had read her note. Tears sprang up in her eyes and a burning sensation shot across her chest until she bent over her knees to catch her breath. She had thought their unexplainable bond had been forever lost, and remembered when she could read Angie's mind, speak Angie's unspoken words, and finish Angie's sentences.

Vangie rushed for the front door. The locked security screen, caked with dust, stood between her and a breath of fresh air. She stared at the dismal scenery like she would a still life and turned her eyes to the sky. To the west the sun set the sky ablaze. To the east dark clouds assembled. The imagery represented the crossroads of her life, the calm before and after a storm, though she wasn't sure which side of the storm she was on anymore.

Then came the melodious jingle of an ice cream truck, drawing Vangie's weary gaze to the street that suddenly came alive. One neighbor, several houses down the way, had parked his lower-rider on the lawn. Spanish music played loudly through the open doors as he went about detailing it. Another neighbor thought it might be a good day to lug her household junk onto the lawn and have a garage sale. Kids played in the street and sirens went off.

On a normal day, the sights, sounds, even the smell of the neighborhood would've insulted Vangie's senses. Faced with spending the rest of life in prison, however, brought on odd sense of homesickness for her.

Kids came from all direction and assembled around the ice cream truck. Vangie kept an eye on a tenacious toddler who couldn't have been older than three or four, her hair wild and uncombed, her feet bare and soiled. The toddler ducked her way through the mob, tugged the shirt of one of bigger boys, and got a boost to the window. Minutes later, the toddler ran off, holding up her popsicle like she had the golden ticket.

Vangie chuckled, surprising herself. She had never viewed kids as cute or cuddly. The very idea of having children was a concept attached to another women's body, never her own. If she were the sentimental type, she would have cried over that proverbial spilled milk. But she merely closed the front door, walked to her room, and packed a meager bag. Clarissa would take care of her assets for her.

Night fell quickly, too quickly for Vangie. She hung on to every passing minute as her final hours of freedom slipped away. Clarissa had bought her favorite food from her favorite restaurant as if it was her last meal. It may as well have been, thought Vangie.

She heated up a plate in the microwave, sat on the living room sofa in front of the TV, and ingested small forkfuls of tasteless food, gulping wine to wash it down. She had drained the entire bottle before she realized it and hardly touched the food.

An insatiable desire to dance came over her. Languidly, she picked up the remote control, aimed it at the TV, and found a music channel. A new-school pop song got her off of the couch. Her mother believed music was a panacea for unhappiness; her mother also believed she could 'bottle up happiness and use it whenever she was sad or lonely'.

Vangie laughed out loud as she danced around the living room, letting her imagination run away with her. She wasn't in a little pink house, hours away from going to jail; she was at the club, *turned up*.

In her mind's eye she danced with Wade. He grinned down at her and did that lip-licking maneuver that made her stomach dip. She turned her butt to him, raised her arms to the sky, and swayed her hips seductively against his pelvis, imagining his long arms hugging her from behind, his sweet breath at her ear, whispering, "I love you."

When she turned around, Ronnie had taken Wade's place. He pulled her close and kissed her lovingly. She intertwined her legs with his as they gyrated to the beat, laughing into each other's eyes.

Prompted by treasured memories and the good times she and Ronnie shared, Vangie found her cell phone. If she couldn't call Wade, she could always call Ronnie.

Ronnie didn't pick up. She tried again. No answer. It was that stupid fight they had, she thought. She was probably the last person he wanted to talk to. With nothing to lose, she called Ronnie a third time.

"Ron! It's me!" She yelled into the phone when Ronnie answered. Whatever Ronnie was saying she couldn't hear with the music bumping in the background.

"Hold on a minute. I'm having a private party!" She laughed and lowered the music. "What'd you say?"

"This is not Ronnie. This is Ronnie's father. Ron is incapacitated."

Vangie was laughing again and didn't know why. Zeke the Great's tone, resounding with arrogance and reeking of privilege, had given her a chill.

"Incapacitated?" she repeated. "How?"

"A car accident. It's all over the fucking news."

"You're not serious?"

"Yes, I'm serious. Who is this?" Zeke demanded.

Vangie hung up the phone and withered to the couch. The wine suddenly had an adverse effect, engulfing her in grief.

Vangie couldn't remember how or what time she fell asleep last night. She awakened out of dark sleep splayed out on the couch, the side of her face pressed to leather and her body in a sweat. Mindful of the time, she sprang up and wished she hadn't. Her head split in two.

Pushing past her splitting headache, Vangie showered and dressed in a hurry, giving little thought to her attire. Jeans and a nice but old T-shirt would have to do. Nothing too chic that would draw attention, and nothing that wouldn't distinguish her from a common criminal.

Her wig slipped over her short hair with ease. Dark sunglasses camouflaged her red, swollen eyes. She found an outdated bottle of aspirin in the medicine cabinet and hoped it worked magic, then threw back two pills, which she downed with a cup of coffee.

Vangie locked up, hid the key under an old planter on the porch for Ross to find, and hurried down the alleyway, hugging her travel bag close to her body. Two blocks later she stood at the corner store and waited an hour for her Taxi.

"Can I use your phone? I lost connection," Vangie lied with an apologetic smile.

The driver handed her his smart phone. Vangie thanked him and typed "Ronnie Livingston, Zeke Livingston's son" in the search bar.

The Hollywood Reporter popped up, listing the accident as one of its top stories just twenty-six hours prior. Recognizing what was left of Ronnie's silver Lotus sports car, now crumpled like tissue paper, Vangie pressed her hand to her throat.

Her teary eyes zipped back and forth as she scanned the blurb, skipping to the part faulting Ronnie for plowing into a center divider after losing control of his vehicle. She hoped like hell he wasn't drinking and driving again. How many times over the years had she chastised him about his driving under the influence?

"Take me to Cedars-Sinai. Beverly Boulevard."

Cedars-Sinai Medical Center was well known for providing top-notch medical care to Hollywood's most rich and famous, and so it didn't come as a surprise to Vangie that Zeke Livingston's son occupied a bed there. The ride to Cedars-Sinai proved sluggish. With the exception of normal weekday traffic on the Interstate, a fender bender slowed the ride to a sweat-producing crawl.

When Vangie arrived at the renowned medical center, constructed entirely of tinted windows eight stories high, the lobby clean and grand, she was running on adrenaline. She kept a clandestine watch for hidden cameras and security. When she spotted a guard near the door, she kept up her casual stroll, hoping not to catch so much as a curious glance.

She approached the help desk. "Ronnie Livingston." She kept her voice low.

"He's a popular one this morning. Critical care Tower, room 21B," said the smiling elderly woman.

Vangie's stomach plunged. She rushed off, now not caring who might be watching her.

Locked doors secured the critical care unit and a security guard loitered nearby. Vangie rang the nurse's station and was told patients were only allowed two visitors at a time. She would have to wait. Thinking twice about sticking around, she reasoned she had to plenty of time before her 24 hours were up. She may never get another chance to see Ronnie.

The waiting room had mauve walls and a coffee station. Vangie helped herself to a hot cup, found a single chair in the corner of the room next to a potted tropical plant, and hid her face behind an architectural digest. She wasn't alone. Two kids, their parents, and a grandmother waited with her.

Thirty-minutes later, Vangie was as antsy as the two kids running around the room. The waiting room was filling up, making the situation too risky. She loitered in the bathroom for ten minutes before checking back in with the nurse's station. Finally, the nurse buzzed her into the unit.

Vangie hadn't recognized the two women coming her way until they were upon her. Both had blonde hair and were thinly built and swanked in the subtleness of wealth. The younger woman had to be thirty, just a few years younger than Ronnie. Sarah was her name, Ronnie's sister. The eldest woman was Ronnie's mother. Vangie had never met Ronnie's family, but she had observed them from afar on the occasions she and Ronnie attended one of Zeke's movie premiers. She kept up her hurried steps, praying to go unnoticed, but the tears in Ronnie's mother's eyes were evident and Sarah looked as though she hadn't slept in days.

Vangie's legs turned into logs. The closer she got to room 21B, the stiffer her legs became.

"I need your John Hancock," a man said as she passed the nurse's station in bewilderment. She stopped and scribbled her name. Steps later, she couldn't remember if she wrote Vangie Cooper or her alias, Daniela Silva.

The door to Ronnie's private suite was open. Vangie walked timidly inside and floated over to Ronnie's bed, biting the inside of her lip so as not to cry. A plastic cap covered his head and needles and tubes punctured his arms. She stared down at him. He appeared to be sleeping peacefully, but Vangie knew better. The breathing machine was keeping him alive.

She reached between the bedrail and took hold of Ronnie's flaccid hand, half expecting him to open his eyes and give her one of his slow grins. Coming close to a breaking point, Vangie listened to the hissing and steady beeping of machinery. There was so much she wanted to say to Ronnie and hadn't said to him over the years. Their chance meeting spurred a friendship she couldn't live without. She wouldn't even mind hearing him blast her for disappearing on him again just to hear his voice that always comforted her in uncertain times.

Vangie leaned over the railing and gave Ronnie a tender kiss on the mouth. "I love you, Ron," she whispered.

Ronnie's eyes popped open and stared into hers. Panicked, Vangie immediately rang for the nurse. Apparently, it wasn't uncommon for a coma patient to open their eyes without an awareness of their environment. The nurse also told her Ronnie's condition hadn't improved and that he was slipping deeper into a coma.

"Who are you?" said a deep voice behind Vangie.

After scrabbling to put on her sunglasses, Vangie spun around. Given Zeke Livingston's importance in Ronnie's life, she would've expected to encounter a man larger than life. But Zeke was a small man with silver hair and a full silver beard. His puffy eyes and downturned mouth crowded the center of his face like an angry bird.

"I'm a friend of Ronnie's," Vangie said coolly.

Before she could make a run for it, Gabriel, Ronnie's older brother, was upon her, standing too close and personal. His melancholy blue eyes that reminded her too much of Ronnie's lowered her guard.

"Ron has a stockpile of female friends. Where did he find you?" he said.

When she didn't answer his offensive question, Gabriel turned his attention to Ronnie. "What's up, lil bro?" He patted Ronnie's face tenderly, kissed his forehead, and straightened out Ronnie's cap. "My mother is under the impression that deluging Ron's brain with recorded family stories will help him miraculously recover consciousness," he said to her.

No comment from Vangie.

"I'm paying enough money to this blasted institution to hire a fucking symphony to recover his consciousness," Zeke said.

"Step up and let Ron know how much you really love him, Dad," said Gabriel.

Zeke stepped forward. While the two men stared helplessly at Ronnie, Vangie left the room, fighting back tears.

With less than an hour and a half to spare before her 24 hours of freedom were up, Vangie roamed the area in a daze. As she passed the row of designer clothing stores, chic boutiques and cafés she once patronized, she tried to remember the last time she had spent a day at a spa, went to a hair salon, got waxed, or shopped for pleasure and not for necessity. It all seemed so trivial now.

In a moment of sobering clarity, Vangie stood stark still at the corner of the busy street. She was tired of running, tired of hiding, tired of worrying, tired of lying—just plain beat down. She removed her sunglasses, wig, and cap and found the nearest trashcan to dump them in.

When Vangie arrived at the Century Regional Detention Facility, there was no fanfare. She surrendered quietly.

Part Five

Twenty-One

Vangie merged with the parade of blue jumpsuits being herded like a pack of animals to the pod, feeling a deep aversion toward socializing with a cast of characters she wouldn't give the time of day in the real world. Day one behind bars she came to the depressing conclusion that classism had no place or presence in jail. Other than her physical characteristics, nothing distinguished her from any other inmate, from the common criminal to the most ruthless.

Her tough skin had softened to the plush life over the years, but her survival skills, which came with being birthed by Annette Cooper, were completely intact. Nevertheless, if she had the choice, she would've stayed locked inside her cell, but self-isolation was against jailhouse rules and social hour was mandatory.

Moving about restrictively, Vangie sidestepped the intentional shoulder bumps, overlooked the intimidating stares, and disregarded the flirtatious catcalls. With the presidential election fully underway, the TV area was a popular hangout. Vangie saw no point in discussing politics with her fellow jailbirds when one of the consequences of being a convicted felon was losing the right to vote.

"Whad up, cuz?" Geneva said, pulling up a chair and sitting too close. Maybe in time Geneva would wise up that she wasn't Angie, but for now the mistaken identity worked to Vangie's advantage some days and to her disadvantage most days. She loathed playing dominoes and hated trivial conversation even more, but she played along to get along, grateful Geneva had her back because of her obvious love and respect for Angie.

Mail call came at the end of social hour each day, which was akin to Christmas morning for anyone whose family or friends cared enough to write, send money, a photo, books, or anything else to make the time pass when time was all a person had to look forward to. Today, Christmas arrived for Vangie in the form of an unsealed letter. Her privacy had been invaded, but Vangie didn't care. Overcome with excitement and trepidation, she folded the envelope in half and stuffed it inside the sleeve of her jumper for safekeeping.

When the moment allowed, Vangie hurried into her cell, sat on her bed, and stared at Wade's name scribbled across the white envelope in his doctor's penmanship.

"Is that from your boyfriend?" her cellmate said.

It was bad enough Vangie couldn't remember the girl's name and had an even harder time relating to a sixteen-year-old.

The girl leaned over the top bunk, staring down at Vangie upside down, strings of long, blonde hair curtaining her narrow face and cat-like bright eyes. The most heinous crimes committed by inmates were rarely ambiguous; the girl wore her crime like a badge of courage and recounted the story with spine-chilling pride. Apparently, the girl killed her father and disfigured her mother with a douse of acid.

Whatever the reason the girl found cause to murder, the judge had waived the protection the juvenile court granted minors in cases involving serious crimes, locking the girl up with adults. Vangie sometimes wondered if the girl understood the gravity of the situation. Half the time she bounced off the cell walls and goofed around like she was at summer camp.

Then again, Vangie thought, she hadn't quite acknowledged the gravity of her own situation.

"It's from a friend," was all Vangie said in response to the girl's question. For all intents and purposes, her answer was factual. She placed Wade's letter under the pillow to read at a later time—if she could get a moment of privacy and build the courage.

Throughout the day that dragged on longer than most, a tingle of excitement shot through Vangie's body each time Wade's letter crossed her mind. Then dread turned her stomach inside out as she agonized over the letter's content. Sleeping on a twin bed with a thin foam pad and a mushy pillow aggravated her anxiety. She tossed and turned.

After lights out, Vangie checked to make certain her cellmate on the top bunk wasn't still bouncing off the ceiling. When she heard the girl's soft snoring, she pulled the letter from beneath her pillow, quietly got out of bed, crossed the cell at exactly five paces, sat by the door, and read Wade's short and bittersweet letter under the dim light streaming through the door's window from the pod.

> *Vangie,*
> *Writing you is hands down my most difficult*
> *undertaking. Your twin, doubling as you,*
> *got the long version of my sentiments. Here's the*
> *extremely edited edition. If you're looking for*
> *absolution, I cannot give it to you. What you've*
> *done to my friend and to me is indefensible.*
> *For closure, it's best you not call me or write me.*
> *Let's not make this more difficult than it is.*
> *Wade F.*

Wade's gruff letter did not provoke her tears; neither was she hurt or angry. Caught somewhere between the here and now and bygones, Vangie was numb inside.

Why should Wade care if she got the death penalty? She was a runaway bride who had murdered his best friend; she was getting exactly what she deserved, from his perspective.

She stuffed the letter back into the envelope, clutched it in her fist, and couldn't close her eyes.

The next day, Vangie lay in bed with her face to the wall and her back to the world. A stick of some kind poked her in the back. She ignored it.

"I called your number. Don't make me call it again. You have a visitor," the guard said.

"I'm not taking visitors today," Vangie mumbled.

"And I'm not the butler. Move it!"

The price of murder, first and foremost, was her loss of dignity and respect. Vangie begrudgingly got up and got moving.

There were certain visiting days for attorneys, clergymen, and bail bondsmen, which were more frequent than visits from family or friends. Vangie could count on a visit from Ross and Clarissa once or twice a week, particularly now that the court upheld the indictment against her for first degree murder and the preliminary hearing date had been set.

Clarissa came alone today. She was waiting for Vangie when the guard walked her into the conference room and sat her down. As soon as Vangie took her seat at the table, she made her declaration.

"I'm changing my plea to guilty."

Clarissa's mouth hung open before she shrilled, "You can't! Think about the legal ramifications."

"I've had enough time to think about it."

"To what end, Vangie? Your decision is premature and irrational. You're admitting that you killed Todd with malice."

Maybe I did, Vangie thought.

"You can't talk me out of it, Riss. My mind is made up," she said.

"You'll be imprisoned for life. Is that what you want, to spend the rest your life in this place?" Clarissa looked around the small, drab room, horror-stricken. "As your lawyer and your friend, I won't let you throw away your life."

"What life? My life is over; I've accepted it."

"It's not over!" Clarissa fired back. "Ross is going to win this case, and I can say that with a relatively high degree of conviction. I have faith in him if no one else does."

"I received a letter from Wade, severing all ties," Vangie admitted quietly, refusing to cry.

"Well, the best consolation to a broken heart is revenge. This is war!" Clarissa looked ready to take her fight with the Fitzgerald's to the streets.

Clarissa's argument was persuasive enough to talk Vangie out of her own death sentence. The more Clarissa talked, the more determined to live Vangie became.

He could've made a halfhearted attempt to get my side of the story instead of sending me a heartless letter," Vangie *thought, resentfully.*

Twenty-Two

I woke up sweating and feeling as though a boa constrictor was choking me to death. The snake turned out to be my own hands. Struggling to breathe, I unwrapped my hands from around my neck, but couldn't shake the feeling that my nightmare had just begun.

My psychologist would say my anxiety over visiting Vangie in jail today caused my nightmare. She would tell me to think of things that brought me joy or anything that would distract me from stressing over talking to Vangie in a room full of strangers.

The day my voice was silenced our voices became one. Without Vangie to speak for me then, I didn't have a voice. Without Vangie then, I didn't have a life; and now that I'd found my own voice and a life, what if our relationship changed and Vangie preferred the old me to the one who had died and been reborn?

Vangie and I hadn't seen or talked to each other since she went to jail, and I got released. A jumble of bureaucratic red tape stood in our way. First, visiting days for the general public started on Saturdays and ended on Tuesdays, so I missed out on my first few opportunities to visit her. Second, now that I'd been put on six months' probation, I couldn't visit Vangie without approval from my probation officer, and I wasn't assigned one until after my hearing before a judge. Third, since all calls made from jail were recorded, Ross thought it was best we avoid talking on the phone to prevent the prosecution from finding evidence to use against Vangie during trial. Lastly, I didn't have a valid form of identification. A call home fixed that problem overnight but also caused another major problem. My mother got Douglas Phillips involved.

Tired of over thinking things, I got out of bed, put on a pair of sweats with a Tee, warmed my feet with socks, and left my new room, which was a fraction the size of my room at Mr. Big's place. Here there wasn't a private chef preparing tasty meals throughout the day or a live-in maid. Early mornings, instead of hearing complete silence, I heard the heavy hum of freeway traffic and woke up to the sound of city life that fit Clarissa and Ross's lifestyle.

They lived in a two bedroom, two bath condo on a street where a village of shops, specialty grocery stores, coffee houses, and cafés were steps outside their door. I took a wild guess Clarissa loved the color red and liked to keep her place ultra-clean and organized. I took extra care not to leave behind a mess while I cooked, and Ross and Clarissa slept.

I'd never seen a kitchen I didn't love, and this one looked new and felt unused. The black granite counters were wide enough to spread things out, and I found few useful spices, sauces, oils, and marinades to work with inside the cabinets and refrigerator.

For today's breakfast I repurposed the crispy parmesan cheese potato halves paired with steak for last night's dinner, dicing them and arranging them in a cast-iron skillet around sunny side up eggs overlain with red-pepper sauce and garnished with spinach leaves and plum tomatoes au gratin. I hoped the combination of savory flavors worked like magic because I didn't have an appetite to even do a taste test.

By the time Clarissa walked into the living room I was sitting at the kitchen bar counter, fully dressed and ready to go. Looking half awake, she wore a nice black tracksuit and her long ponytail fell from under a baseball cap.

"I think I might cry. I thought you were Vangie for a second." Clarissa looked as if she just might cry, arousing my own tears.

She then sniffed the air and put her hands on her hips. "Have you been cooking again, Angie?" Her question sounded as though I was guilty of a petty crime.

I replied with an apologetic half smile.

"I'm living with a real Rachel Rey. If you keep this up, Ross will expect me to cook for him every day." Clarissa laughed.

"I heard my name," Ross said as he strolled into the living room dressed in jogging pants and hoodie sweatshirt.

"I was telling Angie we don't need her to cook every day. Take-out tonight, on us. Right, Ross?"

"That's right, baby."

I didn't mind cooking every day. Cooking was my way of repaying Ross and Clarissa for all that they had done for me until I could repay them another way.

Before leaving the house for his morning run, Ross warned me, again, not to discuss the case with Vangie today or say anything incriminating. I nodded my understanding.

Clarissa peeked at my dish. "Looks delicious, Angie. If I had an appetite, I'd pig out. But I need my shot of brain food first." She poured herself a cup of espresso. "We'd better go. I don't want to make you late."

I beat Clarissa to the door.

Clarissa flew down the highway at eighty miles an hour, driving as fast as she talked. Her voice was light and bubbly as she filled my head with funny stories about her college days with Vangie. I managed to maintain a small smile but with a taste of bitterness in my mouth. Clarissa had achieved what was once impossible—coming between Vangie and me. It was easy to see why Vangie liked Clarissa. She was easy to like. But envy still stung me.

We reached the Century Regional Detention Facility. I had thirty minutes maximum to visit with Vangie—just thirty minutes, and I was already feeling deprived. If I was a second late for pre-check, my visit with Vangie was subject to cancellation. I jumped out of Clarissa's car and into the line gathering outside the concrete compound.

After I made it through the first checkpoint, I sat in the front row where benches lined the sitting area, and then read over the clothing restrictions posted on the wall in bold print: No gang affiliated apparel, tank tops, or hoodies. Shirts for women were not to be too low-cut, and dresses couldn't be too short or too long. No spaghetti stringed tops either and no open toe shoes.

Careful not to violate the rules, I'd put on jeans with a mustard colored mock-neck sweater. Out to impress Vangie, I bought ankle boots, black leather ones with a low heel, and a fancy belt to match.

Visitors filled the benches to capacity and the waiting room with conversation and crying kids. Groups of three or four were called at a time. When I heard my group number called, I lined up for the second checkpoint.

One by one we walked through the metal detectors and got patted down. Concealing contraband in jail wasn't easy, even for people who had something illegal to hide, but people still found a way to slip contraband inside to sell or to trade, Geneva had told me. I made it safely through the final checkpoint.

When I reached the visitation room, inmates and their visitors took up the row of booths, and guards roamed around on both sides of the glass-plated partition without an opening to physically connect with the person on the other side.

I took short and quick steps as I walked to the very last chair at the end of the row, where I sat, waiting for Vangie to walk through the security door. Each time the door opened my heart pounded in my chest.

When I finally saw Vangie, I didn't know what to do with the avalanche of emotions exceeding me in height and weight. I pictured myself hugging Vangie so tight no one could pry us apart.

In actuality I was a speechless basket case. Resisting the tsunami of tears storming inside of me, I placed the phone to my ear and waited on pins and needles for Vangie to take her seat. Our eyes never lost connection, and I knew, like me, Vangie was afraid we might lose each other again, if our gaze faltered.

Vangie took her seat before me and picked up the phone.

In unison we placed the palms of our hand on the glass and pressed our foreheads to it. My tears spilled down my cheeks and dripped from my chin.

"I love you and missed you so much I wanted to die!" my teary eyes said.

"I love you and missed you too, Angie," Vangie's soft eyes replied.

As far back as I could remember we had a secret language, communicating by reading each other's minds, eyes, and facial expressions. Only I could detect the tears glistening in Vangie's black eyes. She wouldn't outright cry. She would put on a strong front for me.

When a guard approached us warningly, we pulled away from the glass and sat back in unison. The guidelines didn't discriminate. Stay seated, stay calm, speak low, and be courteous at all times during visits. Any sudden animated moves, hand gestures, and boisterous behavior would give the guards reason to terminate our visit.

I glanced up at Vangie's short hair, smiled, crinkled my nose, and shook my head. Short hair looked way better on Vangie than on me. Everything looked better on her, I gestured

Vangie smoothed back her short curls with the palm of her hand and smiled thinly. "I like mine long, but you look beautiful, Angie." Vangie spoke aloud, her voice lyrical to my deprived ears. When her brows suddenly caved in and her eyes darkened, I defended myself before she could blast me.

"I didn't know what else to do," I whined in silence.

"That almost cost you your life, Angie. You should've been smarter."

I didn't argue. *"I'm sorry."*

"So, tell me where you've been hiding," she hit me with next, drilling her eyes into mine.

When I opened my mouth to explain myself, the snail flew into my throat. I was speechless, again.

"Well…say something. I know you've broken your vow of silence, Angie." Vangie had a calm way of speaking that left a lot to the imagination, but the hurt and disappointment I detected in her undertone went straight to my heart.

"I should've been the first to know," she said.

Shame made me drop my head and it seemed I couldn't lift it. Only ten minutes into our visit and my nightmare was coming true, the sea stretching between us, pulling us apart. I didn't know how to recover from a bad start or if we could recover.

"I'm proud of you, Ang," I heard Vangie say.

I peeked up to see her beautiful smile and broke down in tears, again. "I'm sorry for ever leaving. I'm sorry for everything," I blubbered.

"Me too, Ang. Me too…for more than you can imagine. Stop crying, okay. I hate crying. Mom cried enough for the both of us."

We both had found a reason to laugh. From then on, I talked comfortably in the company of the others around us. I told Vangie about my recent visit home, how well our mother was doing, and about her latest "houseguest," Mr. Young, who I liked better than the rest.

Vangie had nothing to say about Mr. Young or our mother.

When I told Vangie about Wade Fitzgerald the Fourth coming to Mr. Big's house to visit her, her gloomy eyes came alive.

She pursed her lips. "And what did he have to say?"

"Nothing *bad*. He loves you, Van. Who doesn't love you?" I added with dash of salt. If I wanted to bring Douglas Phillips into the conversation, I knew now wasn't the right time.

Vangie sucked her teeth with her tongue and said nothing more about Wade.

I hogged the remainder of our visit talking about jail life. I'd been on the inside and lived to tell my story. I could tolerate the food, the rotten odors, and tiny cell. Vangie, on the other hand, liked caviar from a mother-of-pearl spoon, silk pajamas, and living in a mansion where she could shower morning, noon, and night. She wouldn't be able to stand the endless commotion, to stomach the gnats that lived in the corroded shower drains, the backed-up toilets that stunk up the place, and living with one outfit rather than a closet filled with expensive clothes to choose from. If I could trade places with her again, as stupid as it might be, I would in a heartbeat.

We had just a few minutes remaining of our short visit, and there was still so much I wanted to tell Vangie about my life and so much I wanted to know about hers.

The phones shut off before we could say goodbye. Our visit was over. I left the compound in tears, but my heart beat for two again and I could smell hope in the air.

Twenty-Three

I f I ever got around to preparing my resume, it would read like my short rap sheet: No formal education. No special skills. No references I could use. Sammy handed the only job I'd ever had to me on a silver platter and taught me everything I knew about the bakery industry.

In addition to finding a job, I had to complete my community service hours, another condition of my probation. Eager to do anything work related, I looked forward to exploring the greater city of Los Angeles that spread boundlessly in every direction without a start or a finish that I could see.

Clarissa insisted on driving me to the work site. Navigating heavy traffic, she took side streets and cut through parking lots for shortcuts. A red light gave her time to focus her attention on me. I held my breath, anticipating her next question.

"Just for clarification, Vangie lived in Canada with your dad during summer months and holidays and you lived in Detroit with your mom year-round, right?"

Ross and Clarissa interrogated me about Vangie's life morning and night, their hospitality seeming more for their benefit than for my own. Everything I thought I knew about Vangie I now second-guessed. I only knew the life Vangie and I shared—raised by our mother who did her best with what she had and who loved us the best she could, not private schools, nannies, servants, and a rich, white father.

I cried myself to sleep after learning Vangie wanted our mother and me dead. Why else would she tell Clarissa our mother died and that I died too? Like a fallen angel, Vangie descended from the heavens in my eyes until I saw her with a new set of eyes, but my love for her and loyalty held strong.

"I think so," I said.

Clarissa's expression puzzled. "Where in Detroit did you live?" she pressed

"Different places. We moved a lot." That part was honest.

The light turned green. Clarissa sped forward. "Why'd you move often?"

I couldn't recount all the reasons why our mother packed up in the middle of the night or dragged us off to somewhere new and sometimes frightening. I shrugged my shoulders to Clarissa's question, dreading the next one to come.

Sirius talk radio kept her occupied for the remaining drive.

We went our separate ways at her and Ross's law office in downtown L.A. The atmosphere changed drastically as I walked toward the morning sun. The further east I walked, the high-rise buildings, restaurant chains, and luxury hotels became the scenic backdrop of old-fashioned one-story shops linked by fabric, fashion, and jewelry stores, flower shops, greasy spoons, and flea market alleyways.

Sights and sounds altered drastically when I turned onto 5th Avenue, smells that would've offended anyone who wasn't accustomed to them. Tent houses, for blocks ahead of me, overtook the sidewalk like a campground. Being on the outside looking in hadn't changed my connection to homelessness. As I walked the street, I wanted to know each person's story. Everybody had one, and everyone's story for landing on skid row differed.

I understood now why so many of us wound up living nowhere and why some of us, who had a way off the streets, stayed longer than necessary. Some of us didn't believe we deserved a better life.

I stopped to stare at the two-story stucco building taking up a corner block, worried I had the wrong address. Covered in graffiti, it had boarded up windows and looked abandoned like most of the businesses on the street.

I climbed the concrete steps slowly and then nervously rang the doorbell. Not long later a black dude stuck his head between the double doors. "You from probation?" he said as though he thought I had the wrong address too.

I nodded. He opened the door wide enough for me to squeeze inside. We stared at one another. "Bro, I know you," he said, positively. "The Hookah Bar?"

I shook my head, avoiding his bold staring.

"The Dirty Down?"

I shook my head again.

"What's up? I'm Jay." His hand overtook mine when I shook it. He could be a bodyguard and had the look of someone who lived a hard life in a short period. He wore dusty black jeans and a dusty sleeveless Tee, old Timberland boots, a bushy Afro, and long sideburns. Tattoos covered his arms and neck.

"We're upstairs," he said, pointing his thumb up.

The stairs were wooden, narrow, and steep. On the second floor, there were four small offices divided by a narrow hallway and two offices at each end. Reluctantly, I followed Jay down the hall, curiously staring through the office windows. Old boxes, stacks of paper yellowed by the sun, and equipment and whatnot filled them practically to the rafters.

We entered the end office where more old papers and boxes upon boxes were stacked as though whoever owned the building planned to relocate and never got around to getting rid of the mess.

Jay's laugh burst from his belly. "Meet your fearless leader," he said.

A woman was crouched beneath the desk, mooning us in a pair of jeans. "You bet not be laughing at me, Jay! You know I ain't a techie!" the woman said.

"What's the problem now?"

"The same problem that's been a problem! I'mma kill this old computer!" The woman crawled backward, popped up and dusted off her jeans. The minute I saw her deep-set eyes full of wisdom, tears of happiness rolled down my cheeks.

"No, it ain't Angie Brown!" Mo said.

"What?" Jay looked from Mo back to me.

"This family right here, Jay." Her eyes awash in tears, Mo pulled me into her arms and held me tight. I couldn't say how long we hugged, crying and rocking from side to side, but I didn't want to let her go.

When we could pull ourselves apart, Mo put her hands on her hips and said, "What'd you do to get yo' ass locked up?"

I didn't attempt to explain my circumstances to Mo, nor would Mo have expected me to say anything.

A loud ringing made me flinch.

"Get the door, Jay, since you ain't fixing nothing!" Mo said.

Jay laughed. I laughed too. Mo was still Mo: tall, loud, proud, and beautiful inside and out. But there was something different about Mo too, something I could feel. She still wore her hair in an Afro, just longer and fuller, and pulled off of her face with an African print head wrap, and her smile still lit up the sky.

When Jay left the office, Mo took me by the hand and pulled me toward the opposite end of the hallway.

"There's somebody you gotta see," she said.

My tears were ready to fall by the time we walked into the large corner office. I didn't see Dunk or Mental as I'd expected, but a little girl no older than three or four, lying on a mat, coloring in a coloring book, and watching cartoons on an iPad.

"This is my baby, Angie, my Nubian princess. Imani, say hi to your auntie, Angie," Mo said.

My heart melted. *I'm an auntie.*

Grinning shyly, Imani lowered her head and pretended not to see us.

"Angie is family, baby. Say hi, girl." When Mo helped Imani to her feet by the hand, Imani leapt into Mo's arms, almost knocking us both over. I laughed.

"Girl, you too big to be jumping on somebody," Mo said.

I didn't ask about Imani's dad and didn't have to. Imani had onyx skin like Mo's, rich with bands of gold, and insightful eyes like Dunk's that took over her face and questioned everything. She was a beautiful replica of both her parents.

Imani kept her legs locked around Mo's hips and her face buried in Mo's neck.

"Say hi, Imani and quite actin'. You ain't never been shy, girl."

Imani peeked at me. "Hi"

I peeked back at her and smiled, hardly able to stand the love I already held in my heart for Imani.

As Mo placed Imani back on the blanket, I listened to her praise Imani for coloring within the lines with pure love in her voice and knew what was different about Mo. She was radiant with motherhood.

I didn't get a chance to ask Mo about Dunk and Mental. Four more probationers showed up, all men, and we got to work. The large warehouse was in need of serious restoration. The floors were fractured cement, the walls in no condition to paint, and the ceiling nothing but rotted wood beams.

From what Mo explained to me, the building hadn't been occupied for over fifteen years. The owner of the building sold it to an investor, who dumped it on the next buyer, and so forth. As of a year ago the place was inhabited by the homeless. Mo had been living in L.A. for a few years, she told me, working independently to get women with children off the streets and getting by on welfare.

A man Mo called The Bishop owned more property than he knew what to do with. One thing led to another, and he hired Mo to clean up the building and open a soup kitchen in exchange for free rent and board plus a small salary. If Mo could pull it off, this place could feed up to two hundred hungry patrons in one sitting, I estimated. My mind went wild with possibilities.

While Jay oversaw the other workers, whose assignment was hauling cement blocks and rubbish from the warehouse to the alley, Mo and I swept up after them with push brooms, keeping our eyes on Imani, who found creative and dangerous ways to play. Mo again sat Imani in a clean corner with books and crayons and told her not to move.

"I need to find a babysitter for this girl when she ain't at school, or child welfare gone' snatch her from me," Mo said.

I almost cried at the thought.

"You know how I feel about the system, Angie." Mo went back to sweeping as if trying to collect the ruins of her life.

Mo didn't have to ask. I'd made up my mind. I would babysit Imani until I found a job.

The workers stayed for as long as they were required to stay, and I stayed the night at Mo's place. We walked there. Jay too. I gave Imani a piggyback ride the whole way.

Mo's place was a studio in an old brownstone on Wall Street where remnants of homelessness spilled over from skid row. I smiled with pride when I walked in. She had done up the place nicely, considering where she started. I chose homelessness. But Mo didn't have a choice. Her mother had chosen that life for her before she was born, and the foster care system had ruined Mo's life more than her mother had. Not the system itself, but cruel people who wormed their way through it.

A queen-sized bed and a dresser furnished a section of the room, and a small kitchen, a couch, coffee table, two folding chairs, a kid-sized dining table, and a TV balanced on milk crates took up the larger half.

We feasted on California burritos, cheesy fries, and rolled tacos from a Mexican food spot. Together, Mo and Jay drank several mini bottles of vodka. Both *lit,* they laughed and talked about everything. Jay laughed the most, talked the most, and ate more than me. I wondered about Jay's story like I wondered about everyone's story. He lived in the storage room on the first floor of the warehouse, next to the roll-up door off the alley to ward off the vagrants trying to break in. At age twenty-two, he attended junior college and was studying to become a computer scientist.

Around 11:00, after Imani had finally fallen asleep, the conversation turned serious. Mo and Jay were debating different topics from their different perspectives. Jay made his points pointedly, and Mo was Mo, throwing verbal punches he couldn't beat. I hadn't anything worth saying to add to the debate, and agreed with them both, on everything, for the most part.

When the topic of police brutality came around, Mo shouted, "You can't tell me shit about police brutality after the po-po killed my man!"

My heart jumped into my throat. I didn't want to believe it. Dunk couldn't be dead.

"No!" I cried. "They killed Dunk?"

"Bro, I thought she was mute," Jay said to Mo, and then laughed at me.

"Girl, you've been scheming on me all this time, Angie?" Mo laughed too.

I got up from the floor and ran out of the apartment, down the flight of stairs, and into the cool night. Mo met up with me moments later and joined me on the stoop where we sat in silence for a while. Maybe, like me, she needed to see the stars, the moon, and the heavens, needed to ask God to make sense of all this. I'd lost a brother and a friend in Dunk, and it seemed, whenever my life brightened, there was something evil lurking around the corner to darken it.

"I wanted to tell you earlier, Angie, but I knew you'd be *extra*. You always have been a cry baby. I'm cried out, girl," Mo said.

"Why would they kill Dunk?" I just didn't understand.

According to Mo, Dunk was walking the streets late one night, having one of his night terror attacks, when the police shot him six times, claiming he had a gun. The case was open and shut. I knew Dunk never would hurt anyone intentionally; he was a gentle giant, the gentlest man I'd ever known, but the Golf War had destroyed him mentally.

"Dunk was my Boo. I loved his crazy ass. You know I did, Angie," Mo said.

I loved Dunk too and couldn't stop crying. At least he received a veteran's funeral, Mo told me, with two armed guards, flying doves, and was buried in the military cemetery in Chicago with his father.

"Where's Mental?" I said with a raw throat. If Mental was dead too, I didn't know what I'd do.

Mo gave me one of her funny stares. "Had me thinking you was born mute. Girl! And since you talking, how'd you get locked up? Tell me *that*."

"It's a long story."

"I got time."

On the verge of tears again, I twisted mouth and shook my head.

"I feel you, girl. I got long stories too. But you gettin' locked up just don't feel right to me. Not my sweet Angie."

Mo's thoughts seemed to turn inward. "About Mental...that crazy fool was try'n to blow up the police department, made a homemade bomb that couldn't blow up a damn flea, girl. I got his crazy self out of Missouri and haven't seen my little brother since Dunk's funeral..." Her eyes turned starry and wet. "I found out I was pregnant that *day,* girl. Imani is my faith in unseen things...and now I got my Angie back." Mo hugged my shoulder. "Ain't God good, girl? Ain't He *good!*"

I laid my head on Mo's shoulder and gazed at the stars. I could almost hear Dunk saying from heaven, "Stop crying Lil Sis. Things gone be alright." Dunk took everything in stride.

Twenty-Four

T he man wore slicked back hair and looked to Vangie to be in his early forties. Ross introduced him to her as "Uncle Sebastian." Vangie didn't see the family resemblance. Ross was tall, lean, and had facial features that resembled his African-American father; Sebastian was short and muscular with facial features that resembled Ross's Latina mother.

"Your mug shot doesn't do you justice," Sebastian said.

Vangie and Clarissa shared disapproving glances. Ross, on the other hand, thought his uncle's offensive remark was worth a laugh. In that respect, Ross and his uncle were cut from the same cloth, thought Vangie.

Sebastian Martinez was his full name, an ex-police officer turned private investigator. Acting as the criminal defense investigator on her case, Sebastian had gained access to confidential police records. According to Sebastian, Todd Bryant's maid discovered his dead body, and police removed a strand of long black hair from Todd's summer sweater, evidence that could link her to the crime. Sebastian also reported that the police initially pursued another suspect before naming her their primary.

"The alleged crime took place the night of June twenty-seventh," Ross said. "Walk me through your day. From the time you rolled out of bed and had your first cup of coffee."

For the most part Vangie couldn't recollect the details of that dreadful day and said nothing to that point.

"Well?" Ross said.

"Well what?"

"Well, damn. You went to law school. I shouldn't have to remind you. You took the bar exam that day, didn't you? Can you think of any other mitigating circumstances that merit consideration?"

Among the litany of mitigating factors that could grant her leniency by the courts were some that could prove to be aggravating instead. The court would also take under consideration her character, which wasn't a good look by any stretch of her imagination. So, with six in one hand and half a dozen in the other, why answer Ross's rhetorical question?

When Sebastian announced that he planned to conduct a thorough investigation into her background as a counter-measure to the prosecution's discovery, Vangie took it as a threat.

"What do you want to know?" she said, giving the appearance of cool headedness.

"Do I need to make you a list?" Ross replied.

"Who's your daddy?" said Sebastian, whose smugness suggested to her that he and Ross both knew about her fabricated father and were merely baiting her to prove their point.

Shame could only go so deep before it hardened into defensiveness, and Vangie's defenses now came to a very sharp point. She threw an aggravated look at them both.

Ross stared at her crossly. "Here's the thing, Vangie. I can't effectively defend you if you're not straight with me. If my investigator discovered Tom Blanchard is a figment of your imagination, the DA's office has too and will use it to prove to a jury you'll lie about anything, including murder. And I'll be goddamned if I put a liar on the stand and my reputation on the line."

"God, Ross. You don't have to be so crass," Clarissa said, finally speaking up.

"Pretrial hearings are around the corner."

"I'm waiving my right to a speedy trial," Vangie decided impulsively.

Clarissa frowned and argued that a delay might give the prosecution time to build a stronger case against her.

Ross said it was the best thing he had heard her say since he took her case. A speedy trial would work against her in the short run, Vangie knew. Ross needed to stall for time to mount an effective defense before going to trial, especially after the preliminary hearing proved damaging.

"Give me something I can work with, anything you can think up, and we'll compare notes." Ross sat back and stroked his goatee.

"Start with your family history." Sebastian flipped to a new page of his note pad, pulled a pen from behind his ear, and watched her through dilated brown pupils. "Whenever you're ready," he said.

Where do I start?

Speaking humbly, Vangie chronicled the lighter side of her upbringing, opening with her mother, Annette Cooper, born the only child of Della May Watson, who died never having married her grandfather, Joseph Cooper, the man she suffered a heart attack over.

Joseph Cooper's ears were deaf to any words God had to offer. He labored solely on the side of evil. Even murder and recruiting drug dealers to carry out his cause weren't beneath him.

She never called him Granddad or anything respectable. Her mother called him "a good-looking devil," a description she agreed with. He was sentenced to life in prison and was ultimately paroled for good behavior. It would stand to reason to a jury, in her mind, that the capacity to murder ran in her blood.

As her story unfolded, Vangie omitted whole chapters of her life. Why paint a vivid picture of Detroit's lower East Side or describe the low-income rundown tenements she and Angie called home? She definitely didn't want to recount the number of days they endured hunger pangs or recall the humiliation of scrounging for loose change around the house, hoping to strike gold. She also made no mention of her mother's frequent unwelcome houseguests. Those shameful aspects of her childhood she kept sealed in her memory bank.

After telling the revised version of her life's story, Vangie hadn't anything more to say and dared anyone to cross-examine her with an icy gaze.

No one dared.

When she returned to her cell she vomited into the sink.

"You puke like every day. Are you knocked up?" the girl said.

Vangie rinsed her mouth, ignoring the girl.

"If you are, I know how to get rid of it. It's easy."

On this rare occasion, the girl had Vangie's attention. Vangie patted her neck and face with cold water and then faced the girl, raising an eyebrow.

"How?" she said for the hell of it.

The girl performed a half-cartwheel, then popped upright. "I ate like a shit load of green pineapples," she said, her pale eyes flashing. "My dad never found out. It only works in your first trimester. My friend, she like waited too late, and had to like put her baby up for adoption and shit."

Now the girl was doing jumping jacks, making Vangie seasick. She stared at the girl in mock observation.

"Thanks for the advice, but I'm not *pregnant.*"

The chance that one night of reckless sex with Ronnie may have knocked her up made Vangie climb into bed like a sick dog and curl into a ball. Tears rumbled inside of her like a developing thunderstorm and stopped just short of pouring from her eyes. She hugged her stomach and rocked. If she wanted to cry for anyone, it was for a baby who wouldn't stand a chance to have a normal life.

It's the crappy food, Vangie told herself.

Twenty-Five

A ngie talked without taking a breath, and Vangie listened without interrupting. Her mind, however, wandered and she couldn't feign interest in hearing another one of Angie's adorable cat stories or think of anything worthwhile to share about her life behind bars. Telling Angie about the latest vomitus meal on the prison menu had gotten old. A fight had broken out in the pod a few days before and they were put on lockdown, but that was practically a daily occurrence. Why bring it up?

"Do you have enough money?" Vangie said for conversation's sake.

"You gave me more than I need."

"Five thousand dollars isn't much to live on, Ang."

"It is for me."

"Did you deposit it in the bank?" Vangie said tiredly.

"Have you called Mom?"

"Lately, no."

"Will you? Please. She doesn't mind you calling her collect. She's just worried about her phone bill."

Vangie didn't bother to ask Angie about the money she left her mother before going on the run. She didn't want to know.

"I started my community service hours," Angie said excitedly.

"Doing what?" Vangie said, halfheartedly.

Monisha Brown had been in and out of homelessness since age thirteen and now lived near skid row while refurbishing a rundown warehouse to open a soup kitchen. Angie planned to work with this Mo person, babysitting her three-year-old daughter, from what Vangie gathered from Angie's horror story.

"When'd you met Monisha, Angie?"

"Mo? Oh. A long time ago."

"Where, Ang?"

"Back home."

"Back home when?"

"When I was homeless."

Vangie mulled over Angie's response, trying to put it into perspective. Maybe *homeless* wasn't what Angie meant to say.

"You were never homeless, Angie," Vangie said adamantly.

"I was." Angie didn't blink her eyes nor lower them.

"I thought you lived in Colorado." Vangie challenged, her voice horse and dry, her emotions on the fence between anger and despair.

"After I got off the streets, I did."

"Then, tell me where you lived between homelessness and living in Colorado? I don't understand."

"I lived a lot of places."

"Which *places*, Angie?"

"That all depended on which freight trains we hopped and what direction we were going."

Vangie's tears brewed, as did her anger. When she could close her mouth, she frowned with her whole face. "That's how you were living, hopping trains like a hobo? What hell, Angie?"

"Homeless people aren't hobos, Van. That's offensive."

"I'm not debating the fucking definition of a hobo! I thought you were dead!"

Angie's eyes jumped around the room. "We're not supposed to raise our voices."

Vangie took in the deepest breath she could muster and gritted her teeth. She shuddered to recall who she had slept with to pay her way through college, let alone Angie's, and this was how Angie repaid her for her sacrifices?

Finding a calm center, Vangie was determined to maintain an even keeled voice if it killed her. "Where'd you live when you weren't *hopping* trains, Angie? In a fucking tent?"

"Sometimes, but we slept in our bags, mostly, unless we made enough money to stay at a motel. We usually didn't make enough." Angie said this without shame.

"How'd you make money?" Vangie dared to ask, "And who is *we?*"

"Oh. Mo, Dunk, Mental and Me, but that was before I lived at Roxy's."

"Who in the hell is Roxy?"

Angie giggled.

"This isn't funny!"

"Sorry. Roxanne's House for Women; it's a shelter for women like me."

"You're nothing like those women, whoever the hell they are."

"I'm more like them than you, Vangie," Angie said softly.

Refusing to fall for Angie's self-debasing game and diversion tactic, Vangie pressed the issue. "How long did you live at Roxy's, or whatever it's called?"

"Years ago, before I graduated from the program."

At least you graduated from somewhere...

"How many years ago, Angie? Don't look at the clock. Look at me. How many?"

Angie's mouth twisting and eye wandering infuriated Vangie to her core. No amount of deep breathing could untie the knot in her chest, relax the folds of her forehead, or keep her anger at bay.

"If you won't tell me how long you lived at a damn shelter, tell me when you decided to change your name to Angie Brown."

Angie's eyes enlarged before dropping again. "Sorry."

"Stop apologizing. You're not fucking sorry. You didn't want me to find you. Why, Ang...?"

~

I could count on one hand the number of times I'd seen Vangie shed a tear or display her vulnerable side in public. Seeing her cry tortured me, but how could I tell her that being homeless was the best thing that could've happened to me, that living outside the shadows of her golden light allowed me to find my own light, that if I hadn't left home, I would never have found my voice again? I couldn't tell Vangie, knowing how the truth would hurt her.

And I couldn't tell Vangie Mr. Reese attempted to rape me. My windpipe shut down when I tried. Reasonably, what could Vangie do about it now, but live with the disgust and anger I'd lived with for years? I hoped Mr. Reese burned to the ground with Cambridge Heights, but even in my darkest hopes for him I prayed for his deliverance and asked God's forgiveness for my cruel thoughts.

"You haven't told me things either," I said in meek defense.

"What haven't I told you, Angie?"

"Everything!"

"I didn't tell you things you didn't need to know and wouldn't understand."

"I'm not helpless anymore."

"You've never been helpless, Angie. You just act helpless."

"Well, I know more than you think I know."

"You don't know shit."

"I know you kicked Douglas out of my life!" My tears came down as my voice went up.

"Is that what he told you? When'd you talk to Douglas?"

"He's coming for Thanksgiving," I said in a hurry, figuring now was as good a time as any to tell Vangie about Douglas, since she was already mad at me.

Vangie's brows stood high. "He's coming where?

"To California."

"To see whom?"

"Me!" I shrieked.

Vangie's eyes turned as dark as our mother's when one of her spells came on. We had a few minutes left to visit, minutes that we always milked to the very last second.

Vangie hung up on me.

It rained last night, gentle and steady, the first sign of the fall season I'd seen in California. I listened to the rain slowly drip off the roof and ping against the old paint cans in the backyard, beating myself up for telling Vangie about Douglas's visit, knowing how the holidays depressed her.

When I heard scratching outside my bedroom door, I got up and let Butterscotch inside. She was the friskier of the two orange tabbies and hogged all the attention from Peppermint. She scampered into my room, curved her long spine, dove for my bed, and made a soft landing. I laughed, took Butterscotch into my arms, and stroked her orange-striped coat.

My undying love for cats was the reason I fell in love with this place, which had been converted from a one-car garage into a room with a private bathroom tacked onto it. It came with a full-sized bed, chest of drawers, and gray painted cement floor.

Clarissa frowned at my new place and called the neighborhood "bad." She said I should've moved to a better area of town. I couldn't afford better than 400 dollars a month, and so far, nothing bad had happened around the neighborhood that I hadn't seen before.

Plus, the location couldn't have been better. I walked to my weekly visits with Vangie now and no longer relied on Clarissa or had to risk missing out on our visits because of slow public transportation.

Clarissa hated to see me leave, but Ross had seen enough of me. They had both been so kind, however, and as a housewarming gift bought me towels, sheets, and a fancy comforter. I bought a clothes hamper, floor heater, TV tray, and microwave oven—all that I needed for now.

I jumped to answer my cell phone when it rang.

It wasn't Douglas, but I was happy to hear my mother's voice just the same. We talked most days now, making up for the years I didn't talk. She did most of the talking, and mostly about Mr. Young who had become her live-in houseguest. He seemed to make her happy in ways most other men who had passed through her life hadn't. She complained about him out of one side of her mouth and smiled about him out of the other. I hoped he didn't turn out to be another creep.

Whenever Vangie came up, my mother always argued Vangie's innocence as if the police had tapped her phone. "I know my girls!" she would say.

After we hung up, I showered and dressed nicer than other days. Ms. Culpepper had given me permission to use the kitchen and to come and go through the front door of the house as I pleased. We were like two ships in the night, Ms. Culpepper and me. I saw Cleveland, her son, more often. He collected the rent and took care of repairs around the house. I hadn't decided if I trusted him yet, so I stayed in my room most days and nights, closed off from the main house.

I left the house through the side door. While passing the old car parked in the driveway, sitting on two flat wheels, I ran into my probation officer. I had been told to expect routine drug tests, warrant checks, and surprise visits, and wasn't surprised to see her walking up to the house, only nervous. I stood at attention.

She was the embodiment of a drill sergeant but with a candy soft center she couldn't hide. Wearing black pants, a white long-sleeve button-up under a bulletproof vest, and her Afro cut close to her head, she cut across the grass toward me.

I let her into my room and stood by while she sniffed around like a bloodhound, making notes on the sheet clipped to her clipboard. She then asked me a sequence of routine questions, mostly about my social life and employment situation. Both were easy to answer, seeing that I didn't have a social life or a job.

She made notes and told me the rate of unemployment for probationers was 27 to 30 percent higher than for the rest of the population and that I shouldn't get discouraged that I hadn't found a job.

I told her I had my first interview today. Afraid of getting my hopes up, I hadn't told anyone else. She wished me good luck and told me to stay in compliance if I wanted to stay out of jail.

By the time I walked into Burger Buff, I was in no condition to interview. The Metro ran slower than usual today, and I got caught in a downpour and was five minutes late for the interview that had started without me.

But I took an immediate liking to the contemporary rustic aesthetics. The location was perfect too, in the Downtown Art District and within walking distance of the warehouse. If I worked the late shift, I could continue babysitting Imani and request Saturday mornings off to visit with Vangie.

I'd never been a line cook and had never coordinated orders for timely delivery to customers, but I had prepared high quality food, could follow recipe guidelines, was committed to the craft, and was over the age of 18.

"Name?" The interviewer said.

"Angie Brown."

He marked my attendance on a sheet of paper and told me to have a seat.

Hair dripping and clothes wet, I sat at the nearest table outside the circle.

I shouldn't have gotten my hopes up. There were six of us interviewing for the job, five males and me, and of the six, I was a guppy in a pool of sharks. I never answered a single question asked by the interviewer, even though I had all the right answers and understood the importance of quality customer service. Two of us out of the group were asked to stay for second interviews. I wasn't one of them.

Twenty-Six

Thanksgiving Day began with dense, dark clouds, but by noon the sun beamed brightly.

I was standing in the front yard of the gray trailer house, taking in a balmy breeze that had turned especially warm, when I saw the black sedan coasting toward me. I was nineteen years old, awkward, clumsy, and impressionable when Douglas last saw me. I wondered how he would see me now. Glancing down at myself, I regretted wearing a pink chiffon dress with bold red flowers just to impress Douglas. I should have dressed like myself, not like Vangie.

Douglas parked neatly and stepped out of the car wearing his big smile, a pair of khaki pants, and a plaid dress shirt. The gray whiskers sprinkled throughout his sideburns and mustache made him more cute, cuddly, and lovable than I remembered.

While Douglas stared as if he didn't recognize me, I felt like a million imperfect particles. "Angie, Angie, Angie. You're beautiful."

Should I tell him how beautiful he looks and that I still itch for him on lonely nights?

He planted a moist kiss on my forehead. The imprint of his kiss lingered. I couldn't take my mind off of his honey-brown lips. I peeked up and into his eyes. They were just as I remembered—hot chocolate with a soft marshmallow center.

"Is that the seven layer chocolate cake you've been bragging about?" He said jokingly, regarding the Tupperware cake dish I held.

I laughed. I hadn't *bragged* about anything, and it was a three layer cake, not seven. But I'd baked it with Douglas in mind and love in my heart.

"I'm looking forward to Thanksgiving with Vangie's attorney. Maybe I can get my questions answered." Douglas opened the car door for me, and then climbed into his seat. "I brought you something." He reached into the backseat. "Your mother wouldn't let me leave the city without them. One's for you and one's for Vangie."

Tears filled my eyes when I saw my mother's homemade sweet potato pies wrapped in saran wrap. The golden crust oozed with peach juice.

Douglas wiped a tear from my cheek with his thumb. "You know your mother would be here if she could. I think under the circumstances, she's holding up pretty good. You should be proud of her."

My mother hadn't left the state of Michigan since birth; I didn't expect she would be here and didn't fault her for it. I cried for Vangie. She was miserable today, and no matter how hard I tried to dismiss her, she stayed on my mind.

The car idled. "What's the address?" Douglas asked me. *Oh!*

I opened the car door, prepared to race back to my room. I'd written it down somewhere. Douglas reached over me and closed the door before I could. He dawdled for what felt longer than all of time, staring at me with his chocolate eyes.

"Still Angie," he said, and then he chuckled as if I was still pitiful. "I think I have it in my phone."

We slugged through heavy traffic on the highway, the navigation monitor in the dashboard screen displaying red for miles ahead.

"You may want to let them know our ETA will be closer to 2:00," Douglas said.

I called Clarissa and told her we were stuck in traffic. She told me dinner wasn't nearly ready and to take our time. That seemed to relax Douglas. I couldn't relax or decide how to sit. I bent my left leg under my right one and turned my body halfway toward Douglas. If I didn't look like an oddly shaped pretzel, I felt like one.

Douglas played one of his favorite old school songs from the nineteen eighties. We bobbed our heads in unison and laughed, loosening me up for the ride.

"How's your driving these days?" Douglas said with a laugh.

I cracked up, reminded of how I confused the brake with the gas pedal sometimes, jerking us for miles.

"Much better," I said.

"How's Vangie?" he said. "She hasn't called me *yet*. We'll see if she approves my visit. You know how your twin can be." Douglas winked at me, as if we both understood Vangie's particular ways.

I turned avocado green and got quiet.

"I love hearing you talk, Angie. Your voice fits you," he said, as if sensing my jealously.

Now I was raspberry red. I hoped my voice was like a cool breeze on a sunny day. To my own ears, I sounded like a mouse afraid to come out of hiding.

I smiled to myself the remaining ride.

I met Courtney, the friendliest and funniest of Clarissa's two younger sisters, when she answered the door with a big smile and eyes as big and bright as Clarissa's. Celeste, her other sister, reminded me of Vangie at that age: too serious for seventeen.

Clarissa's mother had gone to Aspen with her third husband and had left Clarissa in charge of her sisters and cooking Thanksgiving dinner. I sat at the kitchen bar watching Clarissa frantically run around as though she didn't know how to cook or what spices to use. I would've offered my help, but I was too afraid to after hearing Clarissa snap like an alligator at Celeste for offering.

Clarissa shoved a serving spoon at my mouth. "Tell me what you think, Angie."

I tasted Clarissa's stuffing. "It's not bad," I lied.

"It sucks!" Courtney said and laughed.

"She didn't ask you, Courtney," said Celeste.

Clarissa turned back to me. "You think I'm a bad cook, Angie?"

"I'll say it. You're a bad cook."

"Be quiet, Courtney!" Clarissa snapped.

"You're not a *bad* cook," I said, sincerely.

Clarissa took off her fancy apron and handed it to me. "The kitchen's all yours, Angie. Have fun." After pouring herself a class of wine, Clarissa took over my seat at the bar counter and I happily took over the kitchen.

I added bell pepper, onions, celery, garlic, and canned mushroom soup to Clarissa's stuffing, and whipped up garlic mashed potatoes and gravy, roasted Brussels sprouts wrapped in bacon and braised in balsamic vinegar and honey. I shaved corn from the cob and creamed it, repurposed the canned string beans by adding bacon and bouillon to spice them up, and doctored up a simple salad with candied walnuts, dried cranberries, and shaved parmesan cheese. The fried Turkey and candied ham were store bought. If I had time, I would've baked a batch of cheesy biscuits.

Douglas had stopped by the grocery store and bought a bottle of wine, a six-pack of soda, and a six-pack of beer to share. I'd bought cans of jellied cranberry sauce and contributed dessert.

By the time we sat down at the table set nicely with candles and a festive tablecloth, we were all starving. As we ate, I watched their satisfied faces, getting my own sense of satisfaction.

They all licked their fingers over my three-layer chocolate fudge cake glazed in white chocolate ganache.

After dinner, Ross, Douglas, and Clarissa talked in the living room while Courtney, Celeste, and I played Uno. I couldn't hear the conversation in the next room, but I got the impression that Douglas was under interrogation. The interrogation went on for an hour before Douglas and I packed up leftovers and said our goodbyes.

The highway was free and clear as we drove back to the city.

"You know what my mother would say about you, don't you?" Douglas said, glancing at me and smiling.

I shook my head, smiling too. I'd never met Douglas's mother, his father, or any of his eight brothers; but if I ever got the chance, I hoped they'd only have nice things to say about me.

"That girl can burn!" he said, and then chuckled. "Dinner was delicious, Angie. You know, the culinary industry is a growing field. I think you could go far. Have you given any thought to professional training?"

I shook my head quickly, batting back my uprising tears.

"Why haven't you?" he pushed. Douglas always saw greater things in me than I saw in myself.

Sparing myself the shame of admitting I'd blown my chance to attend culinary school this spring, I said, "Okay. I will," and left it at that.

"So, what do you think of Ross? Is he any good?"

I shrugged. I hadn't formed an opinion of Ross, probably because I sensed he didn't have a high opinion of me.

"That's what I thought," Douglas said. "I'll run Vangie's case by a few attorneys I know, good ones, and see what they think. What do you know about the case? Anything?"

What I knew I couldn't share with Douglas or anyone. I shook my head.

Douglas withdrew into his own thoughts for a mile or so. "I'm not trying to be in your personal business," he said finally, "but Clarissa told me something I hated to hear, Angie. What is this business about you being homeless? Is that true?" He glanced at me wearing a frown.

I'd never been ashamed of being a homeless person until now. My face burned, more from hurt than from embarrassment. Vangie and my sacred relationship had changed, our secrets no longer our own, obviously.

"I feel like I failed you," Douglas said.

"Oh no! It wasn't your fault. It wasn't anyone's fault."

"Why didn't you call me if you needed somewhere to stay?"

I said nothing to defend or explain my choices in life.

Home now, I grabbed the bag of leftovers from beneath the glove compartment, ready to jump out of the car when Douglas parked.

"Can I walk you inside first?" he said, turning off the engine.

Goosebumps popped up on my arms, but knowing Douglas, he was just being polite. "I'll be okay."

"Your boyfriend must be home."

"No! I don't have a...boyfriend."

He chuckled as if my having a boyfriend was a real joke. "Do you have plans tomorrow?"

Dismissing my plan to take Thanksgiving leftovers to Mo and them, I shook my head.

"You like to shop, don't you? What woman doesn't like to shop."

It took Douglas calling me a woman to remind myself I was one.

"It's Black Friday. Great deals," he said as if I needed convincing. Vangie loved shopping, especially for clothes. I would rather shop for food or for nothing at all, but I wasn't going to miss a chance to spend another day with Douglas.

I smiled, in a sort-of, kind-of way.

Douglas chuckled. "Okay. We don't have to shop, but I would like to sightsee while I'm here. I'll text you when I'm on my way."

I lit up like a Christmas tree. Before I could jump out of the car, Douglas grabbed my hand. My goosebumps returned, followed by a heat wave. I hoped he changed his mind and planned to stay with me tonight.

"I had a great time today, Angie. Great hospitality. Thank you."

We ended the night without kissing goodbye.

Twenty-Seven

D ouglas and I ate a late breakfast and then drove to Hollywood, where we loaded up with a bucket of buttered popcorn and slushies and found the last two seats in the front row of an IMAX theater. Sitting in a beautiful place close to Douglas was like old times.

We sat through a movie full of action and gunfire and left the theater when the streets were packed with holiday shoppers. The Hollywood Walk of Fame was something else on Douglas's list of things to do. I hadn't seen much of the city and happily tagged along as we walked the mile of stars, stopping to read the names we knew and using Douglas's smart phone to research the ones we didn't.

When our hands accidently brushed, I got an electric shock. Douglas must've felt it too because he smiled down at me and then feathered his fingers against mine intentionally. We played pinkies before he grabbed my hand and held on.

From Hollywood we drove to Venice Beach, where we strolled the boardwalk, hand-in-hand, until the sky turned red velvet and was frosted in gold.

"Are you cold?" Douglas said, obviously noticing my goosebumps.

I smiled softly and shook my head. Just the opposite, I was toasty inside, despite the chill in the air.

"I thought you were getting soft on me, living on the west coast," he teased, as he placed his windbreaker on my shoulders." Just in case…"

I snuggled in the scent of him, smiling inside, down to my toes.

"That east coast time is catching up with me. I can't keep my eyes open." He yawned.

The night was still young, and it seemed my day with Douglas had just begun before it ended.

During the drive from Venice Beach, he said, "It would be a big help if I take you home in the morning, on my way to see Vangie—if you're comfortable with that."

I nodded, thirstily.

Not long later, when we drove into the hotel's parking lot, butterflies tickled my stomach. On the elevator ride up to Douglas's room, I kept my eyes on the iridescent white numbers that climbed too quickly to the 6th floor.

His room had a city view, king-sized bed, and enough space for a love seat and a desk. Without pausing at the door, I passed up the bed quickly, leaned against the desk, and crossed my arms and feet.

"There's a room service menu somewhere over there."

I buried my burning face in the menu and peeked around it, watching as Douglas removed his shoes, socks, watch, and the keys from his pants pockets.

"If you're anything like your twin, you'll want to shower first," he said with a smile.

I wasn't anything like Vangie and never showered before bed. I hurried into bathroom and closed the door anyway. It wasn't until I was soapy and wet that the thought of sleeping next to Douglas, naked, brought an itch down there.

After showering, I wrapped up in a towel and opened the door a fraction, intending to ask Douglas for a T-shirt or something to wear to bed. Suddenly feeling overexposed, I closed the door and waited for my voice to reappear, hating myself for being weird and childish.

I sat for so long Douglas finally knocked on the door. I jumped up from the toilet seat.

"In case you need it," he said, handing me a wife beater through the slit of the open door.

I smiled. Douglas knew me like no other man ever had or likely would. "Thank you so much." I slammed the door in his face and inhaled the shirt, getting drunk off the residue of his spicy cologne. I loved Douglas. I was sure of it.

Modeling the shirt before the mirror, I struck a pose, going for sex appeal—but there was nothing sexy about me. Awkward is my middle name. The too-big shirt exposed the flesh of my breasts around the armpits and hung too long on me.

Douglas barely looked at me when I walked out of the bathroom and he entered it. I tugged at the hem of the shirt, hurried to the bed, jumped under the covers, and drew up my knees, pulling the shirt over them until I looked like a turtle hiding in its shell.

A short time later, Douglas walked out of the bathroom wearing a towel around his waist. I peeked up to see his honey-brown, furry chest, hairy legs, and large, wet feet.

My itch returned.

Douglas climbed into bed. "I promise to stick to my side and keep my hands to myself," he said and smiled.

He doesn't want to touch me.

"Did you find anything good to eat?"

Oh!

I hopped out of bed, grabbed the menu from the desk, and hopped back under the covers.

Chuckling, Douglas put on a pair of wire-rimmed eyeglasses and scooted closer to me. We looked over the menu together.

"You think I'm an old man, don't you?" he teased.

I peeked at him curiously and shook my head.

He laughed. "I understand. Those young boys you go out with hang all night. It's 8:00, if it's that late, and I'm going to bed on you."

"I don't go out," I muttered,

Douglas stared at me. "I can't believe that, Angie."

I scoured the menu, too humiliated to look at him again.

When he reached over and turned my face toward him, my eyes strained not to run from his. His mouth inches from mine, he whispered, "Angie, Angie, Angie," before kissing me so deeply I felt as if I were drowning in his love for me. His mouth tasted of the sweetest honeycomb dipped chocolate. I got lost in his chocolate-coated eyes and floated on air when he pulled me atop him.

He then rolled me onto my back and lowered himself down on me, kissing me for eternity and even that wasn't long enough. Eager to experience the magic we shared years ago, I shut my eyes tightly and held my breath.

That magic moment never came. Douglas rolled off me and sat up suddenly. I sat up too, worried I'd done something wrong. He wouldn't even look at me.

"I'm sorry, Angie. My conscience won't let me take advantage of you again," he said.

"You never took advantage of me. I wanted to be with you." My voice sounded quiet and shaky, which wasn't my intention. "I still want to be with you," I said, my voice much stronger.

"I'm engaged," I thought Douglas said. I prayed he hadn't. "I've been trying to tell you and didn't know how. We work together and have for a long time. I'm not getting any younger and neither is she. The timing lined up for the both of us. One day, when you're older, you'll understand."

I am older and I understood perfectly. He doesn't want to be with me. What man would? I'm not even a woman. I should've touched him down there, kissed him back, done anything but lie here like a stupid lump on a log.

My years of fantasizing about this night rolled down my cheeks in a flood of tears.

Douglas rocked me in his arms. "This hurts me more than it hurts you. Believe me." He released me, grabbed the room service menu from the bed, and stuffed it into my hand. "Here. Order whatever you want on the menu."

I wasn't hungry, not for food anyway. Even when the food arrived, I hardly touched the French fries or the buffalo wings. My hunger for Douglas filled me with an unquenchable appetite that left me feeling starved.

After Douglas fell asleep, I dressed quickly and left his hotel room.

∾

"Girl! You blowin' up my doorbell, waking up my baby. Who try'n to kill you?" Mo said."

I ducked under her outstretched arm without being invited inside. Mo slammed the door behind me. She wore a robe over shorts, a T-shirt, fuzzy socks, and her hair wrapped up like an African Queen.

"And where our leftovers at? Left me and my baby starving over here," she continued.

I burst into tears.

"What? Did somebody F with you? Who was it?" Mo looked ready to swing into action. She was excitable that way and hated being caught off guard.

I gasped for air I couldn't catch, one breath chasing after the next.

Mo shook the air out of me. "Angie! You better tell me what's wrong with you, girl!"

"I'm...not...a...woman!" I cried out.

Taking a step or two back, Mo placed her hands on her hips and stared at me sideways. "How you ain't one? You transgender? Is that what you try'n to tell me, Angie?"

I shook my head. "No...man...wants...to...be...with... me," I stammered in tears.

"Girl. I thought something was wrong with you. Don't be scaring me like that. You know how I am."

I followed Mo into the kitchen. "You don't understand. I'm a freak of nature."

My declaration made Mo laugh. "I understand you're trippin' too late at night."

Mo wouldn't understand even if I could find the right words to explain myself. Men didn't see me, not in the way they saw Vangie. I've lived on the fringes my whole life,

unable to speak my mind or express my feelings to any man
I loved or liked.

"You know what you need? And don't tell me you saved.
I'm saved too, girl. Been *saved*." Mo pulled four mini vodka
bottles from a kitchen drawer and handed one to me.

I gulped too much too fast and regretted it. My throat
burned and eyes watered, but one bottle took the edge off.
The second bottle made me talk more than usual.

We sat on the area rug, drinking and talking. I loved that
I could talk to Mo as easily as I talked to Vangie. I told her
about Douglas, not everything but enough to paint a clear
picture.

"So, this dude flew to California, on a *plane,* to get with
you, knowing he gettin' married?"

"Sort of," I said, on the verge of telling Mo everything.

Mo smacked her lips. "He about to make me start using
the N word again, girl." She grabbed Imani's play cell phone
from the floor and held it up. "See this, Angie. Men are
just like kids. When they finish playing with one toy, they
go looking for a new one to play with. Be his toy and get
played like one, girl."

"I'm a useless toy."

"Quit trippin' with all that. Is this dude your first?"

"My first what?"

Mo cracked up laughing. I laughed too, once I figured
out the joke was on me.

"How many seconds have you had, Angie?"

Turning red, I shrugged. I could not bring myself to tell
her none.

"So, then how you gonna know if the first is any good
if you ain't compared it to nothin'?"

If compared to eating the same meal every day, without a variety of spices, I understood Mo's argument. The memory of Dr. Laurence's kiss on a moonlit night warmed me inside like a shot of vodka. He was the only comparison I had to Douglas.

"Before Dunk," Mo continued. "I needed to be loved so bad I was try'n to please every dude that pushed up on me. Dudes try'n to get pleased, Angie. Know what I mean?"

Having limited relationship experience, I shook my head.

"I'm saying, have some seconds and thirds and see if this dude's worth crying over."

I pondered Mo's advice, wondering if I would ever lose my appetite for Douglas. I could still taste his kiss on my tongue. Not even vodka could wash it out.

Mo started digging through the trash bag she apparently had been digging through before I showed up. "I need to find my marriage license."

When Mo told me that the military needed a copy of her marriage license in order for her and Imani to receive survivors' benefits for Dunk's death, including back pay, I helped her dig.

We dug through years of crumpled, ink smudged, discolored papers, and receipts Mo had stored in a 13-gallon trash bag like a mobile file cabinet until we found it.

When the sun beamed through the African print fabric tacked to the window the next morning, I vowed to myself never to drink again. My head felt swollen, my mouth extra dry, and my eyes ached.

A soft hand stroking my faced pried my eyes open. "You came back," Imani whispered, leaning over the couch and staring at me with Dunk's eyes, her face so close to mine I could smell her baby breath.

"I'm back," I said, smiling up at her. I wrapped her in my arms and pulled her close.

"Where's our food at?" she whispered in my ear.

I laughed through a residue of tears.

Twenty-Eight

I f the gloom in Clarissa's eyes foreshadowed what she could expect from their face-to-face attorney-client conference today, Vangie assumed all was lost.

"Have you heard the news?" Clarissa asked.

Vangie's heart skipped a beat. "No. What news?"

"About Diego Del Rio?" Clarissa said this as if the name should ring a bell. "He's one of L.A.'s highest-ranking members of a Columbian drug cartel." Clarissa went on to say Diego Del Rio had recently made the headlines when he was arrested for distributing truckloads of cocaine and methamphetamine into the U.S from Mexico.

Swallowing hard, Vangie said, "What does any of this have to do with me?"

"Ross got the case," Clarissa announced. "You know what that means, don't you?"

At this point Vangie didn't care what it meant. She sighed out of sheer relief that Diego Del Rio wasn't somehow connected to the Columbian drug dealer who smuggled her out of the country.

"I'm lead counsel on your case," was Clarissa's caveat. "I'm freaking out. I'm not qualified to sit First Chair." Terror

218

resonated in Clarissa's voice. Sitting First Chair in a possible high profile trial would terrify most any newly sworn-in attorney. This Vangie understood and knew better than to stoke Clarissa's doubts with her own.

"You're the best representation I can hire, Riss," Vangie said, sincerely.

Clarissa took tight hold of Vangie's hand. "This is serious, Vangie. You've been indicted by a grand jury in a case that qualifies for the death penalty. If I don't know what happened that night, I don't have a case."

Vangie heard, "death penalty," as if Clarissa had said, "pass the salt." She couldn't wrap her head around being indicted by a grand jury for murder.

"How was Thanksgiving?" she said to change the subject.

Clarissa sighed tiredly, and then released her hand. "A disaster. But Angie is a great cook." Clarissa paused. "I met Douglas, by the way. Between you and me, I think Angie has a thing for him."

Holding her tongue, Vangie reflected on her visit with Douglas the past Saturday, when she sat through his pathetic confession. She tried not to frown, futilely.

"You don't like Douglas, do you? I think he's too old for Angie too, honestly."

Vangie let Clarissa's assumption stand.

Douglas's age didn't concern her so much as Douglas himself. Douglas fell into another category of men she had long ago ascertained, the kind that rode in on a white horse to save poor damsels in distress but couldn't be counted on when the damsel really needed him. She had counted on Douglas to watch over her sister not to sleep with her.

"I thought Douglas was a family friend," Clarissa continued. "He told me he mentored you throughout high school.

Is that true?" Clarissa's casual inquisition raised Vangie's guard. She wondered what more Douglas said about her.

"Yes. It's true." *He did more than mentor me*, she wanted to say.

"Can I ask you something that's bugging me?"

"Is this another cross, Riss?"

"Not a cross. A question. Just one. About our friendship. Have I ever given you the impression that you had to lie to me about your status in order for us to be friends?"

Vangie struggled to look into Clarissa's hurt eyes. She had told so many lies to so many people she couldn't sort them out. A million apologies couldn't make up for her deceit.

"That's a complicated question."

"Well, have I?"

"No, Riss. You have never given me that impression," Vangie said, hoping to end the inquiry. Inevitably, her fictionalized life would be aired in the court of public opinion, and Clarissa might understand what ultimately drove her to murder.

"You can't deny I was a pretentious bitch back then, preserving the Fitzgerald family birthright that *some* people in that fake family think I'm not entitled to." Clarissa shook her head, stood, and picked up her attaché case. "I'm sorry I wasn't a better friend to you, Van, and I'm sorry I can't help you. Let me know when you want to help yourself."

Clarissa called for the guard to let her out, leaving Vangie in the prison of her own mind.

Twenty-Nine

A few sips of caramel flavored coffee dissolved the rock in my stomach, but I couldn't loosen up, worried something had gone terribly wrong with Vangie's case. Why else would Clarissa want to meet with me today?

The second Clarissa walked into the office I leapt to my feet.

"Angie. You're here," she said as if surprised I would be. "I'm glad one of us made it on time. Finding a place to park in this building after eight is murder. I bought muffins if you're hungry."

While Clarissa fussed over the disorder of the reception area, opening the blinds to let in the sun and rearranging the magazines on the coffee table, I grabbed a lemon poppy seed muffin from the box she set on the credenza, then stood around, waiting to hear the bad news.

"We'll meet in my office."

I followed her past Ross's office where he sat behind a large desk. Clarissa's office, though smaller, had a cheery area rug and a calming lavender scent diffuser.

The phone rang as soon as we sat down for our meeting. "Ross E. Lewis and Associates. How can we help you with your legal needs today?" Clarissa said into the receiver.

While she talked on the phone, I chewed small bites of muffin on a nervous stomach, checking out the perfect order of things. Neatly stacked files and documents were on the corner of Clarissa's desk, law books were perfectly arranged by size on the shelves, and artwork hung perfectly on each wall.

Ross walked into the office, passed by me and stood over Clarissa desk. "Riss, I need that transcript?"

"Which one?" Clarissa said when she hung up the phone.

"For Jones."

"The request is in, Ross."

"What about the legal analysis. Murphy. DUI."

Clarissa massaged her cranium with all ten fingers. "I'll get it done."

"By when, Rissa?"

"By 11:00 if I can."

"I'm in court at 11:00."

"When do you expect me to review it, Ross? It's almost 9:00."

"I expected you to review it two days ago, baby. Can I get it by 10:00?"

"Fine, Ross."

"Let me know when you're ready to meet."

When Ross walked out, Clarissa jumped up from her seat. "Shoot! I forgot about our meeting." She grabbed the papers from her printer, placed them in a folder, and handed the folder to me. "Angie, do you mind reviewing a legal analysis for me?"

"You want *me* to review it?" I repeated for confirmation, holding the folder limply between my damp fingers. The office turned hot, cold, and then hot again.

"You can edit on my computer if it's easier for you. Here, sit at my desk." She cleared space for me at her desk. "Don't worry about the legalities. Just check grammar, syntax, spelling inaccuracies... You know, the basics."

I found myself tossing my half-eaten muffin in the trash and sitting at Clarissa's desk before I could find my voice to say, "No thank you!"

"You're the best, Angie." Clarissa hurried out of the office.

Before I touched Clarissa's nice laptop, I swiped my hands clean on my jeans, and then read through the document. My heart hurt when I read Henry Murphy had been arrested for his third DUI and killed an eleven-year-old girl this time. Taking my assignment more seriously, I did a thorough review, making grammatical changes and correcting spelling inaccuracies as I read. After proofing my proof, I took my chair again.

Clarissa returned to the office twenty minutes later. "You're done already?" She sat down before her computer. I watched for her reaction as she read.

She looked up. "Have you found a job, Angie?"

"Not yet," I said slowly, ashamed to admit I hadn't found one.

"I might have one for you. Do you type?"

"Not very fast."

"Do you have basic computer knowledge?

"Sort of."

"You can answer a phone professionally, can't you? We can use a paralegal slash legal assistant slash glorified secretary." Clarissa laughed.

I hoped she was joking, and that I proved I wasn't cut out for the job.

"Our last two temps the agency sent over didn't work out," Clarissa said, seriously. "One was an honest to god Monica Lewinsky type..." Clarissa shook her head, disgustedly. "Anyway, are you interested in the position, Angie?"

Just the thought of talking on the phone all day, to total strangers, intimidated me.

"I've never been a receptionist, just a pastry chef," I said.

"You don't want to be a cook for the rest of your life. No offense," she said.

I tried not to take Clarissa's question offensively.

"Vangie told me you graduated high school with a 4.5 weighted GPA and can read 450 words a minute, and with comprehension."

"That was back in high school," I said.

"Your high school diploma is sufficient. How much do cooks earn? I'm just curious."

"Ten or eleven an hour, I guess." At Sammy's I was up to twelve dollars an hour and proud of it.

"The pay here is sixteen-fifty to start, with benefits and great opportunities in the legal field. Paralegals can earn up to seventy-five grand as base salary."

"Thank you so much..."

"So, you're accepting the position?" Clarissa said, excitedly.

"Oh. No! I mean...thank you for offering. Can I think about it?"

"I can hold the position for another week, but I can't make any promises after that. I need a trustworthy candidate at the front desk like yesterday," Clarissa said.

It was rude of me to stand. "I will." I headed for the door.

"Hold on, Angie" Clarissa said, stopping me before I could run out. "I need to talk to you about Vangie's case—in confidence."

My stomach clenched as tight as a fist.

After I left Clarissa's office, I didn't go home and didn't go to skid row. I took a short train ride and made it to Pasadena, California in no time. I had been here before, not physically but in my dreams. The setting was beautiful. The street I walked, under the pretense of being a leisure shopper, was quiet, peaceful and clean, shaded with full, leafy trees planted in front of charming Ivory buildings and unique shops.

A block later I hurried past the three-story building taking over the corner of the street, afraid to stop, to stare too long or look too longingly. There wasn't a chance anyone would recognize me, but I worried they would somehow know that I was the student who, come January, wouldn't show up on the first day of classes.

I intended to keep walking, but instead I crossed the street and parked myself on the steps of a building where I could dream a little. I'd read everything about the Culinary Institute of the Arts. It's the largest and most prestigious culinary school in the business worldwide, where top chefs trained students to become culinary artists, pastry artists, even restaurateurs.

I watched students enter and exit, wondering if their passion for food gravitated them to the field as well.

Clarissa's question had opened my eyes. Maybe I hadn't thought enough about being a cook for the rest of my life and had only done what came naturally to me and easiest.

I hadn't taken Clarissa's offer seriously, suspecting Vangie was pulling the strings behind the curtain. She didn't have faith that I'd find a job on my own and worried joblessness would put me in violation of my probation. I worried too.

I went straight to the warehouse. We all did our fair share of the work today: sweeping floors, scraping walls, gutting rooms, and hauling away junk. Jay oversaw the probationers and made sure hazardous waste got dumped, Mo handled the business side, and I helped out wherever I was most needed.

This morning Mo had to run down to the Veterans Administration for an appointment. I kept an eye on Imani. We ate cereal from the box, drank milk out of straws, and watched cartoons while coloring together in her Disney coloring book.

Jay appeared in the office doorway. "I thought I knew you from somewhere," he said with the look of someone who uncovered a dead body.

I threw down my crayon, told Imani I'd be right back, and met up with Jay at the other end of the hallway.

"Does Mo know you got pinned for murder?" he said and laughed.

"It wasn't me!" I said but not too convincingly.

Jay's laughter revved up. "This ain't you?" He showed me the photo displayed on his cell phone.

Explaining that I was arrested as Vangie Cooper and placed on probation as Angie Brown, would only rouse Jay's curiosity and provoke more questions, so I told Jay the truth.

"No. She's my twin."

"You got an identical twin?"

I nodded.

"That's dope," Jay said.

My rigid body sighed involuntarily as if all the air had been let out of me. My big secret was finally out in the open, and I couldn't have been more relieved.

Thirty

I arrived at the compound in time to see a busload of inmates steal away into the early morning light. The frost had burned off with the breaking sun, but a chill stayed with me.

On the inside, I took my usual seat at the furthest end of the visitation booths, acutely aware of the hard chair as I waited for Vangie to walk through the security door. I didn't see how I could convince her to talk about the night Todd Bryant was murdered, but if I didn't try to find out what happened that night, Clarissa couldn't build a solid case in Vangie's defense, she had told me.

Vangie was late. I chewed on a fingernail, my stomach tossing and turning.

When she finally walked in, I choked up. I'd never seen her look depressed, even when she had a right to be. Her golden skin was sunless, her eyes were without a speck of light, and her hair was a bird's nest. She was miserable, and I was miserable for her.

"How was your Thanksgiving?" Vangie said the second she sat down and picked up the phone.

Caught off guard, I lost my train of thought and blinked to get it back on track. "O-kay."

"Just okay? What did you do?"

"Went to Clarissa and Ross's house."

"What else did you do, Angie?"

"I cooked and played Uno with Clarissa's sisters."

"What was Douglas up to while you were cooking and playing Uno?"

Vangie had a skillful way of leading me to a dead-end and pressing my back against the wall when I least expected it.

"Watching a football game with Ross," I answered deliberately.

"Is that all he did?"

I didn't fall for Vangie's trick question this time.

Vangie sucked her teeth in response to my silence "What'd the two of you do after Thanksgiving?" she pushed.

"Nothing," I said too fast and too nervously.

"You're too smart to play dumb."

"I'm not playing dumb."

"Then don't insult my intelligence. You have a lot to learn about men, Angie. If you want to screw Douglas, that's your business, but keep him out of mine."

Tears climbed to my eyes that swam around in their sockets.

"I didn't *screw* him," I said under my breath. "I have to go…"

"Don't go, Ang. Please. I think I might be pregnant."

I suddenly felt as if I was pregnant too, and suffering from morning sickness. "Oh, no! How?"

"How do you think, Angie?"

"Is it...?" I didn't have to say Wade's name before grief eclipsed Vangie's face like a gray mask.

"I said I might be."

"Does Clarissa know?"

"No, and don't tell anyone. Please."

"I won't. I promise. What're you going to do?"

"I don't know."

"What can I do to help? Just tell me."

"Ship me a shit load of green pineapples. That'll help."

I stared at Vangie as if she had lost her mind. In response to my petrified starring, she laughed until tears rolled down her cheeks.

"You're acting like Mom having one of her spells," I whispered.

Vangie's laughter cut off. "Grow-up, Angie. I'm not the crazy one in this fuck-up family. And Mom suffered from severe depressive disorder; they were never *spells,* which you would know if you hadn't been hopping trains."

Jail had gotten to Vangie and nothing I said would alleviate her misery, brighten her day or put a smile on her face, but I tried my best to anyway.

"Our life wasn't as bad as you make it sound. There were happy times, Van."

"We grew up in the same fucked up, shitty household. What *happy* times do you remember that I don't, Angie? Tell me."

"The times when we crowded in bed with Mom, watching movies and eating junk food all day..."

Vangie sucked her teeth to that.

"Our girl parties...Remember, Van, just the three of us dancing, singing, and having fun? And when Grandma was alive and baked us anything we wanted—cookies, cakes, pies…Those were happy times…to me."

"You know what I remember…? Mom being too drunk and depressed to get out of bed and get herself dressed…I remember taking care of the bills and buying food when she dragged home a drunk who ate us out of house and home. Do you remember how I paid the bills, Angie, or are you delusional about that too?"

I sat in silent shame for a long while.

Our visit never recovered. I left jail without asking Vangie about the night of the murder. I didn't need to ask what I knew. The truth was there, a spiral of guilt swirling in Vangie's black eyes. She killed that dude and I may never know why.

At home, I stood in the breezy walkway, staring at a beautiful vase of flowers placed at my doorstep. After my depressing visit with Vangie, even hearing from Douglas couldn't excite me. I read the small card:

> *Angie, I hope one day you'll understand.*
> *Please call me if you ever need anything.*
> *Love, Douglas*

Maybe I will call Douglas someday…

Thirty-One

T he slamming steel doors sounded like death to Vangie. Each time a door slammed she died a little more inside. There seemed never a quiet moment or an opportunity to find a semblance of peace. Most days she passed the excruciatingly sluggish hours listening to classical music on a CD Player. Lately, however, Bach's tender organ couldn't quiet her fears.

Tonight, sleep came in no great hurry to put Vangie out of her misery. She couldn't turn off the memories that played in her mind like one of her mother's scratchy CDs. She only saw her past, and now, in the darkest light. A sense of foreboding awakened her every morning and put her to bed late at night. Her sleep patterns were random. Some days she couldn't keep her eyes open from weariness, and other days her mind ran on a twenty-four-hour schedule.

Vangie reflected on her last visit with Angie. They often argued over something or other growing up, but these fights were different. Angie was different. She worried Angie would disappear again—so worried she broke down and called her mother collect, a call she now regretted. It was easier to let go of her old life than to coexist in two worlds. The sound of her mother's voice was the heart of home for her. With all its sorrow, unfulfilled hopes and dreams, and catastrophes there was always love wrapped in her memory of it all.

Her mother hadn't talked to Angie in a few days. A few days for her mother may be of little consequence, but it was a lifetime for her these days.

Tears burning her eyes, Vangie sat up in bed, placed her feet on the cold floor, and leaned her head between her knees, waiting for her nausea to pass.

Early this morning, Vangie dressed before the water turned cold, the offensive alarm went off, and lights came on.

The girl woke with her, talking nonsense about trivialities rather than using her high energy constructively.

"I got my period," she said, stringing her legs over the top bunk. "Can I borrow one of your pads?"

Vangie didn't need to be reminded of her period. She would give her right arm to trade places with the girl at that moment. She reached inside her pillowcase, then handed the girl a sanitary napkin from her stash.

"I'll pay you back."

"You don't need to."

She didn't expect the girl would reimburse her anyway, neither a sanitary napkin nor the money she put on the girl's books. The girl's account stayed empty, and Vangie found herself pitying the girl who, from what she had gathered, didn't have family or friends on the outside that cared

234 I Sheryl Mallory-Johnson

about her. The friendships the girl had established on the inside appeared to have corrupted her.

When social hour came around, Vangie walked into a modernized open room with maple wood bookshelves covering the burnt orange walls, activity tables, and computer stations throughout. She was pleasantly surprised that the library wasn't a dingy establishment with limited resources and tattered old books.

Several inmates huddled around a table. Other's roamed freely. A few sat with their heads buried in a book or a magazine. Vangie noticed them all with a quick sweep of her eyes.

"Can I help you find anything?" a white woman said with the demeanor of a librarian and the suspicious tone of a guard.

Vangie supposed she had stood around unsupervised for longer than a minute, contemplating if she should've come to the library, knowing the risk she was taking. Also knowing her fundamental and constitutional rights of access to the courts and right to due process, she told the librarian she was looking for the legal references.

"Your pass please?"

Vangie handed the librarian her pass that allowed her movement from one zone to another without supervision. The librarian walked her to the kiosk and gave her an overview of the high-security, touchtone screen device used for legal research.

"Tell me what you're researching, and I'll help you get started," the woman said.

"Case citations."

"Which category?"

"Habeas corpus." Her lie was swift and irrelevant.

"Habeas…corpus," the librarian said as she typed it out. "Here we are."

When the librarian walked away, Vangie reviewed civil action cases, wasting time she didn't have to waste.

She glanced over her shoulder for the last time before typing "women prisoners and reproductive health" in the search bar. A list of references and case citations populated the screen.

The first she read was of a Jane Doe who was refused off-site transportation for an elective medical procedure without a court order, obstructing her right to an abortion in her first trimester. The woman sued the county in question.

The second she read was about a woman who elected to deliver her baby in jail. She was shackled to the bed during the delivery process, putting both her and her baby in danger.

Yet another case file was of a woman who went full term, and when the time came for her to deliver her baby, the jail's nurse and staff refused to provide urgent and proper medical care, resulting in a stillbirth.

She read of other Jane Does kept in medical confinement, in miserable conditions, and left near starvation.

The last Jane Doe case she read said the woman committed suicide to terminate her pregnancy after the courts ruled against her request to have an abortion.

Vangie had read enough and knew what she could and could not do.

First things first, she thought. She had to tell Clarissa about the night of Todd's murder, which only nicked the surface of her past. She deliberated for two days.

When Clarissa sat down in her designer, pinstriped skirt suit, primed for their attorney-client conference, Vangie simply said, "Todd raped me, so I killed him."

Vangie had no tears to offer Clarissa, nor did she expect pity from her friend. No stranger to sexual violations, she just wanted to put the memory behind her like every memory of its kind, to bury it so deep it couldn't lay its filthy hands on her again; but the memory was persistent, taunting her with jade-colored eyes, out to destroy her life.

Part Six

Thirty-Two

F ree to leave California, I caught out early Thursday morning. As the train increased speed, that old feeling, like the wind free to blow in any direction I wanted to go, came over me.

I watched Mother Nature's mysterious hand mist over the earth as far as the eye could see, then spread the mist like clay across the Great Plains and mold it into snow-covered mountains.

As I stepped down from the train, Colorado Springs embraced me with a typical spring day of fifty-eight-degree weather. I zipped up my lightweight bomber jacket and stepped back in time.

Arriving at my first stop of the day by metro, I walked the city block of brightly painted restaurants and businesses, passing the coffee shop that competed with Sammy's for business, their bagels and plump muffins almost as good, the print shop Sammy used for ads, and other businesses I once patronized, enjoying the laidback atmosphere.

I missed each pebble in the cobblestone where snow-flakes melted in the sun. I missed every person I'd ever met here. Here, I was lost and then found. Here, I planted seeds that bloomed. Here, I shined in my own light. It seemed nothing about Colorado Springs had changed except for me.

The chime over the door to Sammy's Bakery rang when I walked in, alerting the staff that a new customer had entered the store. Time suddenly stood still. I waited to be criticized, condemned and ridiculed by my co-workers. Maybe no one recognized me. In solidarity with Vangie, I had let my hair grow out and wore it in a bushy ponytail at the nap of my neck.

I removed my beanie and took off my sunglasses. As though someone flipped on a switch, the hustle and bustle of the pink and white bakery returned, and I took in a heavenly whiff of baking bread. Sammy stared at me from the opposite side of the service counter where she displayed all things delicious. I stared back, searching her pale eyes for empathy.

After ringing up a customer, she said, "Hey Angie," as if I hadn't gone missing for six months. She raised her chin and nodded toward the back of the bakery. Nervously, I followed her through the commercial kitchen, passing the refrigerated wall preserving our perishable desserts, a seven-layer decadent wedding cake under construction by Marie, one of the cake bosses, and the convection ovens baking baguettes, inundated with sweet memories. My former co-workers gawked at me, and a few actually spoke to me.

In the bakery business there's little time for office work and less space to get it done. The office was a neat, corner spot inside the inventory room. Sammy didn't close the door for privacy. She sat on the desk and swung her feet in her pink tennis shoes. Sammy's trademark style—jeans, pink tennis shoes, and fire red hair—had not changed. She remained forever young. We were alike in that way, Sammy and me. She wasn't in a rush to grow up either and could eat a whole pound cake and not gain a pound.

"How are yah, Angie?"

My response came slow as I contemplated my state-of-mind. "I'm okay," I said with a shrug.

She tilted her head like a curious cat's. "You could've come to me about anything. I hope you know that."

I wondered what she meant by "anything" and if she knew about Vangie's case.

"I'm sorry."

"How can I help you?" Her question sounded promising. Maybe I still had a life here. Knowing I turned out to be a big disappointment to Sammy and to myself, I didn't get my hopes up.

"If you're here about your old job, Casey is my new lead," she said. "I couldn't continue to hold the position open. I'm sorry, Angie."

"Oh, no. That's okay. I have a job."

"That's great!" Sammy reached into one of the desk drawers and handed me an envelope I recognized as my paycheck. "If you have a problem cashing it, I'll have a new one cut for yah."

I stuffed the envelope into my bomber jacket pocket. "Thank you for believing in me, Sammy."

She swatted the air like I was being a pest. "You were one of my best employees. I wish I had ten of yah. Hey, have you seen Aunt Floe?"

I shook my head.

"She's in here every week asking about yah. I'll fix up a box of treats for yah to take over to the girls. Stop by anytime, Angie."

I took the hint and left the bakery, feeling the cool air kiss my wet cheeks. If I thought facing Sammy and my co-workers was hard, I knew facing Roxie's House would be.

The two-story brick house with turquoise shutters, the place that took us in off the street, fed us, clothed us, and gave us a new lease on life, still stood strong. I trudged up the hill. The automatic gate drew back and Susan's Volkswagen Beetle rolled up beside me.

Susan rolled down the passenger window. "Angie?" she said in her cheerful, twangy, inquisitive voice. "Hop in. I'll drive you down." I hopped into the passenger seat but could've walked down the hill just as fast.

The Lead House Counselor at Roxie's, Susan's big brown eyes were always packed with questions. I expected her to fire them at me, one after another.

"It's awesome to see you. I didn't know you were back."

"Just for the weekend."

"Well, welcome back!" She turned off the engine and glanced at the pink bakery box on my lap. "What'cha got there?"

"Treats for the girls—from Sammy."

"The girls will love it!"

My timing couldn't have been worse. When I walked into the ocean blue recreation room, coaxed by Susan, a house meeting was underway. Floe, the House Mother, Deloris, the Night Mother, and Jamie, the Senior Case Manager were all there, gathering near the notorious circle of chairs. Even Betina, the cook, stepped into the room to see me.

"Well, look who came to visit us this morning. If it isn't Angie Brown, our star graduate." That was Floe, one of the nicest people I'd ever met, who never judged anyone without giving them the benefit of the doubt. She was the only person in the room I could look directly in the eyes.

I received caring hugs, smiles, and curious stares from Deloris and Jamie.

"Graduates are always welcome in the circle," Susan said suggestively.

"Oh, thanks, but I can't stay that long," I said quickly. I wasn't the best example for the girls in the house to look up to anyway.

Betina made a hacking sound, flicked the dishtowel in her hand at me, and walked out of the room.

"I heard yah never collected your scholarship and walked out on your job," Floe whispered in my ear. "Why don't yah stick around? Dr. Slater would love to see yah." Floe had wrapped her arm around my shoulder to keep me from running, again.

I decided to stick around.

Dr. Slater's soft black eyes smiled when she found me waiting outside of her office door. "Floe told me you came for a visit. Come on in, Angie. I have a few minutes."

When I walked into Dr. Slater's purple office and sat on her loveseat, my shoulders released built-up tension. We called this the Purple Room for a reason. It comforted us and gave us a safe space to pour out our hearts. Sitting in her overstuffed chair, Dr. Slater asked me her usual warm-up questions about my overall mental well-being. If

I was going to talk to anyone about Vangie's case, it would be with Dr. Slater, and only in confidence, now that the presiding judge over Vangie's case had issued a gag order to ensure she received a fair trial.

I tried explaining to Dr. Slater that Vangie was everything I wasn't and would never be, that if Vangie died, I would die too; but whatever I said sounded incomprehensible through my tears, nothing but fragmented sentences and breathlessness.

Dr. Slater listened with quiet contemplation, and then said, "The Citizens of Colorado Against the Death Penalty have been fighting to have that draconian law abolished since 1977, which I'm certain was the year the last execution took place in the state. I don't know about the state of California, but your twin's chance of receiving the death penalty is extremely low. There is still such a thing as innocent until proven guilty... I'd like to read something to you, Angie, if that's okay." Dr. Slater opened the newspaper in her hand. "From homeless to culinary school...," she read from an article in the local newspaper that made Jim Mahoney, an otherwise cantankerous old man, proud to be the founder of Roxie's House. The article called me hardworking, resilient, and an inspiration.

Dr. Slater handed me the paper. "I want you to keep it as a reminder of how far you've come. We all take wrong turns in life. That's how new roads are paved." She smiled at me in her mothering way, but I couldn't see a speck of optimism in her soft black eyes.

"What the heck, Angie. Could you have returned one of my phone calls?" Ashley came right out and asked me. She had picked me up in her crimson Hyundai Electra, waiting only until she rolled down all the windows, lit a cigarette, and we were speeding away from Roxie's House before she spoke.

My explanation stammered from my mouth. "I lost my phone with all my contacts. I'm sorry."

"Where were you?"

"It's a long story. I'll tell you everything, one day."

"Tell me everything about what?"

"Nothing really," I said.

Ashley glanced at me skeptically. "You didn't run off with Dr. Laurence and screw his brains out, did you?"

Heat rushed to my cheeks. "No!"

At the next stop light, Ashley gave me a prolonged stare as she tapped ashes into an empty Starbucks' cup. "Too bad. I would've."

We ate lunch at our favorite pizzeria and salad bar three miles from Roxie's. Time slipped away as I listened to

Ashley talk about her new boyfriend, her promotion from case aide to case manager at Roxie's Teen House, and her plan to receive a master's degree, as only Ashley would talk—with modest pride.

I soaked up her success, which tremendously dwarfed my own. I was proud of Ashley, and envious of her too. She had changed in every way, even dying her hair and cutting it in a short, flirty style. The color red brought out her hazel eyes once dimmed my meth.

Ashley and I both had grown by leaps and bounds since our early days at Roxie's, except while Ashley continued to shoot for the stars, I had dropped from the sky like a meteor and smashed into earth. I couldn't see how I would get back on track or imagine what new roads I would pave.

I spent the rest of the day with Ashley and stayed the night at her apartment. From the couch, where I'd slept, I heard playful laughter coming from the other side of the wall. Her new boyfriend showed up late last night and was still hanging around. Ashley didn't seem eager for him to leave.

So, I left the couch, folded my blanket, showered, dressed and left Ashley's apartment quietly. She lived in the heart of Colorado Springs, within walking distance from where I once lived. New construction had sprung up, and a few of the old apartment complexes were being renovated. Pineview Apartments, the oldest building by far, took up a small piece of land on West Bayou Avenue.

I cut across the grassy courtyard, dipped between one of the two-story green buildings, and caught a gust of wind as I walked down the corridor toward the parking lot. Rationally, I didn't expect to see my car, but I stared at the empty parking space once assigned to me, hoping it would magically reappear.

The manager, Neil Nabors, didn't look glad to see me waiting by the rental office door when he walked up. He grumbled hello and let me inside and out of the cold.

"What do you need?" he said.

"I'm here to pay my back rent." I handed him a cashier's check.

Grumbling, Mr. Nabors sat at his desk and watched his slow computer power up. He then scrutinized me with his bold green eyes as if I were a perfect stranger.

"Unit?"

"Unit twenty-five. Angie Brown."

"I remember. Second floor. Corner unit. Quiet. Paid on time. Most don't. A new tenant moved into your unit thirty days after you skipped out. Your deposit took care of the rest." He handed me the check back.

"Oh. Thank you."

"It's not my personal policy. It's the law of the land. That would've cost you in late fees and interest. Anything else?"

His abruptness stopped me from asking him about my car, furniture, clothes, etcetera.

"Nothing else. Thank you."

I returned to Ashley's place and told her of my plans to leave early. If I caught out now, I could be home before work Monday morning. Vangie's trial was set to begin soon and I had to be there.

"That kind of sucks," Ashley said. "Aren't you seeing Dr. Laurence today?"

I had a ready excuse. "Oh. I forgot the clinic is closed weekends, and I don't know where he lives."

"Google him," Ashley said, as if the solution was that simple. It wasn't that I didn't want to see Dr. Laurence; I was afraid to see him. Before I could overreact, Ashley grabbed her laptop and sat next to me at the dining table.

"Is Laurence his last name or first name? That's always been hella' confusing."

My relationship with Dr. Laurence had progressed to a first name basis and hadn't gone much further. Laurence was his first name; Toussaint his last name. I knew his full name by heart and committed it to memory each time I walked into his office: *Dr. Laurence A. Toussaint, DMD.*

I bunched my face into an expression of confusion, as if I couldn't remember my own name let alone his.

"Duh!" Ashley exclaimed. "He's listed on the clinic's website. Right here."

Google listed a number of people who went by the name Lawrence Toussaint, but only one person listed had a middle name that began with the letter "A" and only one was a dentist.

A list of Lawrence's possible relatives displayed first, followed by his current and past addresses. He once lived in Florida and New York before moving to Colorado Springs, and he currently lived on North Pike Drive, in the Aspen Meadows Townhomes.

"You're chickening out, aren't you?" said Ashely.

I stopped biting my nails and sighed. With a few hours still to kill before the next train departed for Los Angeles, I made a spontaneous decision. If Laurence wasn't home, I could leave Colorado guilt free.

∼

During Colorado's winter months, the cherry trees leaves turned white as snow before falling off. I noticed that first about North Pike Drive, how the weeping cherry blossoms were beginning to blush, signifying the start of spring.

Loitering near the Aspen Meadow Townhomes, I kept a close watch on the security gate surrounding the quaint complex. When a car approached, I left the metro stop and hurried across the street, slipping through the gate behind the car to gain access.

Leerily, I walked up one road and down another, searching for Laurence's street among the rows of two-story brick townhomes with forest green rooftops. When I found the street and the building number, I realized I didn't know if he lived in unit A, B, C, or D.

As I approached the first unit, I removed my beanie and smoothed out my hair. A boy with big curious eyes stared up at me when the door opened. A woman came to door seconds later, warned the boy about opening it to strangers, and then told me Laurence—apparently, she was on a first name basis with him too—lived next door. My heart beating ten times faster than normal, I trudged up the next walkway.

I couldn't remember if I rang the doorbell or knocked before I was hypnotized by Laurence's golden-yellow eyes wrapped in long, curly lashes. My eyes fell away from his. The sweatpants he wore with a matching hoodie hung nicely on him. His running shoes were nice too.

"Angie?"

My eyes jumped back up. The keys in his hand jiggled, jarring me out of stupefaction.

"Oh. You're leaving? I can come back later," I croaked.

He looked to my right and then to my left. "Are you're alone? When did you get back?"

"Yesterday."

"I'm on my way to get a quick bite. Are you in a hurry to get somewhere?"

I shook my head, disregarding the time.

"Take a ride with me."

Seeing how Dr. Laurence lived when he wasn't at the clinic fulfilled my wildest fantasy. I entered his townhouse with roving eyes. Everything jumped out at me, from the obvious to the most personal, like his running shoes with muddy soles that lay in the tiled entryway as if he had kicked them off coming through the front door, the nice electric guitar standing against the brick fireplace in the living room, a laundry basket of unfolded clothes that sat on the gray couch, and the bare grey walls. I caught a whiff of chocolate chip cookies in the air and imagined a woman baking in his kitchen.

We walked through his white kitchen and into his garage where his black Jeep and an expensive looking black sports car I'd never seen him drive filled the tight space. He backed the sports car out of the driveway, making room for me to hop into the passenger's seat.

Consumed by the poetic lyrics of Kendrick Lamar, we eased over speed bumps and shot through the security gate, the car roaring like a lion. Halfway up the next block, Laurence lowered the music.

"Talk to me," Laurence said in a way that I loved, as if I had something worthy to say. I told him about finding Mo and being a godmother to Imani, the only worthy aspect of my life worth sharing.

"Where'd you find her?"

"Oh. In Los Angeles. I live there." I held my breath, waiting for him to connect the dots.

"How's culinary school?" he said with little interest in my answer.

"I decided to wait. I work at a law firm now." I made it sound like I'd made an intelligent decision for myself. He stared at me briefly, as though finding my choice plain stupid.

"How's your dental hygiene. Are you flossing every day?"

I ran my tongue across my teeth and glanced at him guiltily.

"Make it a point. I'm still you're dentist of record. I wouldn't want you to lose your golden smile." He said this to his patients routinely, but he said it now without his usual chairside manner. It was a nice reminder that our relationship remained professional, that I had overstepped my bounds by coming to his house unannounced, and that our kiss meant nothing to him.

"How'd you know where I lived? I'm just curious."

Dread filled my stomach. *He thinks I'm a stalker.*

"Google," I said coyly.

The crease in his brow deepened.

I sank lower in my seat. "I should've called before I came. I'm sorry. I lost my phone with all my contacts," I said to justify everything.

A new Kendrick Lamar song played. Laurence turned it up. We sped onto the highway, heading toward the south side.

"I have to make a quick stop before we eat. Do you mind?" he said above the loud music.

I shook my head. I didn't mind at all.

On the south side of the city, we stopped at a white and gray house of average size. An inflated jumper, filled with bouncing kids, sat on the lawn, and colorful balloons tied to the porch post blew in the breeze.

The pregnant Hispanic women who answered the door welcomed Laurence with a hug and told him he could find Julio out back. He introduced me to Ruby before she guided us through the house overtaken with delightful scents, chatty women, and playful kids. I kept my eyes low and feet moving.

The backyard resembled a small used car lot. Most of the cars in the yard were custom lowriders or under construction. I stared at a beautiful mustang shimmering under the gloomy sun in its pearly white coat. Two black striped decals ran down its hood, it sat on large tires with nice rims, and had a spoiler kit tacked on.

Choked up and nostalgic, I floated toward it while Laurence talked to the dude, Julio. Through the darkly tinted window I peered into, I noticed that the seats were red leather, like my old car, just not shabby. With a good yank, the driver's door on my car would open even locked. I reached for the handle and yanked. It popped right open.

Oh my God!

I ran to the front of the car, checked the license plate, and stomped my foot. Mo was right when she said, *Men are like kids. When they finish playing with one toy, they find a new toy to play with. Well, it's my toy and I want it back!*

Laurence walked up to me, smiling.

"You stole my car?" I squawked.

"Stole?" He leaned away from me. "That's loaded language. Let me explain the situation before you jump to crazy conclusions."

Frowning, I waited for him to explain why my car was sitting in a used car lot with a "For Sale" sign in the front window. I wanted to cry, not over my car but over realizing I didn't know this dude and evidently never knew him. He was just my dentist. He made that clear to me.

"I stopped by your apartment looking for you. The manager had it up for sale. I bought it for more than it was worth, thinking I was doing you a favor."

Oh. It was a favor to me? I wanted to say. I accidently rolled my eyes at him.

"You can't be serious?" he said.

"What if I hadn't come back?" My sarcastic question shot out of my mouth before I could stop it.

"You left without notice and never returned my calls. Admit you're in the wrong, woman."

I opened my mouth to explain myself and then clamped it shut when Julio walked up.

"What does she think, Doc?" Julio said.

"We didn't get that far, man. Meet Angie, the friend I was telling you about."

Julio shook my hand. "Doc, here, is a car man. He takes good care of me and my family. I give him the best deals."

Laurence handed me a car key. "It's yours."

Shame tugged at my neck, pulling my head and eyes downward. I peeked up contritely. "It's beautiful. But I can't..." I handed Laurence the key back.

He scolded me with his beautiful eyes. "Take it, Angie," he insisted "You can pay me back."

I threw my arms around his neck. "Thank you! Thank you!" I turned to Julio and thanked him profusely too.

Julio removed the "For-Sale" sign from the window. I hopped into my new car. My cheeks hurt from smiling so hard as I listened to my engine purr like a newborn kitten.

We drove our separate cars, Laurence and me. At an antiquated mini-mall a few blocks away from Julio's place, Laurence and I parked our cars side-by-side. As we walked into a greasy spoon, he reached back and took my hand into his, which took me by surprise. His pulse beat between my legs, turning my face all shades of red.

The menu was limited—cheese steak and pastrami sandwiches, burgers, fries, and soft drinks—but I wasn't thinking about eating. When our orders came up, we grabbed two empty seats at a small round table.

I channeled my sexual energy into eating, biting into the juicy steak and pastrami sandwich on soft warm bread smothered in melted cheddar cheese. Once I got started, I couldn't stop.

Laurence reached over the table and wiped the side of my mouth with his napkin. "You had a little cheese right there…"

"Sorry…it's *so* good," I said through a mouthful.

Even his laugh was beautiful, a deep wave on an ocean night. "This is one of my spots whenever I'm on this side of town."

I wondered how many "spots" he had and if he was a "foodie" like me. Nibbling my hot cheese fries, I watched his beautiful lips rotate. When his lips curled at the corners, I looked up and caught him watching me too.

I read once that male cats can detect a female cat's desires, and wondered if Laurence detected my desires for him, itching between my legs.

"Are you coming home with me?" Laurence said, smiling at me.

He knows!

Thirty-Four

We returned to his place. The second we walked
through the door Laurence kissed me, his tongue
swirling around mine repeatedly, sending my
stomach on a thrilling ride. I fell back against the closed
door, and when I did, he lifted me clear off my feet, supporting my weight with his hands cupped under my butt.

Suddenly, I floated off. I kept my legs and arms locked
tightly around Laurence's waist and my lips fastened to his,
as he carried me up a short flight of stairs.

Inside a bedroom, he spread me across a large bed and
removed my sweater, my tank top, and then my sports bra.
When he suckled my breasts, first the left and then the
right, an unbelievable sensation overtook my body, spreading like wildfire.

I braved him removing my tennis shoes and socks, and
I couldn't stop giggling while he kissed all ten of my toes.
When he peeled off my jeans, I trembled uncontrollably
and almost lost my nerve as he slowly slid off my panties.

Incredibly aware of my own nudity, I lay, quivering,
timidly watching Laurence strip for me. I skimmed over

every inch of his cinnamon brown skin, from his chiseled chest to his ripped stomach and to his slightly bowed legs. I no longer had to imagine what my dentist looked like nude. He was all mine to behold and I itched to do things to him I never thought I would want to do to any man.

Laurence and I made delicious love—at least it felt like real love making to me. Afterward we rested in comfortable silence, our arms and legs wrapped in a tight hug. From his bed, the white shutters opened onto a magnificent view of the downtown skyline and Rocky Mountains. I was sure it was a dream: the view, me here with Dr. Laurence in Colorado Springs. All of it.

I gazed over at Laurence. "Tell me your story," I said before I could bore him with silence.

Laurence crooked his lips and said, "Isn't this where we left off?"

Color rushed to my face. My eyes briefly fell away from his. "I'm really sorry I didn't call you." I spoke softly, doing my best to hold his beautiful, scolding gaze.

"So, what's your story? You've kept me waiting long enough."

"Yours first. Please."

Laurence sat up. I did too, and I snuggled in the blanket, under his arm wrapped around my shoulder.

His story began off the coast of South Florida, on a dingy boat packed with Haitians at a time when Haiti was at war with itself. Met by the United States Coast Guard, many Haitians were incarcerated for seeking asylum, including his parents. His mother was eight months pregnant at the time. Weak and sick from the sea, she died in jail giving birth to him. Born on U.S. soil, Laurence was declared a citizen of the United States. His father was deported.

Teary eyed, I clutched my aching heart. "What happened to you," I breathed.

"Nothing so bad. Haitians take care of Haitians, you know. I got passed around from poor household to poor household and was eventually adopted."

"Were you a baby?" I said, breathily.

"I was nine and headed for big trouble."

Oh...

"Your family, they live here, in Colorado?"

"In various places, doing their own thing. I have three adopted brothers..."

I have an identical twin. She's locked up for murder, I badly wanted to confide in him.

"You'll be surprised to know we all attended medical school." He smiled warmly. "I have altruistic parents."

Many more questions about his fascinating life crossed my mind as I hung onto to his story.

"What else?" I said.

"What else...? I graduated from Columbia, completed my residency and was offered an opportunity I couldn't turn down. It came with nice Fringe benefits." He smiled at me, but as if to himself. "That's when you showed up. Do remember that day, when you first walked into my office, on crutches?"

Feeling myself turn red, I nodded. How could I forget one of the worst days of my life?

"You were my first patient as a private practitioner," he said.

"Was I?" I laughed embarrassingly loud.

"You had me sweatin', and not just because you're beautiful and sweet. I was interested. I'll admit it."

I wanted to believe I was beautiful in Laurence's eyes, but couldn't see myself through his eyes or anyone else's but my own. I crinkled my nose. He kissed the tip of it.

"I'm sorry for making you sweat over me," I said, coyly.

"So, it's like that?"

"It's like that."

I giggled as he spread me out on the bed and mounted me again. He grinned down at me. "What should we do next?"

The greedy cat woman in me wanted more of him. But I had an incredible urge to feel the Colorado wind at my face and the fresh air in my lungs. "Go running?" I suggested.

"I like how you think."

I raised up on my elbows. "Can we?" I said, excitedly.

"Let's go!" Laurence hopped out of bed immodestly.

I wrapped myself in the blanket and scooted off the bed. Remembering I left my backpack inside my car, with my running clothes, I bent over to scoop up Laurence's hoodie and sweatpants from the floor. "Can I wear these to my car?" Feeling a slap on my butt, I squealed and shot upright.

"Don't get too comfortable in those," he said.

I laughed nervously and dashed into the bathroom. Does he want me to leave? I didn't know what he meant and was back to feeling like a nineteen-year old virgin.

Great sex had me looking like a wild-haired cat. I snickered, admiring my reflection in the mirror. There was definitely something womanly about me.

I peeked inside one of the vanity drawers and found evidence of another woman: lipstick case, hairpins, mascara, and whatnot. I imagined her genuinely beautiful and wondered if she was one of his 'fringe benefits' too. My stomach dropped ten feet.

I closed the drawer quickly.

The ten-mile Legacy Loop at Pikes Peak Greenway was a short drive from Aspen Meadows Townhomes and a breeze to run. I'd run it before and run more challenging trails. If I were brave, I would challenge myself to conquer Pikes Peak at over 14,000 feet above sea level. Many marathon runners had conquered it. Laurence was one of them.

"You think you can keep up?" Laurence said, as if worried I couldn't keep up with him. I worried too and felt dressed like an amateur compared to his professional running gear. He had scooped his locks into an adorable ponytail and wore a handy water bottle holder strapped around his waistline.

I wore nothing more than a warm windbreaker, plain white tee, and a pair of old biker shorts. But the day was perfect for a run: crisp, cool, and sunny.

After our warmup, we hit the dirt trail, keeping a steady pace, slow enough to talk although neither of us did. Laurence listened to his music; I listened to my thoughts, tortured by guilt. Every so often he reminded me to watch my form. To impress him, I followed his instructions by keeping my head level, back straight, and eyes forward. His running form was perfect. He was perfect. I couldn't stop glancing up at him and wishing he was all mine.

We ran through an isolated part of the trail bordered by pine trees and weeds and inhabited by the homeless. When we came to a stop light, we jogged in place, waiting for the light to turn green, and then picked up the trail on the other side the street.

We ran for a long stretch, stride for stride, crossed under a bridge, passed the picnic area with glorious trees, and ended our run at Dorchester Park. Bent over my knees, I struggled to catch my breath.

"You good?" he said, looking worried.

I guzzled water, took a deep breath, and said, breathlessly, "I have to tell you something about me."

"Are you married?"

"No!"

"Are you into girls?"

"No!"

Laurence knitted his brows and studied me. "Talk to me."

"I have a twin sister. She's locked up for murder and it's my fault."

"You're shittin' me," he said.

Eyes wet, I said, "I can't tell you more; there's a gag order. But I can show you. Can I see your phone?"

He handed me his cell phone and regarded me with a smirk.

A woman pushing a stroller approached us.

"When we're alone, okay," I whispered.

We returned to his townhome. His home office had French doors, a built-in office unit, and boxes of dental supplies. Laurence sat in his office chair and logged into his desktop computer.

I sat on his lap and Googled Vangie's name.

"Let me see your twin who's locked up for murder," he said with a laugh, attempting to peer around my shoulder.

I stood and stepped aside. Tears filled my eyes as photos of Vangie loaded. Laurence glanced up at me, turned back to the photos of Vangie, and glanced at me again. Even the photos of Vangie posted by people intending to show her in her worst light were beautiful snapshots of her.

Clarissa warned me about the court of public opinion, but I wasn't prepared for how cruel people could actually be. Social media was cruelest. People, with their opinions and suspicions about Vangie, called her names I couldn't stand to hear or read.

I tried to read Laurence's reaction and couldn't decide if he was shocked or repulsed by my confession. He washed his hand over his face and then swiveled his chair in my direction.

"Which twin are you? Vangie or Angie?"

"I'm me! Angie."

"So, you and this identical twin were supposedly arrested for killing that man and you got off. Is that what you want me to believe?"

I opened my mouth, but it just hung open. I had said more than I should've said.

"I'll leave." I tried to slink off, but Laurence stood in my way, staring at me curiously.

"Where're you going?"

"Home."

He brows arched dramatically. "To California?"

I nodded.

"If you plan to drive, it'll be safer to leave in the morning." He stepped out of my way.

He hates me.

I stayed the night, never broaching the subject of Vangie or the murder again. Neither had Laurence. He treated me nicely and cooked me a nice dinner. We watched movies and slept together, but we didn't make love, hug, or even kiss goodnight.

At dawn, I crept downstairs and found eggs, butter, a jar of peanut butter, sugar, flour, and chocolate chips in the kitchen. Within twenty minutes, my peanut butter chocolate chips bars were ready and fresh out of the oven, and I was ready to leave Colorado Springs. I arranged the bars on a plate, covered them with plastic wrap, and pasted a sticky note to the wrapping:

> *Thank you for making me feel beautiful.*
> *Love, Angie*

I left eighty dollars cash as the initial payment toward my car and left the house. I hoped it all compensated for the love and gratitude I couldn't verbally express last night.

With sixteen hours ahead of me and mostly open road, I filled up the gas tank, bought coffee and a breakfast sandwich at a drive through, and hit the highway, cruising toward marshmallow skies as the sun rounded the Rockies.

Thirty-Five

"Wall! Wall! Wall!" the guards yelled.

Inmates hit the wall, placed their hands at the back of their heads, and spread their legs, as ordered. Tangible fear tasted like blood inside Vangie's dry mouth. She thought by now she would've grown accustomed to these random search and seizures provoked by one act of violence or another, but they only seemed to build up her intolerance.

A high-pitched howl, like the eerie sound of an injured dog, echoed through the pod. Vangie twisted her neck slightly to the right and peeked over her shoulder. From the furthest corner of her eye she saw the girl's stringy blonde hair sweeping dust off the floor as two guards carried her away.

The girl didn't return to the cell that day. She was sequestered in the hole for allegedly crafting a shank out of her asthma inhaler, which she purportedly used to slice open another inmate. The girl's life was altered by her own volition. Vangie's life had been altered too, subsequently.

An additional bed had since been crammed into her cell to accommodate her two new cellmates. This move was a product of overcrowding she was told. Was it then that she realized the severity of her own situation or was it a Friday around the turn of the new year inside a cold, sterile room with a lone doctor? Vangie reflected on her abortion like she reflected on certain days of her childhood, with deep sorrow, shame, guilt, and great misgivings.

Her deepest regret was that Ronnie would never know she had carried his baby. She wondered, if he had the choice of keeping the baby, would that have altered her decision. Her mother's pregnancy with her and Angie had been unplanned and unscripted; that terrified Vangie most about motherhood: being unprepared for a child and unwilling to be selfless with her love. Realistically, what kind of life would her and Ronnie's child have had if she has made a different choice?

Her public trial had since begun. In a public statement, Kimmy announced her intention to seek the death penalty.

Today, when Clarissa arrived, Vangie knew there wasn't a chance in hell Clarissa had come to share good news about her case. Vangie saw it in her friend's fatigued eyes the moment she walked into the conference room.

Clarissa got right down to business. As her defense attorney, Clarissa had filed countless pre-trial motions, including the defense's latest motion to have the charge in the indictment reduced from first degree murder to voluntary manslaughter.

Kimmy was willing to cut a deal with her if she pled guilty. In exchange for her guilty plea, she would have to accept a life sentence without the possibility of parole in order to avoid death row. If she didn't accept the deal, she could maintain her innocence and face a jury trial in a case wherein the deck would be heavily stacked against her.

If accepting a plea meant life without a chance of parole or death, Vangie would rather take her chances on liberty.

The first day of trial, Vangie didn't need instruction on how to dress for court or to be reminded to sit forward at all times with her feet firmly planted on the ground and her hands placed on the table. Pandering to the jury, she wore a charcoal pants suit to hide her golden legs, a crewneck blouse, concealing her cleavage, and low-heeled conservative pumps. For jewelry she wore simple pearl earrings with a coordinating dainty pearl necklace. Her make-up was translucent, her lips lightly glossed, and her hair wrapped in a conservative bun.

Clarissa sat to Vangie's left, making a fashion statement in her black and white striped, pencil skirt suit and cream-colored pumps. Rebecca Macheto, the firm's new junior attorney, sat to her right, propping up the defense team. Wearing a plain black dress and black-rimmed eyeglasses, Rebecca was in her early forties and had only recently decided to forgo her teaching career for the legal profession.

Kimberly Fitzgerald and Mario Hernandez sat at the prosecutor's table across the aisle from the defense table. Both Kimmy and Mario, senior prosecutors in the district attorney's office, were in their mid-thirties and highly ambitious, and neither of the two gave Vangie comfort or assurance that Clarissa was prepared for the fight ahead or qualified to properly defend her in this case.

Angie was the one person Vangie had counted on to comfort her today. Listed as a potential witness for the prosecution, Angie was not permitted to be inside the courtroom until it was time for her to testify. Nevertheless, Vangie felt Angie's presence and clung to the sensation.

"All rise!" the bailiff called out.

Everyone in the courtroom stood to their feet for Judge Kelsey Papadopoulos. In preparation for the trial, Clarissa had dedicated an entire case file to Judge Papadopoulos history on the bench and the cases she had presided over. Clarissa contented that a young female judge would be more favorable to her client's defense than an older male judge.

Judge Papadopoulos, dressed in her black judge's robe, wore her long brown hair down and swinging freely, but the judge's bright round eyes and straight set lips provided no glimpse of her emotions that Vangie could read, favorable or otherwise. When the judge took the bench, the court retook their seats and court was in session.

Clarissa knew, as did Vangie, that jury selection, or voir dire, would be critical to the defense's case. Kimmy fought covertly to disqualify as many women as possible from the jury pool.

Clarissa tried her best to select more women for the exact opposite reason that Kimmy wanted to disqualify them— men would likely vote to convict her, a common belief in the legal profession. In the end, Kimmy got her way. Seven men and five women with the power to exonerate her or sentence her for life without parole or death were selected as the jury.

After the jurors were seated in the jury box, the Judge gave preliminary jury instructions. The Court then turned to Kimmy and said, "The People may proceed with an opening statement."

Since the state had the burden of proof, Kimmy took no prisoners in her opening statement, shocking the courtroom with a gruesome image of Todd's murdered, blood-soaked body vividly displayed on the courtroom screen in a PowerPoint presentation.

Todd's jade eyes spooked Vangie most and seemed to follow hers. She tried to find empathy for killing Todd, but the only emotion she felt was disbelief. Turning her attention back to the American flag, Vangie kept her face as blank as a sheet of paper. What she couldn't hide from the jury was her tapping foot. While her foot tapped under the table, Clarissa's knee jittered.

Kimmy began, "Ladies and gentlemen of the jury, this is a capital murder case. The murder in question took place on June 27 at about 10:00 PM; when the defendant, Vangie Cooper, arrived at Todd Bryant's home with murderous forethought. The evidence will prove that she carried through with those bloody thoughts.

"You may question, why would a well-educated and seemingly respectable woman commit this vicious and merciless crime? I'll tell you precisely why." Without as much as glancing over her shoulder, Kimmy pointed to the defense table and said, "The person you see sitting in this courtroom today is not the real Vangie Cooper. The real Vangie Cooper lies, swindles, manipulates, and murders to obtain the things in life growing up underprivileged did not afford her.

"The real Vangie Cooper targets and seduces wealthy men, and then uses them as a meal ticket. The real Vangie Cooper knew that if Todd Bryant had lived that night, he would have exposed her and destroyed the life she had lied, swindled, and manipulated to gain. That, ladies and gentlemen of the jury, is who the real Vangie Cooper is. Greed got the better of her, and the overwhelming evidence in this case will show that the defendant, Vangie Cooper is not the victim in this case, but that Vangie Cooper is a cold-blooded murderer who knowingly picked up a steak knife and brutally murdered Todd Bryant in cold blood!"

While Kimmy painted her as a gold-digger who murdered for greed, Vangie had stopped listening before Kimmy concluded her opening statement.

The Court then turned to Clarissa and asked, "Is the defense prepared to make an opening statement?"

Clarissa responded, "Yes we are, Your Honor." Clarissa put on a brave face, and walked across the courtroom floor, tugging at the hem of her cropped suit jacket. She then stood stiffly before the podium.

Good morning, members of the jury," Clarissa humbly began. "I stand before you today as one of the few people in this courtroom who knows the truth…that my client, Vangie Cooper is innocent of the charges that have been brought against her today. I'm one of the few people who knows the truth about what happened the night of June 27. By the conclusion of this case, you will too…

"Yes, it is true that Vangie killed Todd Bryant on that fateful night. That fact is undisputed. And yes, Vangie has not always been honest about her life. We do not contest that fact, either. However, your role throughout this trial is not to judge my client's honesty about her life, but to determine if the evidence to be presented by the prosecution proves beyond a reasonable doubt that my client committed the charged criminal offense. In other words, has the prosecution met its burden of proof that Vangie Cooper murdered Todd Bryant with willful and malicious intent?

"I submit to you, ladies and gentlemen of the jury, that the prosecution will not be able to meet its burden and that my client is not guilty of the charge of murder in the first degree!" Clarissa said, her voice becoming more confident.

"The evidence presented by the defense will show instead that the victim in this case is my client. Yes, my client, Vangie Cooper, did not commit a premeditated act but acted in self-defense to prevent being raped by Todd Bryant. That is the unsullied truth about this case."

The court rustled in their seats and low groans shouted in Vangie's ears.

"And the defense can and will prove, beyond a shadow of doubt, that Todd Bryant plotted to sexually assault Vangie Cooper the night of June 27, and that Vangie Cooper was within her absolute right to use the degree of force necessary to defend herself against bodily harm!"

When Clarissa retook her seat at the defense table, she grabbed Vangie's hand and almost squeezed the life of it. Vangie squeezed back.

Throughout the first day of trial, the prosecution presented evidence linking her to Todd's murder. First, a female forensic pathologist presented trace evidence, including fingerprints, DNA, and hair follicles extracted from the crime scene. In painstaking detail, Dr. Burman demonstrated how the positioning of the knife punctured Todd's abdominal aorta, causing Todd to die of exsanguination—the slow and painful process of losing over 40 percent of his blood. Kimmy then used a life-sized mannequin to demonstrate how Vangie allegedly stabbed Todd, an overdramatized scene that riveted the courtroom and sickened Vangie.

Clarissa cross-examined the coroner about the wounds found on Todd's forearms, just above his elbows, and the scratch marks found on the right side of Todd's neck. The coroner agreed that the scratch marks could've been caused by a person defending him or herself against the alleged victim's aggression.

"In your expert opinion, Dr. Burman, would Todd Bryant still be alive today if the defendant had made a simple 911 phone call before fleeing the scene of the crime?" Kimmy said, during re-cross.

"Objection! Cause for speculation," cried Clarissa.

"Sustained," said the Judge.

Kimmy then called Detective Sergeant Carter to the stand. Detective Carter's scrutiny of the bloody crime scene, the surveillance camera footage that tracked her cross-country flight by car, and text messages exchanged between her and Todd a week before she killed him, Vangie felt positive, left a lasting impression on the jurors' minds.

Clarissa questioned Detective Carter about the shattered dinner plate on the floor, spilled champagne, and the overall dishevelment of the dining table. "Are these not clear signs that a struggle took place, Detective Carter?"

"They are not clear signs, but it is possible that a struggle took place between the victim and assailant," Detective Carter said.

Vangie knew this may or may not influence the final outcome of her case, but, in any case, Clarissa had planted a seed of doubt in the jurors' minds.

The excavation into her past had begun, and this was only day one of her trial, Vangie thought wearily.

Thirty-Six

T odd's housekeeper, Valeria Sanchez, discovered Todd's dead body two days after the murder. Delivering an emotional testimony, Valeria told the jurors that she had known Todd since his childhood, when her mother provided housekeeping services for the Bryant family. Valeria described Todd as "a very good person." Clarissa did not risk cross-examining Valeria Sanchez.

Betsy Leaf, a gray-haired elderly woman whose vision impairment should have excluded her from the prosecution's witness list, described herself as a God-fearing Christian. Betsy testified that, on the night of the murder, while taking her dog Max out to "expel himself," she witnessed Vangie fleeing the scene of the crime.

"Will you please point out the person you saw running from the victim's home?" Kimmy asked. Betsy pointed a finger straight at Vangie.

"Can you describe the defendant's physical appearance that night for the jurors, Mrs. Leaf?"

"Well, I believe she wore shorts and high-heeled shoes. I never could walk in heels that high and wondered how she could run in them. She raced by me so fast she would've run me down if I had taken another step."

Vangie couldn't remember seeing Betsy Leaf or Max that night, try as she may.

"Based on your observation, what was the defendant's demeanor?" Kimmy pressed.

"Well, she was in a panic. That I could tell."

During Clarissa's cross-examination of Betsy, Clarissa wasted a great deal of time trying to pinpoint the exact area outside Todd's house where Betsy allegedly saw Vangie "race by," and demonstrated for the jurors why, given Betsy's poor vision, that it was highly improbable for Betsy to have had a clear view of Vangie's demeanor on the dark street. But Vangie knew, once the bell had been rung, the description of her fleeing the scene would be etched in the jurors' minds with a permanent marker.

Vangie badly needed a recess before Cameron Calloway sashayed into the courtroom in supermodel fashion, but there was no recess to be had. Tall, lean, her neck long and proud, her beauty seemingly shaming the room, Cameron took the witness stand, her vivid almond shaped eyes appearing willing and eager to testify for the prosecution.

Mario Hernandez, wearing a neutral colored suit, conducted the direct examination of Cameron, a strategic move by the prosecution to avoid any appearance of bias by Kimmy, Vangie suspected. After all, Cameron was in bed with Wade, figuratively and literally.

"Tell us about your relationship with Mr. Bryant," Mario said.

Flipping her long tresses, Cameron explained that she and Todd had been close friends since high school, embellishing her story ad nauseam with tales of the three-some's—Wade was the third member of their group—summers on Martha's Vineyard.

"Last Christmas you attended the defendant's engagement party, did you not?" Mario said.

"Yes, I did."

"Can you tell us where the engagement party was held?"

"At my boyfriend's grandfather's home in Beverly Hills," Cameron stressed.

"Your current boyfriend is the defendant's ex-fiancé?"

"Yes."

Not to look as if she wanted to kill Cameron, Vangie took a slow sip of water. She hated Cameron. She mostly hated that Cameron was free to be with Wade and that Wade had elected to be with Cameron and abandon her.

"Did you witness the defendant and Mr. Bryant interact at this party?"

"You mean did I see them hugged-up?" Cameron's intended joke infuriated Vangie all the more.

"Can you be more specific?"

"In the dining hall, after dinner, I specifically saw Todd with his arms around Vangie's waist and her arms around his neck. They might as well have been kissing."

"Motion to strike, Your Honor!" Clarissa shouted.

"Overruled."

"Did you say anything to the defendant or to Mr. Bryant?"

"It wasn't my business."

"When did you last speak to Mr. Bryant, do you recall?"

Cameron cut her eyes toward the defense table. "The day she killed him."

If Carissa didn't object to Cameron's flagrant violation of the rule against coming to such a conclusion, Vangie was prepared to. She nudged Clarissa's elbow.

"Objection!" Clarissa shouted.

"Sustained. The jury is to disregard the witness's last statement," said the Judge.

"The day the murder took place, do you recall what you and Mr. Bryant talked about?" Mario continued.

"Yes. We talked about Vangie. I mean Todd talked about her."

"What did Todd say about the defendant?"

"That he and Vangie had dinner plans that night."

Clarissa's hearsay objection was quickly batted down by the judge.

To substantiate Cameron's testimony, Mario asked that Cameron's cell phone records be placed into evidence. Cameron had, in fact, talked to Todd that fatal day, a conversation that lasted thirty-six minutes.

"Did Mr. Bryant say anything more about his plans with the defendant on the day he was murdered?"

"He told me he would tell me more later."

"But later never came around, did it?"

Cameron batted her long lashes, calling for Mario to hand her a tissue lest her runny make-up ruin her façade of perfection. "No. It didn't."

"No further questions, Your Honor," Mario concluded.

Clarissa marched up to the witness stand. "Good afternoon, Ms. Calloway. You testified that you attended the defendant's engagement party. Were you listed as an official guest of the bride and groom to be?"

"I was the guest of the groom's best friend."

"Yes or no?"

"No."

"So, it's fair to say that you crashed the party?"

"I wouldn't put it that way."

"How would you put it, Ms. Calloway?"

"Objection. Argumentative," Mario said.

"Sustained."

"At my client's engagement party that you unofficially attended, you and my client's fiancé argued over his engagement to my client, isn't that right?"

"We debated."

"You debated because Wade chose to marry my client and not you! Vangie is the one woman who came between you and the man you've loved since high school and you hate her. Isn't that true, Ms. Calloway?"

With another flip of her hair, Cameron said, "I hate or envy no one, and to set the record straight, Wade and I are getting married."

"You have a lot to gain if my client is found guilty, don't you, Ms. Calloway?"

"Objection! Counsel is badgering my witness," Mario interjected.

"Sustained. You have exhausted the subject. Please move on, Counselor."

"Yes, Your Honor." Clarissa held up her index finger. "Let me back up for a minute. You testified that you witnessed Todd and the defendant embracing, just after dinner in the dining hall. Was it a pretty big party?"

"I don't know. I wasn't counting the number of guests."

Because you were too busy trying to get with Wade, Vangie thought, digging the point of her pen deeper into the notepad. She'd handwritten a paragraph of unintelligible notes.

"Were there servants at this formal party?" Clarissa asked, seeming to regain her point.

"Yes."

"So, immediately following dinner, at a very formal engagement party, you alone bore witness to Vangie and Todd's alleged interaction. Don't you think that's a little odd, Ms. Calloway?"

"I honestly don't know who else saw it."

"Because it never happened, right, Ms. Calloway?"

"Objection!"

"I withdraw the question. I'm done with this witness."

Clarissa couldn't hide her gloating when she retook her seat. Vangie might have gloated over Clarissa's performance too if the news that Wade and Cameron were getting married hadn't caught her by the throat. Her blood curdled.

Thirty-Seven

M y first day on the job two dudes walked into the office, one with a glorious ponytail and a grisly scar slashed across his face and the other wearing a seriously mean mug. They each wore black business suits and gold chains around their thick necks and refused coffee and muffins when I offered. Ross treated them like kings. Clarissa called them thugs behind their backs. I learned later they were associated with the firm's biggest client.

Legal Secretary is my official title. I caught on to the lighter duties of my job pretty quickly, answering phones, taking messages, greeting visitors, keeping up with Ross and Clarissa's schedules, sorting mail and whatnot. As the weeks progressed, so did my job duties. I had gotten the feeling Clarissa was putting me through another test. Worried I would fail, I arrived early each day, turned on the lights and opened up the blinds, dusted off the coffee table and receptionist console, arranged the magazines perfectly, and restocked the coffee flavors, muffins, and granola bars. I even cleaned the bathroom.

Taking calls and greeting clients challenged my people skills. But being close to Vangie's case made up for

278

job duties I hated. I read every document that came across my desk relating to *The People, Plaintiff, vs. Vangie Annette Cooper*, researched legal references, and rarely offered my opinion on the case, even when Clarissa asked. I was too afraid to speculate.

This morning I clocked in for work fifteen minutes late. The office lights were on, the blinds still shut, and I could smell the remains of Clarissa's expensive perfume. I stuffed my backpack beneath the receptionist console and rushed down the hallway and into Clarissa's office, where I found her inspecting her oversized bulletin board filled with sticky notes.

"I'm late. Sorry," I said, nervously. "Is there anything you need me do?"

"There's a lot I need you to do, Angie. Start with getting me another cup of coffee." She handed me her coffee mug and I noticed her puffy bloodshot eyes. "Make that two cups, please. I'm sorry for being snarky. I had a rough night."

I prepared Clarissa's coffee and warmed a muffin for her. I did the same for Ross when he arrived at the office.

I worked straight through lunch and skipped dinner. I would've worked all night on Vangie's trial if I had to and didn't care about the overtime pay.

That same week the prosecution called me to testify against Vangie. More terrifying, the court had given the prosecutor permission to treat me as a hostile witness, which meant Kimmy Fitzgerald would be more hostile toward me than she had been previously.

For my protection, the bailiff sequestered me inside the children's waiting room at Superior Court. The yellow walls decorated in Disney characters, bins filled with toys, and shelves stocked with children's books were designed to alleviate kids' anxiety before they testified. A tranquilizer couldn't relax me.

With nothing left of my nails to bite and no more snacks to eat, I paced the room off and on until the bailiff, carrying a gun and dressed like a police officer, walked back into the waiting room.

I made it to the witness stand without passing out and promised to tell the whole truth and nothing but the truth, so help me God.

I could feel Vangie watching me. If I looked at her, the jurors may think we were conspiring, Clarissa warned me.

The prosecutor approached me. "You've had a name change recently. How would you prefer that I address you? Ms. Cooper or Ms. Brown?"

"Angie is okay."

"Okay Angie. Are you and the defendant identical twins?"

"Yes."

"Is your mother's name Annette Cooper?"

"Yes."

"Do you know a person by the name of Tom Blanchard?"

"No."

"Does your twin sister know of or has she ever met Tom Blanchard?"

"Objection. Calls for speculation," Clarissa said, saving me.

"Sustained. Rephrase the question."

"Is Tom Blanchard your biological father, Angie?"

I swallowed hard. "I don't know."

"Because you've never met your biological father, isn't that correct?"

"Yes," I stammered.

The prosecutor then questioned me about Vangie and my childhood and about the quality of our upbringing. I didn't understand what she meant by "quality" until she played the recorded argument Vangie and I had during one of our visits in jail. My stomach pushed up into my throat.

"Is that your voice on the recording, Angie?"

Teary eyed, I said, "I think so."

"Yes or no?"

"Yes."

"Do you recognize the other voice? Is that Vangie's voice?"

"Yes."

"How would you describe your twin's attitude toward her life growing up?"

"I don't know."

"You don't know?" she repeated disbelievingly. "The defendant described her life as, and I quote, 'fucked up and shitty,' but you don't know her attitude? That's hard for the jury to believe, don't you think?"

"Vangie just wanted us to have better lives."

"Vangie wanted a better life!" the prosecutor shouted. "And in her pursuit of a better life, has your twin ever lied to you, Angie? Remember that you're under oath."

I twiddled my thumbs in my lap. "Sometimes."

"Can you please tell the jury what your twin lied about sometimes?"

"Nothing big."

"Nothing big!" she echoed. "So, lying about the identity of her biological father, fabricating her own mother's death, and claiming you, her twin, died at birth isn't that big a deal to you, Angie?"

I chewed my lip not to cry. "Kind of."

"Those are kind of big deal lies, aren't they?"

"Yes."

"You love your twin, don't you, Angie?"

"More than anything or anyone."

The prosecutor smiled at me sinisterly. "I don't think anyone in this courtroom would deny that you love your twin, Angie. You love your twin so much that you would do anything to protect her, including obstruct justice. Isn't that true?"

In the middle of a full-blown meltdown I heard Clarissa ask for the judge's permission to approach the bench. The next thing I knew I was being escorted from the courtroom.

～

Helplessly, Vangie watched the bailiff walk Angie out of courtroom. She had expected Kimmy to renege on their backdoor plea deal even if it meant winning in the short run and losing in the long run; but knowing that ahead of time couldn't alleviate her rage. She bore down on her jaws so tightly she worried her teeth would shatter like glass.

The judge called a recess in order to meet with the lawyers in her chambers. Vangie had hoped like hell the judge would order Kimmy to recuse herself from the case and cite

Kimmy for professional misconduct, but Kimmy's liberty to bend the law in her favor won out. The judge gave Kimmy a slap on the hand and court was back in session one hour later.

So much for a young female judge being favorable in my case.

The prosecution elected to postpone their examination of Angie for the time being, which meant Kimmy would be merciless the next time Angie took the stand. Vangie would bet her life on it.

Thirty-Eight

Throughout the trial, Kimmy paraded character witness after character witness who spoke to
Todd's morality and those who spoke to Vangie's
immorality.

The majority of their lives, Vangie and Angie kept to
themselves. There were no childhood or high school friends
that followed them into adulthood, no aunts, uncles or
cousins they grew up with; their grandmother died years
back and their grandfather was estranged. That left a limited
pool of character witnesses the prosecution could subpoena
to testify against her. To strengthen the prosecution's case,
Kimmy stopped at nothing, including digging Mrs. Reese
out of the ashes of Cambridge Heights Apartments.

Using a cane and the help of the bailiff, Mrs. Reese
hoisted herself into the witness chair. Growing up, Vangie
never knew Mrs. Reese's exact age, but in her young mind,
Mrs. Reese was an old woman even then. She now realized
how relatively young Mrs. Reese must have been. Evidently,
marrying a despicable man whose greatest achievement
was managing a decrepit apartment building had taken its

toll on her. The stress showed in Mrs. Reese's disillusioned blue eyes.

Mrs. Reese testified to the number of times Mr. Reese served her mother an eviction notice and the number of times she had to call the police because of Annette's loud parties and houseguests who had no business in their apartment. This, of course, led to Kimmy's inquiry about the night Vangie threatened to hit Mr. Reese with a hammer.

"What did you do when the defendant threatened to bludgeon your husband with a hammer, Mrs. Reese?"

"I called the police. Had to or she would've killed my husband as sure as I'm sittin' here talking to you. I never trusted neither one of them girls, especially that mute one. Their mother had mental problems too, you know."

"Don't react," Clarissa whispered into Vangie's ear. "We knew this was coming."

Vangie didn't know how much longer she could stomach Mrs. Reese. But she told herself that finding out Mr. Reese was buried six feet underground was worth her suffering.

Clarissa cut right to the chase during cross-examination. "You didn't witness my client threaten to hit your husband with a hammer, did you, Mrs. Reese?"

"Didn't have to. The hammer was in that girl's hand."

"Yes or no, please."

"Then, no."

"Isn't it true that the police found your husband in the wrong for locking my client out of her apartment?"

"I know what I saw."

"Yes or no, please."

"Yes, but…"

"I have no more questions of this witness."

Kimmy went for the jugular next. In any other case involving a sex crime, Rape Shield Laws banning prejudicial testimony would have protected Vangie. But Rape Shield Laws almost always related to cases involving the plaintiff, and since she was the defendant and there was no physical proof that Todd raped her the first time and attempted to rape her a second time, Kimmy straddled the legal line, cleverly injecting Vangie's sexual history and irreparable reputation into the court record.

As far back as Vangie could recollect, she had been called a ho', even by her own mother once. Add money-grabbing whore, gold-digging-slut, coldhearted bitch, sex-crazed lunatic, lying cunt, sugar-daddy vixen, poor black trash, and murderer to the mix and what difference did it make what people called her, publicly or privately, she once thought, before her thick skin thinned.

Angelica Moretti, the scorned ex-wife of Antonio Moretti, first testified that Vangie seduced her husband and that Antonio paid her large sums of money and gifted her expensive jewelry in return for sexual favors. If Vangie ever took the stand, she couldn't deny or refute Angelica's claim, particularly since security cameras at both Angelica's Boutique and the Moretti Jewelry stores had caught them in compromising positions.

Clarissa cross-examined Angelica about her use of the word "seduced" and pointed out that her client was only seventeen years old when she first met Antonio, and that Antonio was a grown, married man with children at the time of the alleged affair in hopes of swaying the jurors' minds in the right direction. Clarissa also brought into question the quality of the video and mentioned Antonio's history of affairs with other young, female employees.

Jacob Stein's sole flight attendant, Ingrid Peterson, also testified to Vangie's "immoral character." Kimmy belabored her examination of Ingrid, inquiring about where, when, and how Vangie met with Jacob and how "generous" Jacob had been compensating her for sex.

Vangie suspected Ingrid had secretly hoped to become the first Mrs. Jacob Stein someday, but women over thirty didn't suit Jacob's palate. He had a taste for the young, the bold, and the ambitious, girls that he could mold, not marry.

Vangie couldn't recall half the times she hooked up with Jacob, but their documented trips to the Cayman Islands, Paris, and Atlantic City corroborated Ingrid's testimony, not to mention Ingrid's recount of the night her and Ronnie Livingston flew to Florida for Jacob's "play party." This inquiry opened the door to a salacious world, and Kimmy pounced.

Clarissa's only counterattack was objecting to Ingrid's hearsay testimony that Jacob had paid her client's way to college. The judge sustained the objection.

Jacob, though listed as a potential witness for the prosecution, never took the stand. Vangie wouldn't put it past Jacob to have threatened to file a defamation lawsuit if the prosecution called him to testify. After all, he could very well face statutory rape charges.

Vangie was too afraid to speculate why Ronnie hadn't been called to testify.

Most well-intentioned criminal defense attorneys try to prepare their clients for the prosecution's most damaging witness. But try as Clarissa may, nothing could prepare Vangie for Wade.

When Wade took the oath, she glanced up from her notepad, taking mental note of his tailored charcoal gray suit worn with a burgundy tie, the perfection of his haircut, his smooth-shaven face, the tightness of his jaw line, and the way his piercing brown eyes avoided hers.

During direct examination, Mario questioned Wade extensively about his level of education, prestigious awards, and physician status as a way of establishing Wade's credibility. What juror wouldn't find Wade credible? Vangie wouldn't be surprised if one or two female jurors hadn't already made up their minds about her guilt. In their eyes, she was ghetto trash who didn't deserve a man of such distinction and decency.

Contemptuousness rang in Wade's voice when he talked about their six-year relationship, explaining to Mario how they initially met in college and the years that led up to their engagement.

"What can you tell us about the defendant, Dr. Fitzgerald?"

"I can't tell you anything about Vangie."

"Would you say the woman you planned to spend the rest of your life with is pretty dishonest?"

"I bought her lies, so yes, I guess that would make her dishonest."

"What facets of her life has the defendant not been truthful to you about, Dr. Fitzgerald?"

"Name it."

"Is it your testimony that you don't know the real Vangie Cooper?"

"That's my testimony, yes."

"What was your relationship with Todd Bryant?"

"We were best friends."

"Did you know the defendant and Mr. Bryant had a sexual relationship?"

"Objection. Leading," Clarissa said.

"The question speaks to motive, Your Honor," Mario said.

"Overruled. The witness may answer the question."

"No, I wasn't aware of their *sexual* relationship."

"Were you aware that Vangie had dinner plans with Mr. Bryant the night of June 27?"

"I wasn't aware of that either."

"And after the night, did you hear from the defendant?"

"No. I didn't."

"Did you attempt to contact the defendant?"

"Every day. Up to our wedding day."

Vangie knew Wade so well, every note in his shifting tone, that she didn't have to look at him to see his furrowed brow and injured eyes. She struggled to hold back her torrent of tears determined to break free. A lone tear escaped her right eye. She dabbed it with a quick finger before it could fall.

"Do you believe your ex-fiancé is capable of malicious murder, Dr. Fitzgerald?"

Wade cleared his throat. "I don't know what Vangie is capable of."

"Is it your opinion that Vangie Cooper is capable of anything?"

"Yes."

"Even murder?"

"I respectfully decline to answer that question."

"Just yes or no, Dr. Fitzgerald?"

"I respectfully decline to answer that question," Wade repeated.

"Thank you for your time, Dr. Fitzgerald. I have no further questions, Your Honor."

The courtroom crawled with the Fitzgerald's today and Clarissa had something to prove. Not only had Wade's parents showed up to support him, Gerald Fitzgerald, Wade's uncle and Clarissa's estranged father, made an unexpected appearance too. When Clarissa's turn came to cross-examine Wade, Clarissa shot from her seat and accosted the witness stand eagerly.

"You're a trained neuro-ophthalmologist, Dr. Fitzgerald, correct?" Clarissa fired off.

"Yes."

"So, it's safe to say you've performed numerous eye surgeries?"

"Yes."

"Roughly, how many eye surgeries have you performed, Doctor?"

"I can't say,"

"Throw out a number."

"Roughly, a hundred," Wade said sarcastically.

"So, on one hundred occasions you've used general anesthesia to put your patients to sleep. Is that your testimony?"

"Have I? No. Has a trained anesthesiologist? Yes. However, general anesthesia is rarely used to perform eye surgeries when local and topical anesthesia can be used."

"Okay, but you have performed surgeries on patients when general anesthesia has been administered," Clarissa said as if regaining her point. "Therefore, based on your expert knowledge, you would've known that Vangie was unconscious when you asked Todd to drive her home the night of the engagement party, correct?"

"I knew she was drunk," Wade said, his voice full of agitation.

"I would like to call your attention to this video." Clarissa entered into evidence surveillance footage of Wade's grandfather's Beverly Hills mansion that captured Wade carrying Vangie to Todd's Porsche.

"Does your ex-fiancé appear conscious and alert to you, Doctor?" Clarissa said.

"Not by appearance, no."

Vangie struggled to watch the footage of Wade placing her into the passenger's seat of Todd's Porsche before Todd hopped into the driver's seat and sped off with her.

"When you returned to my client's home that night you found her unconscious, in bed and nude. Isn't that right?"

"Yes."

"And you didn't find that unusual, Doctor?"

"For Vangie? No, I didn't." Wade's response got chuckles from the crowd, prompting the Judge to bang her gravel and order decorum in her courtroom. Vangie tapped her foot faster, aggravated like hell with Wade.

"Did you have sexual intercourse with Vangie that night?" Clarissa continued.

"Me? No," Wade said crossly.

"But Vangie was under the impression that the two of you did have sex that night?"

"I can't recall."

"I'll refresh your memory. 'You must've had a wet dream. You were out cold when I got in last night.' Quote, unquote. Do you recall saying those exact words to Vangie?"

Wade cleared his throat. "I may have said something like that, yes."

"Then, if you didn't have sex with Vangie while she was *out cold*, who did, Doctor?"

"I can't answer that question."

"Were you not also aware that Todd explicitly expressed interest in having sex with Vangie? In fact, you and Todd bet over who would be the first to sleep with her. Isn't that right, Doctor?"

"It was a harmless bet."

"Todd Bryant *raped* your fiancé! That is not a harmless bet!"

Vangie shut her eyes and forgot how to breath.

"Objection!" Kimmy spoke out of turn. "Assumes facts not in evidence and badgering!"

"Objections sustained."

"I have no further questions of this witness."

Clarissa sat down next to Vangie, breathing laboriously. Vangie had yet to find a stable breath. Throughout Wade's testimony, if she thought she heard any expression of love or compassion in his tone, she dismissed it as wishful thinking.

Thirty-Nine

ate mail arrived today, this one addressed to Clarissa for defending Vangie. The other hate letters were addressed to Ross for defending Diego Del Rio. Clarissa kept the letters and emails for evidence for the same reason Ross kept a gun around. Just in case.

Vangie's trial seemed to bring out the worst in everyone, even in Cleveland. He had taken the key to the main house from me and confined me to the garage. To store my food, I broke down and bought a mini-fridge and cooked on a hotplate. I figured he would kick me out altogether soon.

I spent time at the office as much as I could and helped out wherever I was most needed. Whatever work I wasn't qualified to do, Rebecca handled. Rebecca and Dulos Crenshaw, our newest junior attorney, shared the small office across from the bathroom just until Ross located a larger space for us.

While I was in the middle of drafting a letter for Dulos, Ross called me into his office. He had upgraded his furniture, laid out an indoor putting green, and bought a fancy fish tank, expenses Clarissa said the firm couldn't afford.

Ross said we had enough money to spend and that he expected money to come rolling in now that the firm was getting exposure.

Ross gestured for me to take a seat. "Close the door," he said.

After closing the door, I sat near the window in one of the six leather chairs surrounding the beveled glass conference table. Ross sat at the head of the table.

"How's your day going, Angie?"

"It's going okay," I said slowly. Ross never called me into his office to ask me about my day. I sat on the edge of my seat, my hands clasped in my lap, and mind turning with questions.

"The prosecution is prepared to rest their case against your twin," he said. "I know we've been over this before, but I'll ask you again. Did your twin say anything to you about the alleged assault?"

Looking thoughtful, I shook my head.

"Nothing, huh?"

I shook my head, again.

Ross frowned. "Here's the thing, Angie. Rissa is getting her ass kicked. I'm not saying your twin wasn't sexually assaulted but based on the preliminary evidence—no police report, no rape kit, no bodily fluid or DNA from the attacker—the jury will likely convict. If Clarissa had listened to me, she would've avoided a trial and taken the plea deal. But Rissa doesn't listen…and the firm can't afford to take an L on this one. Know what I mean?"

I nodded.

He studied me for an uncomfortable second. "Let me know if you think of anything."

"I will. Right away. I promise."

"You do that."

When Clarissa walked into the office, I immediately told her I wasn't feeling so well and asked if I could leave work early. With her reluctant permission, I left the office and sat in my car, shivering, crying, and feeling alone again, lost and scared without Vangie.

Leaving my car behind, I walked to skid row. Short lunch breaks and late work nights kept me from spending as much time with Mo, Imani, and Jay as I would've liked. But not visiting also allowed me to avoid questions about Vangie's case I wasn't legally allowed to discuss.

The soup kitchen was coming along. Jay had the bright idea of doing up the cement floors in abstract graffiti, Mo planned to make a section kid friendly, and I had big plans with the kitchen once it shaped into one. But money for the renovation had run out, possibly for good unless the funds for the homeless the bishop requested from the city came through. Jay had a fulltime job now, and Mo got by with the help of Dunk's military pension and working for the bishop for free. I saved a portion of my bi-weekly salary to help out however I could and sent Laurence money toward my car debt.

Hiding my emotions from Mo wasn't easy. As soon as I walked into the warehouse, she saw right through me and wanted to know why I looked like I'd been crying. I could talk to Mo about anything and told her something had come up on Vangie's case and she could get convicted.

"Stevie Wonder can see that dude was shady," Mo said comfortingly.

I hugged Mo, left the warehouse, returned to the office, and got back to work. Before leaving for the day, I knocked on Clarissa's office door to say goodbye. "I'm leaving now," I whispered, peeking my head inside the room.

"Can you stay a few minutes longer, Angie? I need to ask you something."

I eased into the office and sat on the edge of the chair, gripping my backpack straps.

Clarissa sat at her desk, her eyes bloodshot, again. "I don't know why I'm telling you this." She laughed lightly. "Well, I do know, actually. You're the next best thing to having Vangie to talk to." Talking to the still red liquid filling the wine glass she held and not to me, Clarissa said, "What would you do if you found some chick's pathetic pair of thongs at your boyfriend's house, where he spends too much time *clearing his head*, quote, unquote?"

Hit with a question I was unqualified to answer, my eyes got big enough to light the dark sky. "Ummmm," was all I could manage to say.

Looking directly at me, she said, "And he had the unmitigated gall to say the thong belonged to you when he should know, based on your history together, that you wouldn't buy low-budget anything made by a subpar designer?"

I bunched my mouth to one side of my face.

"If he's screwing that temp, I will torch that shithole, I swear on my grandmother's grave, I will! His loss, not mine, right? It's not like we're married with joint assets or have kids to fight over. Burning that house down would be an easy resolution to a dead-end relationship..." Now Clarissa was full-on crying. I cried too.

"This is so unprofessional. I'm sorry, Angie."

"It's okay. I understand."

"It's not okay!" Clarissa slammed her wine glass on the desk. "I'm supposed to be a friggin' criminal defense attorney!" She blew her nose with tissue. "I'm losing Vangie's case and I don't know how to turn it around."

I listened to Clarissa's sniffles, afraid to speak without Vangie and afraid that if I didn't speak up Vangie would be convicted. But what if the truth hurt Vangie's case more than my silence? What if no one believed me and Vangie got convicted anyway?

"Maybe I can help," I heard myself say from a tiny place inside of me.

Forty

Vangie lined-up to be counted, ate a tasteless break-fast, and called Clarissa when her chance to use the phone came. They talked long enough for Clarissa to tell her new material evidence about her case had come up. The abruptness Vangie detected in Clarissa's voice unsettled her.

After, Vangie ran into Tamala Jackson at the library. To her pleasant surprise, she had found camaraderie with Tamala, a civil litigation attorney serving a 90-day sentence for criminal contempt of court. Tamala, who wore her afro like a statement of freedom and filled the room with unapol-ogetic discourse and unorthodox legal theories, actually got a laugh or two out of Vangie, somedays.

Today, Vangie wasn't in the frame of mind to listen or talk to anyone. She headed straight for the research kiosk. She had taken a greater interest in law than she had while she was in law school, but unlike Tamala, she wasn't inter-ested in playing jailhouse lawyer to the other inmates. She was just passing idle time and trying to keep her sanity.

Late that afternoon Clarissa showed up with Ross and let Ross do the talking, unsettling Vangie all the more. She listened quietly as Ross recapped the strengths of the prosecution's case against her and emphasized the weaknesses in the defense's case.

"What's your point, Ross?" Vangie said with unambiguous agitation.

"We're putting Angie back on the stand, bottom line."

"Over my dead body," Vangie snapped.

Ross chuckled. "You got it twisted. That's my name on the marquee; my cases pay the bills. Your case is racking up billable hours."

"I'm not your charity case, Ross, so fuck you."

"No, fuck you, Vangie. This is my call."

Vangie looked to Clarissa for solidarity. "Are you my counsel or not?"

"Let me talk to Vangie, Ross. Alone. Please," Clarissa said.

Ross departed reluctantly and much to Vangie's appreciation.

"What's going on, Clarissa? You know how I feel about putting Angie on the stand."

Clarissa sighed heavily. "You're right, Van. I shouldn't have made a unilateral decision without discussing it with you. But Angie is our best chance to get a favorable ruling."

"How?" Vangie demanded to know. Clarissa's pitying stare raised Vangie's defenses all the more. "What?"

"Angie told me about your stepdad, Van, and I'm so sorry. That's just horrible!"

White noise suddenly filled the room. Her nerves on the edge of collapse, Vangie shot from her chair. "Guard!" she screamed.

The guard entered the room, hand at his holster. "Is there a problem?"

"Everything is fine, officer. She's just upset," Clarissa said calmly.

"Everything isn't fine. I'm ready to leave."

"Van, please sit down. Can we discuss it?"

"There's nothing to discuss."

"You need to sit down," the guard ordered.

Vangie dropped down into her seat and folded her arms. The guard left the room but kept watch on her through the door's glass window.

"I'll take the stand but not Angie," Vangie said grudgingly.

"We both know why that's a bad strategy."

"Because I'm a cold, unfeeling bitch? Oh, yeah, and a trick. Is that how you feel about me too, Riss?"

"My opinion of you isn't what influence's a jury; the public's opinion of you will. You know this, Van."

"Just say it, Clarissa. The jury will empathize with Angie and not with me."

Clarissa took in a deep breath and exhaled. "Do you know how many women are acquitted for killing in self-defense? Do you, Van?"

Vangie didn't need Clarissa to recite the statistics nor did she want to be reminded that her chance of being acquitted was extremely low.

"It's my life and my constitutional right to testify on my own behalf."

"And it's my first case and my reputation as a criminal defense attorney on the line." Tears brimming Clarissa's eyes, she whispered, "Ross and I could've been arrested and disbarred for life!"

Vangie swallowed the hard truth.

~

I was up with the sun and feeling its initial blaze as I ran up my block and rounded the first corner. Against Clarissa and Ross's warning not to visit Vangie before the trial concluded, I decided to take my chances.

My heart beat faster than normal and I was sweating excessively within a few miles. I removed my windbreaker, tied it round my waist, and walked the remaining distance to the detention facility.

The line to get inside wrapped around the building. The entire hour and fifteen-minute wait, I worked up my courage to broach the subject of Russell King with Vangie.

The moment Vangie sat before me and our eyes met, she said, "Is Ross forcing you to do this, Angie? Because if he is…"

"No! I volunteered to testify. I promise."

"Be smarter, Angie."

"It's the smartest thing I've ever done."

"It's not *smart!* The court could grant the prosecution the opportunity to rebut your testimony and call that man to the stand. Mom could be subpoenaed too."

"Clarissa said we can still press charges against him, since there isn't a statute of limitations for what he did, not in Michigan there isn't," I whispered.

"Do you really want to relive that shit? Because I don't!"

"I can do it, Van. I have to."

"Not for me, Ang, you don't." Tears stood in Vangie's eyes.

I held back my own tears. "I'm not doing it just for you…"

For a long while we stared into each other's eyes before coming to silent agreement.

"You know what to say," Vangie said, by which she meant I knew what not to say, and then she hung up.

Forty-One

At court, Rebecca and I rushed past the media itching for a story and the usual crowd carrying picket signs calling for Vangie to get the death penalty and others that supported her innocence. A beautiful black lady moving through the crowd caught my attention, not because she looked the friendliest among the rest but because she looked the angriest. The man walking beside her kept his arm wrapped around her waist as if to keep her from killing me. They were Todd Bryant's parents.

The public seats were filled when we walked into the courtroom. Clarissa had reserved a seat for me. She gave me a reassuring hug and took her seat at the defense table with Rebecca. I sat directly behind Vangie, within arm's reach of her. We both wore pale blue dresses, pearl necklaces with matching stud earrings, and our hair in an updo. Clarissa believed, if Vangie and I looked identical today, it would make a better impression on the jury. Vangie sat with her head high and shoulders proud and never looked back.

The next thing I heard was the judge saying, "Is the defense prepared to present their case-in-chief?"

"Yes, Your Honor, we are," Clarissa said.

"You may call your first witness."

"I call Angie Cooper to the stand."

My feet carried me, against a nearly overwhelming force of fear trying to hold me back, to the witness stand. Besides Vangie, Mo was the only person in the courtroom I considered family. Mo sat in the back aisle on the defense's side of the room and steepled her hands when I glanced her way. I noticed Ross slip into the room. He stood in the back to watch. Wade Fitzgerald the Fourth sat behind the prosecutor's table. I avoided his intense stare.

Before Clarissa asked the first question, my hands started trembling. I grabbed the handy cup of water and took a gulp, cooling off my burning skin secreting droplets of sweat down the back of my neck, and then knotted my hands in my lap.

"How far apart were you and Vangie born?" Clarissa said, opening with a warm-up question.

"Eleven seconds," I quickly said.

"Who's the oldest, you or Vangie?"

"Vangie."

"Why did you ask to testify today, Angie?"

"Because people need to know…"

"What do people need to know?"

"What happened to Vangie."

"Did Vangie tell you Todd Bryant sexually assaulted her?"

"Objection!" The prosecutor shouted. "No predicate of sexual assault in this case has been laid."

"Objection overruled. The witness may answer the question."

"No," I said.

"Did you ask Vangie if Todd Bryant sexually assaulted her?"

"No."

"Why not, Angie?"

"We don't talk about those kinds of things."

"What kinds of things don't you and Vangie discuss?"

"Getting raped," I said so faintly I wondered if anyone heard me. The stillness in the room made me afraid to look up again.

"I'm sorry to have to ask you this question, but have you been sexually assaulted, Angie?"

"Objection! There is no probative value to this line of questioning, Your Honor," the prosecutor shouted.

"The probative value is at my discretion, Counselor," said the judge. "The objection is overruled. However, counsel for the defense is advised that irrelevant testimony will be stricken from the record."

"Thank you for the court's indulgence, Your Honor." Clarissa turned back to me. "Angie, growing up, did you witness Vangie being sexually assaulted?"

Tears escaped my eyes. "Yes."

"And who was it that sexually assaulted Vangie?"

"A lot of men."

"More than one?" Clarissa repeated as if I had gotten the number wrong. I hadn't told her about the others. "How many more?"

"I can't remember how many." They were all strung together in my mind.

Before *Russell King* ever walked into our lives with a pocket full of quarters he handed out like candy, before

Vangie threatened to cut any man's throat who stared at us wrong or too long, before we locked our bedroom door at night, before we learned two pair of eyes were safer than one pair, it started with a tickle, a pinch, a grab, or a wet kiss we couldn't wipe from our lips. We were too young to understand but old enough to never forget. We slept curled into one another so tightly no one could come between us and walked linked hand-in-hand like an unbreakable chain. If our mother had known or seen, she warned us without opening her mouth not to speak of it. Or maybe we knew, instinctively, she wouldn't have heard us anyway.

"Is there a specific incident of sexual assault you do remember?" Clarissa said.

"Yes," I croaked.

"Can you please tell the jurors specifically what happened?"

The snail tried to choke me; I swallowed it whole. "Our stepdad... Russell...he sent Vangie to the store to buy vanilla extract for me..."

Two teaspoons of pure vanilla extract were all that I needed to complete my vanilla butter cream frosting and to this day the scent of vanilla extract turned my stomach inside out.

"Where were you, Angie?"

"At home, baking our birthday cake."

"And how old were you and Vangie at the time?"

"We were turning twelve."

Turning twelve meant nothing to Vangie and everything to me; I expected something magical to happen, to feel less awkward, to see my breasts develop into something worth looking at...

"Was your mother home at the time?"

I shook my head. "Just Russell."

"And what happened after Vangie went to the store and left you alone with Russell?"

I knotted my hands tighter. "He grabbed me and he… He tried to… He um…"

"Take your time," Clarissa said.

"He tried to rape me…" I stammered. "But Vangie… She came home and she… She…"

I reimagined it all, thinking if I had screamed louder, fought harder, hadn't worn a dress that day, Russell wouldn't have gotten my underwear around my ankles, lifted me off my feet, and bent me over the kitchen counter with the skill of a burglar. But fear seized me the moment Russell pressed himself hard against me, telling me, in his mean, hot voice to shut up. So, I stopped crying and stopped screaming.

"What did Vangie do when she came home, Angie?"

"She told Russell if he left me alone, that he… He could have sex with her…" I caught spurts of air to catch my breath, my tears warm and salty to taste, my chest spasming.

"What happened next, Angie?"

"Russell, he took Vangie to our room and he…he raped her instead of *me*." My sobbing overpowered my will to be strong for Vangie. I glanced at her. In the twinkling of an eye I saw what no one else could see. Vangie looked small, as small and terrified as I remembered her looking that day. Wanting to hug Vangie and tell her how much I loved her, I hugged myself instead, rocking and crying.

I remembered sitting on my knees, pressing my ear to the floor and peering underneath the closed door through one eye. I wanted to kill Russell, and I meant to kill him when I barged into the room with a pair of scissors in my hand. When I saw Vangie pinned underneath Russell, her breasts out of their training bra, her body stiff and unyielding, her eyes tightly shut, her face, in a rage of pain, drained of blood and teeth gritted as Russell tore into her in a frenzy, my courage to kill Russell was zapped out of me. I shrunk back in a corner, shivering, crying, trickles of pee draining from me. My presence seemed to make Russell hurt Vangie more.

"Do you need a break, Angie?" With tears in her eyes, Clarissa handed me a tissue. I wadded it in my hand and shook my head.

"Who stopped Russell from hurting your twin, Angie?"

"Our mother...she came home from work and she caught Russell...but she saw what she wanted to see and believed Russell's lie."

"What lie did Russell tell your mother, do you remember?"

"That Vangie begged for it and needed a lesson for teasing grown men." I broke down in tears again.

"And how did Vangie respond to her experience?"

"She never cried."

"Never?" Clarissa said.

I shook my head. "We pretended it never happened to us."

"Why did you and Vangie pretend the rape didn't happen, Angie?"

"Russell would've killed us if we told anyone, he said."

I remembered how Russell watched us more closely after that day. If we got near our mother or had the chance to corner her alone, he hovered over us, his black eyes darker, his wide nose flared, and his lips in a big old pinch.

Russell lived and breathed in every corner of our small apartment until the day he disappeared from our lives.

"And how did you respond to your experience, Angie?"

"I stopped talking…to Russell, to our mother, to everyone except Vangie."

"How long did you exclusively talk to Vangie?"

"For eleven years."

"Thank you for your candor, Angie. I have no further questions of the witness."

The prosecutor stood. "The prosecution does not wish to cross-examine the witness," she said.

I left the stand quickly. Mo met me in the corridor, gave me a long comforting hug, and let me sob on her shoulder. Ross told me I represented well and walked me to my car.

Clarissa gave me the rest of the week off from work, but I didn't want to go home and didn't want to stay and listen to the other testimonies, even for the chance to see Douglas testify. He was in town. I knew because I had scheduled his flight to California and booked his hotel room. I also knew he brought his fiancé with him. He wanted me to meet her and thought we'd get along.

The busier I was the better, and the less time I had to reflect and worry. With everyone in court but me, I drove straight to the office and buried myself in a pile of work, drowning my thoughts in the poetry of Kendrick Lamar.

My mind consumed with work and music, I didn't hear the front door open or see him walk in. He was already standing over the reception counter when I looked up. I yanked my earphones from my ear and stood, holding onto the desktop for balance. He wore the same lilac dress shirt and coordinating tie he had worn to court earlier today, and he appeared as shocked to see me here as I was to see him.

"So, you're Vangie's little sister?" he said, as if we were meeting for the first time.

I spoke reluctantly. "Yes, technically."

"Wade Fitzgerald." He stretched his long arm across the countertop. "It's nice to formally meet you."

Meeting him as me was more intimidating than meeting him as Vangie. He looked taller and even more imposing.

Turning crimson, I shook his hand loosely. "Hi. I'm really sorry."

He stared at me thoughtful, and then handed me a manila envelope. "Will you give this to Clarissa and have her call me. Tell her it's urgent." He left the office quickly.

I dropped into my chair and concentrated on the manila envelope, glowering over the red confidential stamp. Before locking up, I sent Clarissa a text message and then placed Wade's envelope on her desk with an "urgent" sticky note.

I waited to call my mother until I got home, ate a spoonful of peanut butter, and settled onto my bed with Butterscotch in my lap.

My mother answered the phone on the first ring. "Angie, baby," she said, and then she immediately told me Mr. Young had bought her a laptop and she was getting the hang of using it. The TV played in the background and I worried Mr. Young was listening to our conversation. He usually did.

"One of them reporters called me again?" my mother said.

"Offered to pay Annette good money too!" Mr. Young shouted in the background.

"*Humph!* There ain't enough good money in the world to tell a dog off the street about how I raised my girls, single parent or not! Have you seen Douglas?" she said before I had an opportunity to jump into the conversation.

"No."

"He's there, in California. Supposed to be testifying for Vangie."

I jumped at my chance. "I testified again today, Mom," I said quietly.

"What for?"

"For Vangie… about Russell."

A beat passed. A lighter flicked. I heard her blow a stream of breath. "What made you go bringing up Russell?" My mother had a way of packing a simple sentence with a paragraph of insinuations.

"The jury needed to know, Mom."

"What business going on in *my* house them people need to know, Angie?"

Silence.

"Some business you don't go telling white folks. Some business can hurt you more than it helps you."

Silence.

"You and Vangie must think I'm blind and dumb," she continued. "I got eyes and ears, and a mouth too when I want to use it. Russell got what's coming to him and I ain't gotta' be God to know it." She flicked the lighter again, puffed and blew. "Vangie came out alright. Both my girls did."

Silence.

"I love you, Angie, baby."

"I love you too, Mom."

"Vangie knows I love her too. I haven't heard from her. Tell her me and Mr. Young planning on driving to California to see her."

"I will, Mom."

I hung up and squeezed Butterscotch tighter in my arms.

Over the years, from time-to-time, I Googled Russell. Knowing his location made me feel safe. He still lived in Gary, Indiana where he owned King's Auto Repair, and he still lived in a nice house on 24th Avenue. His second wife decided to stick around and have his biological kids. To some people Russell seemed normal and lived a normal life, but there had to be others like Vangie and me who feared Russell King in silence.

Forty-Two

With court approval, Clarissa scrambled to find a forensic psychologist who could testify to Vangie's possible state-of-mind on the night of the murder.

After conducting a four-hour psychological evaluation, Dr. Georgette Hamm described for the jurors how Vangie's repressed trauma predicated her natural reaction to being sexually assaulted, and why, given Vangie's history of sexual assaults, she would likely not have reported either of Todd's assaults or recollected the details of her experiences.

Emma Horn, in her late thirties, was subleasing the bungalow next door to Todd when the murder took place. Emma testified that she saw Vangie enter Todd's house around 10:00 P.M. and heard a woman screaming for help shortly thereafter.

Kimmy badgered Emma at length, effectively characterizing her as a confused drunk whose testimony held little credibility.

Douglas Phillips also took the witness stand. Vangie thought she never wanted to see Douglas again, but she was relieved to see a friendly face. As a character witness for the defense, Douglas testified that he had mentored her throughout high school, told of her stellar grade point average, her impeccable attendance record, her numerous scholarships to a list of Ivy League intuitions, her maturity and her dedication to caring for her ill mother and twin sister.

Douglas never mentioned he lusted over her for years, and had she given him the chance, he would have willingly entered into a sexual relationship with a minor, Vangie thought. Had Kimmy asked, Douglas would've perjured him. Kimmy, instead, belabored her cross-examination by questioning Douglas about her impoverished childhood.

Then came Elisa Earwood's testimony, Todd's ex-girl-friend, who the police originally pursued as the prime suspect. Elisa, a professional dancer, pretty, and petite, met Todd in graduate school. They dated for 18 months. Eliza testified that she and Todd had an "on and off again" relationship. She described Todd as having "a mean streak" and said he "shoved her around" more than a few times. Their relationship ended after Todd forced her into having sex with him against her will.

"Todd would've hurt me if I tried to stop him," Eliza said in tears.

Kimmy thoroughly cross-examined Eliza, but with kid gloves.

Next, Clarissa called Sean Aikman to the stand. Sean testified that he and Todd met up at a bar for drinks the night of the engagement party and that Todd boastfully told him, "Wade's blushing bride-to-be just spread her legs for me." Sean apparently wasn't the type to let a salacious statement get by him casually. He interrogated Todd on the details. Todd described Vangie as a backscratching, sadistic sex fanatic who liked control. A photograph of Todd and Sean posted on Sean's social media page, corroborated Sean's story.

During cross-examination, Kimmy got away with calling Sean's testimony hearsay and skillfully turned the tables, using Sean's testimony against the defense and in favor of the prosecution's theory.

Dr. Dennis Bui, the forensic pathologist Ross hired, testified that the steak knife entered Todd's abdominal aorta at an angle. The depth versus the length of the wound suggested that the assailant was left-hand dominant and in a perpendicular positioning to the victim, said Dr. Bui.

Because Vangie was right-hand dominant, Dr. Bui postulated that she would've been in horizontal positioning to Todd, holding the knife in her left hand at the point of contact; and based on the force of impact and the velocity necessary to kill Todd, this suggested that Todd had plunged forward, falling onto the knife and possibly causing his death.

Mario Hernandez cross-examined Dr. Bui vigorously, calling the doctor a "glorified con-artist" and attacking Dr. Bui's trial history as fraught with inaccuracy and incomprehensible scientific findings.

Next Clarissa submitted into evidence the written testimony of Thomas Jones, the owner of Thomas Jones Investment Services, who confirmed Vangie's net worth. It was still hard for Vangie to believe she invested her hard-earned money in stock that made her a millionaire at age nineteen.

"Do you have any more witnesses for the defense, Counselor?" said the judge.

"The defense calls Doctor Wade Fitzgerald the Fourth to the stand."

Vangie's eyes flashed. In a knee jerk reaction, she found Clarissa's hand and squeezed hard.

"What the hell are you doing, Clarissa?" Vangie whispered to the best of her ability.

"I need a moment, Your Honor," Clarissa said to the judge.

"Make it quick."

Clarissa leaned over and whispered in Vangie's ear. "You have to trust me, Vangie."

There was no stopping Clarissa or the proceedings. The bailiff had already called out Wade's name. Vangie turned desperately to Rebecca for answers.

"Please tell me what's happening right now?"

"He's our key witness," said Rebecca.

Vangie grabbed a bottle of water, unscrewed the cap, and sipped continually, trying to get a handle on herself. In a sweep of her eyes, she caught Kimmy's reaction as Wade took the stand and took the oath. Every great attorney knew when to dial down their emotions when caught by surprise, and Kimmy was one of the best. She never even batted her eyes. Vangie was crashing and sure to burn.

Clarissa bound for the witness stand, holding up the document she carried. "Permission to approach the witness, Your Honor?"

"You may approach."

"The defense enters Exhibit K into evidence!" Clarissa practically shouted, and then she handed the document to

Wade. "Doctor Fitzgerald, can you please read the caption on page one?"

"Prenuptial Agreement," Waded said. His response brought Vangie's attention front and center.

"Can you also tell us the date of the prenup?"

"April 25, 2016."

"The twenty-fifth of April, almost two months to the day before Todd Bryant met his death," Clarissa said to the jurors before redirecting Wade. "Can you please tell the jurors who signed the prenuptial agreement?"

"Vangie did."

"So, is it your testimony, Doctor Fitzgerald, that Vangie Cooper signed a prenuptial agreement forfeiting *all* future claims to your assets and the Fitzgerald fortune?"

"Yes."

"So, you had firsthand knowledge that the defendant wasn't motivated to marry you for your money. Is that correct?"

"Yes, I did."

"To your recollection, did Vangie ever express her sentiments about Todd to you?"

"Yes. She told me on more than one occasion that she didn't trust Todd."

"Did Vangie tell you why she mistrusted Todd Bryant?"

"Yes, she did, when Todd and I were roommates. He made a habit of walking in on her undressed; a bad habit."

"Do you believe Todd Bryant raped Vangie that night of the engagement party?"

"I believe he did violate her sexually, yes," Wade said, his piercing eyes boldly meeting Vangie's.

"Thank you, Doctor Fitzgerald."

Vangie hadn't yet decided what to make of Wade's testimony or if she believed he actually gave a damn about her or what Todd had done to her.

The prosecution declined to cross-examine Wade. He left the stand and the defense rested.

To begin her closing, Kimmy displayed a different photo of Todd, this time dressed in a plain black T-shirt against a white backdrop, his smile quirked to one side of his mouth and jade eyes mischievous. Vangie stared Todd squarely in the eyes.

"This was the very last headshot taken of Todd Bryant for his acting career, a career with a bright future," Kimmy began. "But Todd will never grace the stage again, never marry, never have children or live until old age because Vangie Cooper made sure he wouldn't!" Holding fast to her "greed" theme, Kimmy reconstructed a pyramid of evidence presented by the prosecution that culminated with murder.

"You've listened to testimony from many credible witnesses, people who knew Vangie Cooper intimately, all testifying with one accord: Vangie Cooper is a master of deceit and will do whatever it takes to get what she wants—even murder!"

Following her reexamination of the prosecution's forensics, Kimmy hotly disputed the defense's findings, calling Dr. Bui's conclusions "unconscionable and an offense to the court" to even suggest that Todd, in an act of aggression against the defendant, had managed to kill himself. "Anything is possible," Kimmy said, "but plausibility defines the law, good people, not possibility!"

Vangie was left to wonder about her own intentions. Did Todd fall onto the knife in her hand that killed him, or did she stab Todd with hatred in her heart? She knew she would spend the rest of her life staring into a black hole, wondering.

Kimmy softened her hardnosed tone, empathizing with those jurors who may have been swept into sentimentality by Angie's testimony. Kimmy even commended Vangie for her achievements and, for the first time since the trial began, actually looked at Vangie. In her next breath, Kimmy argued that Vangie's tragic life did not give her license to take Todd's life.

"The proof in this case is overwhelming. Vangie Cooper is guilty of murder in the first degree, and it is your job as members of the jury to find the defendant guilty beyond a reasonable doubt!"

Vangie held her composure, but she suddenly felt as if someone had turned up the heat and then dropped the AC to freezing.

Sitting next to Vangie, Clarissa flipped through her notes, apparently making last minute adjustments to her argument. She had put her life in her best friend's hands, now wasn't the time to question Clarissa's legal aptitude, Vangie told herself.

"You may proceed with your closing argument, Counselor," the judge urged.

Clarissa took the mic. "Good morning, members of the jury," she began. "Vangie Cooper's life hangs in the balance because the prosecution could not accept the truth about Todd Bryant. Why? Because accepting that Todd Bryant had a history of sexual assault would have shattered the prosecution's case from the very start."

Clarissa recited California law that granted Vangie the right to defend herself, and then she highlighted the weaknesses in the prosecution's case to show there was indeed reasonable doubt.

"Approximately seventy-five to eighty percent of women who acted in self-defense are convicted or encouraged to plead guilty," Clarissa continued. "Is it because these women are guilty or is it because, in a male dominated society, lawmakers, prosecutors, the law enforcement, and the general public have been conditioned to presume that women, like Vangie Cooper, are guilty from the very start?"

"Each of you must ask yourselves if the prosecution has proven guilt beyond a reasonable doubt or not. I submit to you that the proof in this case falls way short and does not add up to a guilty verdict."

Concluding her argument, Clarissa went on the say, "As you leave this courtroom and head into the jury room to deliberate, I ask you to do what is right, what is just, and what is fair. And, that is, based on the evidence presented to you, that you find Vangie Cooper not guilty of murder, but that she acted in self-defense. To find Vangie Cooper guilty of murder and sentence her to death would be a gross miscarriage of justice! Thank you!"

Forty-Three

W aiting was all Vangie had to look forward to: waiting to use the bathroom, waiting to make a call, waiting to eat, waiting for social hour to end, waiting for mail that never came, waiting for lights out, waiting for judgment day. Her life had been ripped apart and placed under a microscope, and Vangie was tired of waiting. She wanted her trial over and done with, whatever the final verdict, if only to regain a sense of direction in her life.

She worried nearly as much for Angie's future as for her own. She had the discernment and legal intelligence to lower her expectations regarding the outcome of her trial, but Angie had always been irrationally optimistic, throwing caution to the wind. If she left Angie's future in Angie's hands, Angie would never live up to her potential. So, she put Angie's future in Clarissa's hands. Should she be convicted, Clarissa was to create a trust fund for Angie.

Vangie mulled these things over at an unspecified hour of the night while listening to the rain thrash against the compound. She would rather listen to the rain and reminisce about a trip to an exotic island, imagining herself lounging in the sun, absorbed by the sea, than to think about death row.

Yet, remembering the scars and bruising Russell left behind, her days of pain, the blood that flowed from her afterward, and her sadness after realizing she had become a woman before her time surpassed her fear of death row and dominated her thoughts.

Russell King had been revived in the deepest, darkest, damaged parts of herself. If she could just expel the tears bloating her stomach and moistening her eyes, she thought, she would cry herself to sleep. But not a drop spilled from her eyes over what Russell had done to her.

She remembered how her mother lost all sense of herself after that day and spiraled into depression—and how she was put to blame for her mother's unhappiness. In her young mind, she believed she was a 'tease" and somehow deserved Russell's punishment.

At times she wondered who she would have become had she not taken Angie's place that day. Would she have lived an honest life? Could she have lived with herself? What she endured would've destroyed Angie long before it destroyed her. Angie had always been more fragile, since birth. This Vangie felt intrinsically.

When the jailhouse alarm screamed and the lights popped on, Vangie was thankful to put her dark past behind her for another day and to see a semblance of daylight.

She hadn't expected visitors today. In shock to see Ronnie, she slid into the chair, picked up the phone, and stared, affectionately, at Ronnie, choking back tears.

"Hey you," Ronnie said.

"I can't believe I'm looking at you," Vangie breathed.

His shock of unruly curls had returned, and he wore a plain tee under a blue blazer. Reminded of that warm, humid night in West Palm Beach, Florida, so long ago, when Ronnie's persistence eventually won over her heart, Vangie suddenly felt a deep loss for the baby he would never know existed.

"How's the slammer?" he said.

Fingering through her own unruly mane, Vangie said, "What do you think, Ron?"

"Brutal. But you look beautiful."

Vangie's cheeks flushed. She had to laugh to herself for worrying about the condition of her hair, of all things, in front of Ronnie. He had seen her at her worst.

"Seriously, Ron. Are you doing okay?" Vangie asked this carefully, avoiding any reference to the cause of the accident or the extent of his recovery.

"Then you know about my fender-bender?" He put on his slow grin, slower than usual.

"It wasn't a fender-bender. You could've died, Ron." Her voice broke.

Ronnie eyes turned to glass. "I almost fucking did die, Van."

"But you're still here."

"One hundred percent off the breathing tube."

"Well, thank you for always being here when I need you," Vangie said sentimentally.

"Right. So, the dickhead came through in the clinch, I read."

Vangie wasn't so quick to defend Wade against Ronnie's jealous jabs these days. "How long have you been following my trial, Ron?" Her tone was playfully accusatory.

"Long enough to quash a subpoena."

Vangie laughed, coming to the realization that Ronnie's team of sharks had kept him off the witness stand. "You could've written me or something."

"My brain coordination wasn't cooperating with me," he said.

Ronnie's statement sobered Vangie. She didn't know the physical, cognitive, or psychological aftermath of a coma, but she imagined Ronnie's road to recovery hadn't been easy. Right off she had noticed the brass cane leaned against the counter. She never imagined Ronnie having to carry around a walking stick, but then, no more than he imagined her behind bars, she supposed.

Gone was that daredevil look in Ronnie's eyes, which once told her to pack a suitcase and meet him halfway across the world at the drop of a dime. Vangie wanted to cry, as much for her loss as Ronnie's.

"I'm sorry, Ronnie."

"Don't fucking start pitying me, Van."

"How can I pity you? We're two of a pair."

"Right."

"I visited you at the hospital, by the way," she confessed.

Ronnie put on his slow grin, again. "So, I didn't dream you said you love me?"

Vangie didn't hesitate to say, "I do love you, Ron. I always have and always will."

She and Ronnie kept their remaining conversation light-hearted. When it came time for Ronnie to leave, Vangie refused to say goodbye.

"I'll see you later," she said.

The next few days slugged by and still no verdict.

During her weekly scheduled visit with Angie that Saturday, Angie didn't mention the pending verdict, and Vangie did her best not to be consumed by thoughts of the subject.

To avert her thoughts, she listened to Angie's office gossip. When they were young, Angie never could engage her in the gossip she stored up all day at school and unleashed on her at night when no one was in earshot. This gossip she took to heart. She could only imagine Clarissa's devastation after finding out Ross cheated. As for Ross, she wasn't surprised.

Angie moved to her next broadcast. "Mom and Mr. Young are driving to California soon."

Vangie mustered a thin smile. "I'd like to see Mom." Not to get her hopes up, she didn't ask how soon her mom planned to visit.

Angie talked on, telling her about Dr. Laurence, the man evidently responsible for putting the twinkle in her twin's eyes. Angie didn't tell her why she didn't expect to see or hear from Dr. Laurence again, only that someone named Ashely had given him her cell phone number and now she talked to this guy every day.

"What kind of doctor, Ang?" Vangie asked with Wade on her mind.

"Oh. Laurence? He's my dentist." Angie couldn't say his name without smiling. Vangie caught herself smiling too.

"Is he a fine dentist or an okay dentist?" she teased

"A fine one."

"How fine?"

"Really fine."

"What else do you love about Doctor Laurence, besides that he's a *foodie*?"

Angie hadn't stopped giggling.

"Was he that good, Ang?"

"Really, really, really good!"

They giggled together, a history making moment for the two of them. She had never discussed sex or alluded to sex with Angie.

Time flew when there was so little of it to hold on to. They were down to their last few seconds on the clock. Tears pushed up Vangie's esophagus. She raised her hand to the glass. Angie mirrored her gesture.

"I love you with my life," Angie's tearful eyes said.

"Me too, Ang. Me too."

"The verdict is in," Clarissa announced on Sunday morning.

Legal scholars might argue that the jurors' brief deliberations meant she had been found guilty. Presumably, the longer the jurors haggled over the evidence, particularly in a murder trial, the more likely they would rule in favor of the defendant. Vangie was too nervous to hope for an acquittal or to consider the alternative. Clarissa did her best to maintain optimism.

Forty-Four

For her final court appearance, Vangie wore a mushroom colored skirt suit that defined her every curve. She had even taken the time to lengthen her lashes and brighten her lips.

"All rise for the jury!" said the clerk.

As the procession of jurors walked into the courtroom and took their seats, Vangie begin to feel as though she had dressed for her own execution.

Judge Papadopoulos took the bench and ordered the room to be seated. Above her thrashing heart, Vangie noticed the absolute silence in the crowded courtroom.

"Have you reached a unanimous verdict?" said the judge.

"Yes," said the male jury foreperson.

"Will the defendant please rise, along with Counsel, and face the jury."

Vangie and Clarissa stood and grabbed hands simultaneously. Rebecca stood close for support, and Angie's presence nearby gave Vangie added comfort. Suddenly, the weight of an elephant sat upon Vangie's shoulders.

Overcome by extreme exhaustion, her eyes shut, involuntarily, as she waited out her fate.

Judge Papadopoulos instructed the foreman to read the verdict.

Throughout the trial, Vangie had kept her composure, holding her head high and refusing to cry. When the verdict was read, life stopped for her. Her heart raced and then slowed, and her knees fought to keep her standing. A shock wave permeated the room, spurring gasps, moans, and cries.

"Having been found not guilty, the defendant is free to go. Court is adjourned!" Those were the last words Vangie heard from Judge Papadopoulos, words her own ears didn't trust.

Vangie felt herself being swallowed by Clarissa's arms. A hand shook hers, another patted her on back, cameras snapped, and bodies seemed to bury her. Amidst the chaos taking place around her, Vangie's eyes tore through the crowd in search of Angie. When she found Angie, everything in her peripheral vision fell into the shadows. It seemed a lifetime for Vangie before she could take ten steps forward, but no one or nothing, including the seven seas, could keep her from her twin.

When Vangie got her arms around Angie, her tears broke free and her legs buckled. Angie held on tight, keeping her standing.

That night, Ross E. Lewis & Associates celebrated Clarissa's victory at one of the most expensive and exclusive restaurants in Downtown L.A, without Vangie.

Sitting behind the wheel of Angie's souped-up Mustang, Vangie pulled into the private driveway of the Beverly Hills Hotel, handed the valet the key, and casually walked the famed red carpet in a cami dress and flip-flops. Hoping to blend in with the stars, she wore dark sunglasses and a wide-brimmed straw hat.

Vangie spared no expense at the luxury boutique hotel just blocks from Rodeo Drive where she could have anonymity and protection from the press. Standing in the foyer of her junior suite, she admired the timeless beauty of the modern chic décor with warm and inviting colors. She thought about her 6x8 cell, and the suite's extravagance nearly overwhelmed her in contrast. She blinked back tears and went about her routine of ordering room service, booking a spa day for her and Angie, filling a wine glass with a Cabernet, soaking in a tub of bubbles, and wrapping herself in the plush bathrobe. She expected to feel back on top of the world again. Barraged by loneliness, she regretted talking Angie into attending the celebration without her.

She walked from the marble-clad bathroom to the master bedroom with a glorious view of the garden and sat back on the immense bed to enjoy a five-star meal. She didn't have a cell phone or even a laptop. For the sake of company, Vangie turned on the smart-tv.

The hotel's landline rang before she could cut into the juicy New York Steak. She jumped to answer it, thrilled that Angie may have changed her mind and decided to dine with her tonight. When the front desk clerk announced her visitor, Vangie stopped breathing.

"Would you like me to send the gentleman to your room?" the clerk asked.

Vangie freed the breath she had been holding. "Yes," came her raw-throated reply. After hanging up, she sat motionless for a spell, and then jumped up and quickly changed out of her bathrobe and back into her cami dress.

Anticipating Wade's arrival with bated breath, Vangie stood in the foyer, gazing at herself in the vanity mirror and questioning her sanity. What could Wade possibly have to say to her now? If he came to offer her his absolution, she didn't need his pity.

Vangie sighed resignedly. Mostly, she wasn't ready to confront her dishonor in Wade's eyes. Hearing Wade's heavy knock, she drew back the door with a show of great reluctance.

"Have a good night, ma'am," said the hotel security guy before leaving her alone with Wade.

Dressed in a slim fit suit, Wade held a bouquet of beautiful long-stemmed red roses and wore a slight smile. Was he trying to remind her of their first official date on a cold night in an Olympic-sized pool? If so, he had done just that—except she wasn't nineteen anymore or eager to impress him. Vangie kept that in mind as she struggled to hold Wade's unfaltering gaze.

"I didn't see you at the celebration." He said this as if she had broken one of his codes of conduct.

Well, I didn't know you were invited, Vangie thought, and then she thought to kill Clarissa later for telling him where to find her.

"Congratulations are probably not in order..." Wade handed her the roses as if an afterthought.

A boutique of roses couldn't make up for her nightmare, but nevertheless she thanked Wade for the gesture, holding the bouquet with one hand and keeping a tight hold on the door handle with the other, ready to close this chapter of her life as quickly and painlessly as possible.

"Are you inviting me in or giving me a hint?" Wade's thin smile spread.

As always Vangie found him frustratingly irresistible. She wanted to despise him for believing she could plot to kill anyone, hate him for abandoning her for Cameron, loathe him for putting her life in Todd's hands; but she was reminded of all the reasons she loved him.

Disinclined to let Wade back into her life and into her heart, Vangie slowly widened the door for him to enter her suite. When his back was to her, she set the roses on the vanity, grabbed her wine glass, and took a healthy swallow.

Trailing the distinct scent of Wade's enticing cologne, Vangie entered the living room behind him. While Wade sat on the chaise lounge, she sat in one of the two sitting chairs across from him, loosely cradling her wine glass between her fingers for security.

With so much left unsaid between them, Vangie marveled at how few words they exchanged. For the most part, they stared at one another introspectively as if to avoid an inevitably passionate argument about right and wrong.

Wade asked her a question or two about her plans; she gave him a halfhearted reply about taking a long vacation, passing the bar exam and the legal field.

Wade's smile gleamed. "You passed the bar? Congratulations is in order."

Her wine glass needed replenishing. Vangie drained the last of it to dissolve the lump in her throat and walked to kitchenette to pour herself a second glass. The last subject she wanted to discuss with Wade was the day of Todd's murder.

Wade must have realized his gaffe. When she returned to the living room, he apologized. She eyed him over the rim of her upturned glass, longing to ask about his State Medical Board. She was sure he passed with flying colors. He was the embodiment of success, a true "blue blood" through and through, she thought, and then she thought about the number of years she stood on the sidelines, cheering him on. He had lived up to his promise in every way. She wished she could say the same for herself.

When Vangie heard another heavy knock on her door, she rushed to answer it.

Angie came stumbling into the suite with Clarissa hanging from her shoulder.

"We beat those bitches!" Clarissa said drunkenly to Vangie, and then said to Wade, sappily, "Cousin! You're here!"

Wade scooped Clarissa up and carried her over to the chaise lounge.

Angie stood by, staring at Vangie with owl eyes.

"I should go," Wade said.

There wasn't a question in Vangie's mind who she planned to spend her first night of freedom with. She hoped Wade got the hint when she walked him to the front door. Her disinclination to say goodbye to him, however, led her into the warm night on bare feet. They stood in the center of a tropical paradise under a full moon, locked in a staring contest. Now, more than ever, Vangie was reminded of their first date, which ended with Wade's sweet kiss under the arched doorway of Toyon Hall.

Wade cleared his throat. "This is tough. There were no winners today."

She had certainly lost more than she gained, Vangie agreed silently.

"Is this goodbye?" he said.

"Is it?" Vangie's voice rang with hope, while her heart ached to pour out her apologies to Wade. But his plans to marry Cameron stood as her deterrent.

Her stomach clinched when Wade stepped forward and did the unexpected—folded her into a loving embrace. "I still love you," he said.

A heart of steel couldn't hold back Vangie's tears this time. She walked away from Wade before he could walk away from her.

Clarissa had passed out by the time Vangie returned to the suite. Having completely lost her appetite, Vangie topped off her wine glass, well on her way to drunkenness. Angie was the only bright spot in her life. They slept in the same bed as they had as kids and talked into the night.

Angie rushed her with stories about her life that brought Vangie more sadness than joy, but she listened quietly and patiently, and was happy to hear Angie had found real love.

Her love for Wade, however, Vangie kept her to herself.

Once the lights were off and Angie had fallen asleep, Vangie grieved her greatest loss before the weight of her tumultuous experience pulled her into deep, soundless sleep.

Forty-Five

The office suites off the Santa Monica Pier had towering windows that overlooked the cobalt blue water. Wearing a raw silk dress of the same hue with stiletto sandals, her hair falling in soft curls about her shoulders, Vangie took a moment to appreciate the Pacific disappearing into the sunset.

She never imagined she would want to wear the color blue again, and she rarely took the time out of her busy life to reflect.

Now that she was officially sworn in as an attorney, she had a sense of direction. The first case she took on, pro bono, was Carly Ann Tonner's, her former cellmate charged as an adult for stabbing her father to death and disfiguring her mother with acid. At age seventeen, Carly had received a twenty-five-year sentence without the possibility of parole. Vangie took an interest in the case when she ran across a news report. Apparently, the baby that Carly had self-aborted was her father's. From age six on, Frank Tonner had repeatedly sexually violated Carly while Carly's mother observed. Vangie filed an appeal of Carly's case.

Mindful of the time, Vangie pulled her eyes away from the sea. As she was leaving her office, Clarissa entered dressed in a ruffled white blouse, high-waisted pencil skirt, and high-heeled pumps. Clarissa claimed the executive suite down the hall and had a spectacular view of the ocean. Vangie didn't mind. Afterall, Clarissa had earned the higher ranking.

It had taken them nearly a year to officially launch their law firm, after Ross put up a fight over losing Clarissa, losing the prospective clients Clarissa attracted to the firm, and over the money Clarissa had invested in their partnership.

"It's that time." Clarissa's voice rang with nervous excitement.

Vangie couldn't deny the butterflies in her stomach. Taking in exhilarating breaths, Clarissa and Vangie grabbed hands and made their grand entrance. The guests had begun to fill the reception area, charmed by cranberry colored walls, cream leather seating, and cherry wood flooring.

Wearing the hat of receptionist/personal chef, Angie had put her culinary training to good use for the launch party and was charged with the task of greeting guests and passing out welcome packets. Angie's hors d'oeuvre spread from one end of the reception console to the other and smooth jazz played by the DJ flowed through the room.

They held a soft opening, just family, close friends, business associates, and a judge or two were invited.

"Do you need me to turn things up?" Vangie heard in Wade's buttery smooth, deep voice. She turned her head to see him towering over her. Dressed for the special occasion, Wade wore his best tailored suit with an open collar white shirt and his dazzling white smile. One look at Wade swooned Vangie and put a big smile on her face.

"I think Clarissa has everything covered. You know Clarissa." Vangie and Wade exchanged knowing laughs.

"Are you talking about me?" Clarissa said under her breath, holding her smile for their audience.

"We were complimenting you. Nice job, Clarissa," Wade said.

"Yeah, right," Clarissa shot back before bee-lining to greet one of the judges.

Wade took hold of Vangie's moist hand, pulled her into him, and gave her a soft, sweet, lingering kiss on the lips. "You look beautiful and smell delicious."

Vangie gazed into Wade's piercing eyes. "You too."

They were taking their engagement slow, rediscovering each other in new, exciting, and sometimes frightening ways for Vangie. She still worried Wade couldn't love the real Vangie Cooper, that she couldn't live up to his high expectations of her, and that he would return to Cameron's waiting arms.

"I see you invited your boy," Wade said, hitting a sour note.

Vangie chuckled. Ronnie had just walked in with his latest bombshell groupie on his arm. With her secrets out in the open, and her dark past bared, Vangie had nothing left to lose but Wade's trust in her. She kissed Ronnie's cheek and then introduced herself and Wade to Ronnie's guest.

For Clarissa, the celebration hadn't officially kicked off until the matriarch of the Fitzgerald family walked in. Kimmy wasn't far behind Wade the Second and wouldn't have missed the opportunity to silently take credit for

Clarissa's first big win. Vangie learned from Wade, in the strictest confidence, that Kimmy had provided him a copy of the signed prenuptial agreement to enter into evidence. Some secrets Vangie intended to keep.

Chiming her champagne flute, Clarissa called the room to attention. Vangie joined Clarissa before the small gathering. After toasting their launch, Vangie and Clarissa unveiled their elegant signage: The Law Offices of Fitzgerald & Cooper.

Acknowledgments

I am eternally grateful to the following individuals:

To God, you are my glory.

To Rudolph A. Johnson, III, thank you for thirty-one years of love.

To Marcea Lloyd, J.D., retired General Counsel and Chief Administrative Counsel, and Deborah LaTouche, Esq., acting Deputy District Attorney, thank you for your invaluable legal guidance, my sisters.

To Randy Jones, Esq., former Assistant U.S. Attorney and current Partner and Member at Mintz Law Firm, thank you for saving the day and preserving my credibility.

To Michael Mclivren, your suggestions mattered.

To Jamila Goosby, Shawna Cook, and Jacquelyn-Sherman-Rustin, you answered the call and I am eternally grateful.

To Catrina Johnson-Green, thank you for opening my eyes to the penal system, *old pal*.

To my readers, family, and friends, you are my muse!